D1550682

THE AGA KHANS

The Aga Khan's family

The Aga Khans

by
WILLI FRISCHAUER

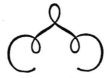

Hawthorn Books, Inc.
Publishers
New York

DELUXE

DELUXE

BUSINESS Advantage

Zeid. Maather@
wamm. het

For business check products *call* 1-800-252-3414

DESIGN: MARTIN J. BAUMANN

1 2 3 4 5 6 7 8 9 10

The author gratefully acknowledges Simon and Schuster, Inc., for permission to reprint from The Memoirs of Aga Khan.

FOREWORD

Whenbeen I first told Prince Karim Aga Khan that I proposed
to write his life story against the background of his family, his
ancestors, and the Ismaili community of which he is the spiritual
head, he suggested that before talking to him I should spend a
year or two reading the literature on the subject. He was not far
wrong. Before I went much further, I met a Muslim scholar in
East Africa who was working on an Ismaili bibliography and
had so far listed some 260 volumes and was still going strong.
In Karachi the "Dr. Alidina Memorial Library" was stacked to
the ceiling with works on Ismaili history, ancient and contemporary. The Aga Khan himself drew my attention to several
learned tomes on related and relevant topics.

Every single phase of the colorful Ismaili story from the first
Ali (A.D. 600–661), Mohammed's son-in-law, to the better known
last Aly (1911–1960), the Aga Khan's father, had found a more or
less loyal chronicler. The quarrel between the Prophet's daughter
and his child bride; his grandson, "the Great Divorcer"; the
turbulent reign of the Fatimids in Egypt; the Ismaili "underground," the notorious (or much maligned) Assassins; the first
Aga Khan, who helped the British conquer Sind; the third Aga
Khan, Prince Karim's grandfather and predecessor as Imam of
the Ismailis (and five-time winner of the English Derby)–have all

provided historians and diarists with ample material for narratives. But although his name is a household word that figures even in pop songs, little is known of Karim Aga Khan except what has appeared in the gossip columns of Western newspapers.

What seemed lacking was one comprehensive account spanning the whole scintillating spectrum from Mohammed to Karim, and this is what I set out to produce. History, religion, war, women, politics, racing, and big business provided some of the raw material. My aim was to trace the story from the very beginning, but with growing emphasis on the last three of the line—the old Aga Khan, Aly Khan, and Karim Aga Khan, whose life takes on a new meaning in the context of his religious and dynastic antecedents.

While it was impractical for me to visit every outpost of the Aga Khan's spiritual empire (his religious subjects in China, Soviet Russia, and other parts of the world are "out of touch"), I did spend some time at Ismaili centers in East Africa and Pakistan and am indebted to Ismaili dignitaries and councillors for much enlightenment. What I saw of Ismaili educational, medical, and social work was so impressive that I often had to restrain my enthusiasm, because my purpose was not to write an Ismaili social history but a treble biography. I have talked at length with the Aga Khan and with members of his brain trust, who answered many of my questions, though by no means all. While I am grateful for the time they spent with me, I have, of course, tried to fill in the gaps from other sources. Though Ismailis no longer practice *taqiya* (disguise, dissimulation), they are reluctant to talk about many aspects of their highly esoteric religion, and even well-educated Ismailis living in the technological age continue the ancient tradition of secrecy. (No secrecy is attached to the Ismaili Constitution, copies of which were freely available.)

Little of this tradition emerges from the many works I consulted, which were nevertheless of invaluable assistance in many respects. Professor Philip Hitti's *History of the Arabs* was an indispensable introduction to the scene; Professor Bernard

Lewis's *Assassins* made fascinating and instructive reading. The (old) Aga Khan's *Memoirs*, discreet and reticent though they are, allowed me to flavor this account with his reactions to many controversial incidents in his life.

Inevitably, I have soaked up a large measure of information from the biographies of the old Aga Khan by my friends Stanley Jackson (particularly good on the racing activities of this prince of the British turf) and Harry Greenwall. Prince Aly Khan was such a flamboyant figure of our time that he obviously stimulated his biographers. British author and journalist Gordon Young, with his intimate knowledge of Aly's social environment, followed his course closely, and more recently the American Leonard Slater published a special study of Aly's love life. The French model Bettina, who might have become Aly's third wife had he lived longer, has written her memoirs and elucidated many points for me in conversation.

The lives of my three principal characters have almost become public property. Press, newsreels, and television attended at many spectacular occasions and have contributed vivid eyewitness accounts. As a newspaperman, I make no apology for consulting the files of editorial offices in Africa and on the Indian subcontinent, in Britain, France, Germany, and the United States.

The people who have helped me are altogether too many for individual enumeration, though their help is appreciated. A number of them, Ismailis and non-Ismailis, who supplied me with information stipulated that they should remain anonymous. Librarians in four continents were generous with their time and advice. I was going to conclude this list of grateful acknowledgments with the usual reference to "my wife's invaluable help, etc.," but that kind of pro forma recognition would be grossly inadequate. Without my wife's assistance in every department of a writer's endeavor, this book might not have been attempted; it would certainly not have been completed.

W. F.
London, 1970

THE AGA KHANS

CHAPTER I

For Dar-es-Salaam, October 19, 1957, was a public holiday. Houses were decorated, streamers with messages of welcome spanned the streets, front page reports in the press described the scene. The city was in a festive mood; Europeans and black East Africans as well as Asians all joined in the celebrations. The Muslims of the prosperous Shia Ismaili community, some twenty thousand of them from all over Tanganyika, were in town to acclaim their new spiritual leader. The were attending the *Takht Nishini*, the ceremonial installation of His Highness Prince Aga Khan IV Shah Karim al-Huseini, twenty-year-old direct descendant of the Prophet Mohammed and the late Aga Khan's grandson and successor, as Imam-e-Zaman (Imam of the Age). He was forty-ninth in a line that started with Hazrat Ali, husband of the Prophet's daughter Fatima.

From early morning people made their way to the Upanga ceremonial area, which was soon packed to the bursting point. Exhausted but excited, one group—a thousand men, women, and children—tumbled from twenty trucks that had taken three days and three nights to bring them from the Southern Province to Dar-es-Salaam. Nothing short of disaster would have kept them away, and they were only just in time to join in the shouts of

1

"Nalle Tagbir! Nalle Tagbir!" ("May Allah bless you!") that greeted the arrival of the young Imam. Dressed in a white high-necked *sherwani,* black trousers, and Astrakhan hat, the slim new leader mounted the dais and settled himself in the heavy ornamental chair. His fixed smile barely disguised the tension and the deep emotion in his eyes as the waves of applause swelled.

The Dar-es-Salaam ceremony, first of a number to be held in East Africa and the Indian subcontinent, was a public pageant, a social occasion, but above all a religious service that emphasized the living Imam's link with the Prophet and his son-in-law. Unlike other Shia Muslims, Ismailis believe in a living, hereditary Imam as the vicar of Allah on earth. Devout Muslims, theirs is an esoteric but progressive and enlightened philosophy, a combina-tion of deep spiritual fervor and a highly developed business sense. They rely on the guidance of a divinely inspired Imam who is in close touch with modern developments in every sphere of human endeavor. They follow and obey him without demur.

The new Imam was deeply conscious of the reason why, to the surprise of many, his grandfather had chosen him as his successor by *nass* (divine ordination, absolute will). As the old Aga Khan had said in his will, "In view of the fundamentally altered condi-tions in the world in the very recent years due to the great changes which have taken place, including the discoveries of atomic science, I am convinced that it is in the interest of the Shia Muslim Ismaili community that I should be succeeded by a young man who has been brought up . . . in the midst of the new age and who brings a new outlook on life to his office as Imam." The descendant of the Prophet was already being hailed as the Imam of the Atomic Age.

Nothing could have been further from the atomic age than Dar-es-Salaam at this moment. Thousands of Ismailis who could find no seats squatted on the sandy ground. Babies slept soundly in their mothers' arms while bigger children played hide-and-seek among the crowd. In the gaily festooned grandstands, leaders of the Ismaili community in high turbans and crimson robes looked as colorful as their womenfolk, who were dressed in flowing saris of a hundred shades, lavishly embroidered with gold and silver thread and sparkling sequins. The gowns of European women brought a whiff of Paris *haute couture* to the Upanga Road.

For the British government, the Colonial Secretary, Alan Lennox-Boyd (now Lord Boyd), was there to pay his respects to the new Aga Khan; the Governor of Tanganyika and his lady headed a large official party. Prince Seyyid Abdulla, bringing the felicitations of his father, the Sultan of Zanzibar, was one of the many African nobles present.

Many eyes wandered from the solemn and lonely figure on the dais to the grandstand and the small group of the Imam's relatives, who included the Mata Salamat (the Ismaili title of Yvette Blanche Labrousse, the late Aga Khan's stately French-born Begum) and Karim's parents, Prince Aly Khan and Tajudowleh (the Ismaili name adopted by Princess Joan, a daughter of Lord Churston). The sophisticated, elegant trio gave no hint of the strains—personal, religious, constitutional—that tested their nerves. Nothing was allowed to dim the glory of the new Imam in this great hour. Presently the noise subsided and the recitation from the Koran was intoned. Everybody rose—including the Imam— and listened intently, after which the leaders of the community approached to play their part in the ceremonial investiture, an ancient ritual of historic symbolism that signified the succession.

As the Imam held out his hand, an ancient signet ring was placed on his finger. Throughout Ismaili history the ring's large engraved stone has served as a seal of communication from Imams to their followers, particularly between the eleventh and thirteenth centuries and whenever they were forced to live in concealment. But even in recent times it has been used to testify to the Imam's authority among followers in Afghanistan, Turkistan, and other countries not prepared to rely on the Imam's signature without additional proof of authenticity. In the next stage of the ceremony, a robe was placed on the shoulders of Prince Karim—it was the one his grandfather had worn at the Diamond Jubilee in 1946. A *pagrina* (turban) was put on his head and the historic chain was draped around his neck, each of its forty-nine links representing one Imam, the last bearing his own crest. Finally, he was handed the same curved Sword of Justice that had symbolized the installation of his predecessor in 1885 as the authentic "Defender of the Faith."

The spiritual successor of his ancestor the Prophet, His Highness Aga Khan IV was now truly installed. As he said on one occasion, "Since my grandfather, the late Aga Khan, died, I have been the bearer of the 'Noor,' which means Light. It has been handed down in direct descent from the Prophet." He was now the Imam of the Ismailis.

The Imam of the Ismailis!

Tradition, history, geography, invest the office of the Imam with a significance beyond anything the Western mind can easily accept. To millions the Imam is King, high priest, supreme judge. No European royalty is the object of such uninhibited adoration. A collection of "significant utterances and writings" of the previous Aga Khan is introduced by a panel that says:

THE AGA KHAN

Direct descendant of the Prophet of Allah, Imam and dictator de facto, whose word is Law to many millions of Muslims . . . A Prince and a Lawgiver.

Writing in *The Fatimid Theory of State*, P. J. Vatikiotis, a student of Ismaili history, says, "The Imam is not a mere temporal executive enforcing the sacred law among the Community of believers and adjudicating their disputes. He is rather an heir to the Prophet's 'ministry' and a proof of God on earth. As the rightful heir to the prophetic mission, he possesses and knows the esoteric meaning of the 'Book' and its interpretation. Thus, the

Imam rules and guides in the name of God . . . the Imam has prophetic attributes which are transmitted to his lawful heir and successor. . . . All Imams in succession are the Light of God."

Bernard Lewis, Professor of the History of the Near and Middle East at London University's School of Oriental and African Studies, writes about the cult of holy men and Imams who were believed to possess miraculous powers: "The Imam is central to the Ismaili system—of doctrine and of organisation, of loyalty and of action. The Imams . . . descendants of Ali and Fatima through Isma'il, were divinely inspired and infallible—in a sense indeed themselves divine . . . fountainheads of knowledge and authority—of the esoteric truths that were hidden from the uninformed and of commands that required total and unquestioning obedience."

To his followers Prince Karim is "Hazar Imam" (Imam of Our Time) or "Imam-e-Zaman" (Imam of the Age). Some address him as "Mowlana" (My Lord) or "Khudavind," which means the same. Others call him "Hazar Jonejo Dhani" (Present Holder of the Mantle), "Dhani Salamat Dani" (The Master Who Is Alive), "Shah Pir" (Great Lord).

"My duties are wider than those of the Pope," the previous Aga Khan said when he was asked how his position compared with that of the Supreme Pontiff of the Roman Church. "The Pope is only concerned with the spiritual welfare of his flock; the Imam looks after his community's temporal and spiritual interests." I asked Hazar Imam—Prince Karim Aga Khan—for an authentic definition. "It is difficult to define the position of the Imam," he answered, "and I have never done so in public." He thought a while and went on, "You look after the community's spiritual and temporal interests—after their temporal interests only as far as you are capable. But a member of the community need not accept temporal guidance if he does not wish to. It is not an obligation. If he turns to the Imam for assistance, it will be given as far as possible, but if the Imam's advice on temporal matters is rejected, no religious sanctions follow." His advice is sought on many personal matters and no loyal Ismaili would dream of disregarding it. That the Imam's holy *firman* (formal pronouncement) on any subject should be disobeyed is inconceivable.

When Prince Karim's predecessor was asked where the Aga Khan's followers were to be found, he smiled and replied, "Everywhere, except *dosakh*"—everywhere, except in hell.

They number some twenty million, and apart from their strongholds in Pakistan, India, and East Africa, live in such remote places as the peaks of the Pamirs and on the plains of China and Russia. The ruler of the mountain state of Hunza and most of his people are Ismailis. In Syria Ismailis form a strong minority. In Iran they are known as Aga Khanis, in Afghanistan as Alillahis, in Central Asia as Maulais, and in Indo-Pakistan as Khojas, Shamsis, Naosaris, and Guptis. Burma, Japan, and Madagascar also have Ismailis. A number now live in Britain, France, and the United States.

To invoke the name of the Imam is common: "With the Imam's guidance . . . ," Ismailis say frequently. But I have also heard immensely wealthy and sophisticated Ismaili industrialists in Africa, India, and Pakistan say humbly and sincerely, "What I have I owe to the help and guidance of Imam-e-Zaman." Many Ismailis, including those educated in the West, implore the Aga Khan to accept a share in their business because they are convinced that they will prosper if the Imam supports them—and they usually do. I asked a young Ismaili university graduate in an important position in a Commonwealth organization to tell the Aga Khan of our conversation, and he replied, "Of course, of course—but being the Imam, he will know anyway."

The Aga Khan's Paris house, a converted old monastery on the Île de la Cité, stands by the Seine on a narrow street that runs alongside the Quai aux Fleurs but on a much lower level. From the quai a few steps go down to the street below, and on the other side, a few steep steps up, is an ornate wooden door. Strong and solid, as if hewn out of rock, the building once belonged to the complex around the cathedral of Notre Dame and was later occupied by a Count Orsini, from whom the street takes its name. It is like a medieval castle behind a protective moat, but the butler in the white coat who answers the bell restores a sense of the twentieth century. The hall is gloomy; daylight hardly penetrates the small windows, and no more than a hint of sun reaches the courtyard, where flower beds surround an ancient fountain. Except for the distant murmur of a few words in Urdu, the silence is unbroken, and the spiral stone staircase seems to wind its way up into another world.

Actually it leads to the Aga Khan's study, with tapestries on the walls, a desk at the far end, a table covered with documents, copies of East African newspapers (his own) on the windowsill, large easy chairs. (A fortnight later, the desk was missing, the furniture had been rearranged, the documents had disappeared. "Things are changed around frequently," said an associate.) When the Aga Khan enters, it is with a burst of youthful but well-controlled energy. He wears a sober dark suit, white shirt, and an unobtrusive tie. He looks elegant no matter what he's wearing, rather like an English squire who sports his shabbiest jacket during weekends on his estate. His mother says that it is a job to get him to buy a new suit, and friends have noticed holes in the soles of his shoes. One of them says, "The Aga Khan wears a French smile and English socks"—not a bad combination.

When he talks, expressive hands underline his words. Idiomatic French phrases supplement a rich English vocabulary that sometimes betrays a Harvard flavor. Without sounding too harsh, he is precise and definite, like someone who is not accustomed to being contradicted. The dark eyes in his oval face are questing, attentive, and sympathetic when he listens, but they sometimes narrow in a distant look that almost removes him from immediate reach. He laughs easily and his gleaming white teeth show up against his slightly swarthy skin, the only physical evidence of his oriental extraction. His receding hairline adds years to his appearance.

At thirty-two he is much more handsome than his famous grandfather, who made the name Aga Khan an international household name. Child of a less picturesque era, he disdains old-fashioned flamboyance and is studious, serious-minded, and dedicated; neither does he exude the infectious, daredevil *joie de vivre*—on horseback, behind the wheel, on the dance floor—that, even in middle age, endeared his father, Prince Aly Khan, as much to Western socialites as to the Bedouins of the Syrian mountains. Prince Karim shuns the limelight and belongs to the age of anonymous technocrats and accountants into which he was born. His restraint and reticent manner owe something to his Anglo-Saxon heritage.

The impression he creates is inevitably colored by the implications of his direct descent from the Prophet and his complicated genealogy, which combines the Syrian, Egyptian, Persian, and Indian blood of his male ancestors with the varying backgrounds of their consorts—high-born oriental women, slave girls of Christian or Jewish descent, widows of conquered foes, Middle Eastern, North African, and Spanish women. He has inherited the contemporary European element from his Italian grandmother and from his mother, whose line goes back to the English King Edward III (1327–1377).

Following the precedent set by Queen Victoria, who honored his grandfather, Queen Elizabeth II of England conferred the style of "Highness" on the young Aga Khan, and this is how most people address him. Among themselves, his collaborators refer to him as "H.H." (His Highness) or "The Prince," but his mother speaks of him as "K" (and of his younger brother, Amyn, as "A"), which dates back to his school days. Prince Karim enjoys the citizenship of three countries—Britain, Iran, and of course, Pakistan, which counts his grandfather among its founders. East of Suez, as a descendant of the Persian Kajar dynasty, he is invariably addressed as "Royal Highness."

More than any Hapsburg archduke, Hohenzollern prince, or Bourbon pretender I know—and their roots go back almost as far in history—this scion of an august tribe remains linked to his origin. The bond is difficult to define. The closer one is to him, the more apparent it becomes. Not long ago in Nairobi I compared notes with Michael Curtis, the former London editor who served the Aga Khan as an aide in 1957 and who now runs a multimillion-dollar East African publishing enterprise controlled by the Aga Khan. "He mystifies me as much now," Curtis confessed, "as he did when I first met him more than ten years ago. He is not English, not American"—a reference to the Aga Khan's years at Harvard University. "More than with any other member of his family, there is about him an element of the East. . . ."

His complex personality is not easy to penetrate. He is proud and humble, friendly and magisterial, at the same time. As a religious leader, he is not unlike Billy Graham with his streamlined sermonizing. Privately, he has a combination of qualities rare in a very rich young man: He is intelligent, erudite, moral, and charming.

From the study on that day in Paris he takes me across the landing to the spacious drawing room with the antique chess table by the door, deep settees, and high fireplace. Only a meticulous, pedantically rigid schedule enables the Aga Khan to cope with the constant stream of people who are anxious to see him—leaders of the Ismaili community from Asia and Africa whose appointments were fixed many months earlier, industrial and financial executives from half a dozen countries, and legal experts who deal with his international interests.

One delegation from Karachi waiting to be admitted has come to consult him on a major educational project he has initiated in Pakistan, one of the numerous colleges, schools, and orphanages that he sponsors wherever Ismailis dwell. They are voluntary workers and have made the trip to Europe at their own expense. The Aga Khan greets his "spiritual children" (many of them twice his age), accepts their homage, and quickly puts them at ease with the trained monarch's knack of remembering names and circumstances of his flock. With the help of an aide-mémoire that has reached him ahead of the delegation's arrival, he discusses the problem. An hour later he gives proof of his astonishing versatility when the Pakistani Ismailis are followed by architects who have come to discuss highly technical plans for a big new housing project in East Africa.

In the last two years matters requiring his personal attention have become so numerous that it is no longer physically possible to deal with them in his private residence. He has taken offices nearby, where one English and two French secretaries cope with the voluminous correspondence. For secretarial work immediately connected with the Ismaili community he largely relies on Guli Noorali, who is Ismaili and is married to Robert Muller, who manages the Aga Khan's stud farms in France (Lassy, Marly-la-Ville, St. Créspin, and Bonneval).

The engine of the Aga Khan's private Mystère jet (since replaced by a Grumman Gulfstream, which has a longer range) started with a low whine that rose to a penetrating scream as the plane took off to carry him to England. With him was Robert Muller and Mme. J. J. Vuillier, widow of the old Aga Khan's racing expert. Their destination was the English racing town of Newmarket, where the party was joined by Major Cyril Hall, who manages the Aga Khan's Irish studs at Gilltown, Sallymount, Sheshoon, and Ballymanny. Four top-class stallions and some eighty equally prestigious brood-mares add up to a formidable establishment.

In 1960 the death of his father, Prince Aly Khan, whose chief hobbies in life were racing and horses, left Prince Karim in control of the studs, about which he knew very little and seemed not to care. As a boy he used to stay frequently with his father on one of the Irish farms. "The first time my father put me on a horse, I fell off," he recalled, "and I haven't been much interested in horses since." On another occasion he said, "Unlike my grandfather and father, I have no interest in horses." But those who thought that he would quickly liquidate the famous racing empire did not realize his loyalty to the family tradition which started with his great-great-grandfather. Aga Khan I owned three hundred fine horses, but it was the third Aga Khan who made his name and horse-racing virtually synonymous and became the English turf's most prominent figure in the interwar years. The only man to win the English Derby five times, he headed the list of winning owners in England seven times. Karim would not in any case have brought such a rare success story to a sudden end, but while he was contemplating what to do with the horses, one of them, Charlottesville, won two major prizes of the French turf, the Jockey Club and the Grand Prix de Paris at Longchamp, the latter worth 404,814F (about $81,000).

It was like a sign from heaven. The young Aga Khan decided to carry on and began to acquaint himself thoroughly with the intricacies of racing and breeding. In 1965 he engaged François Mathet, a strict disciplinarian and probably the best trainer in Europe. "I made up my mind to run the studs and the racing not as a hobby but as a business," the Aga Khan told me shortly after the Newmarket expedition. He devoted himself to the task with his usual thoroughness. He reorganized the administration of the whole establishment, introduced modern accountancy methods, and difficult as it was to reconcile his methodical approach with a sport so full of imponderables, has kept a wary eye on the balance sheets ever since.

From this point of view his trip to Newmarket was a most satisfying experience. The Newmarket December Sales are a major event in the racing world, and 1968 promised to surpass the record turnover of 1964, when over 2 million guineas (more than $5 million) changed hands at the public auction. Although the biggest names in racing were present, many eyes were on the Aga Khan and his advisers. As usual, he was on the lookout for suitable horses to buy, but everybody else was more interested in what the Aga Khan had to sell. He prunes his studs four times a year to make room for new foals, and so four times a year his surplus horses are offered for sale. This time the most useful of his batch was Atrevida, a ten-year-old gray mare bred under Colonel Vuillier's unique points system from an ancestry that included Blenheim, the old Aga's 1930 Derby winner. Atrevida, in foal to the Aga Khan's stallion Silver Shark—the descendant of his grandfather's 1936 Derby winner, Mahmoud—fetched 31,000 guineas ($78,500), becoming the highest priced brood mare of the whole sale. The nine mares and fillies the Aga Khan brought to Newmarket realized a grand total of 106,700 guineas ($268,900). Sales from the studs bring the Aga Khan nearly half a million pounds sterling a year, but sometimes he has qualms about the cost of his private aircraft. "I wonder whether it is not too spectacular," he said. Considering that his racing establishment alone is worth around £3 million and represents only a fraction of his investments which keep him traveling all over the world, the question, though sincerely put, answers itself.

Mérimont, next door to the famous house of Voltaire, is a charming little villa on its own grounds on the outskirts of Geneva and looks like a rich man's retreat. The lovingly tended gardens, the parquet floors, and the elegant staircase reinforce this impression, which is only corrected by the big baize-covered conference table in the ground-floor drawing room. Known as Le Bureau du Dr. Hengel (after the German industrial expert who presides over it), Mérimont is the nerve center of the Aga Khan's industrial empire, a unique head office that does not serve a corporation or a holding company but is adapted to the peculiar position of the Aga Khan as head of a religious community and independent millionaire industrialist.

One characteristic common to most of his ventures is that he rarely concerns himself with enterprises that have no social purpose and from which the Ismaili community does not benefit either directly or indirectly. The emphasis is on tourism and half a dozen related enterprises, industrial promotion in seven or eight largely underdeveloped countries (cotton, jute, textiles, marble, ceramics, cosmetics, pharmaceutical products, clothes, household utensils), real estate in Europe and overseas, publishing in East

Africa, and banks, investments, insurance institutes, and co-operatives in Africa and on the Indian subcontinent. With the community schools, hospitals, health centers, and religious institutions, they add up to an empire believed to be worth at least $300 million, which is under the control of but not necessarily wholly owned by the Aga Khan.

Sitting in his ground-floor office at Mérimont with the bamboo-rimmed desk, the big green plants, and the huge glass frontage, the Aga Khan looks out on the lawn, the bed of tulips, and, in the distance, Mont Blanc. His small flat upstairs is discreetly furnished but has a rather spectacular bathroom. "Not really his style," says an aide. "It was already here when the house was acquired in the early sixties." The Aga Khan's brain trust working in these civilized surroundings and assisted by a dozen multilingual secretaries includes two Swiss experts on hotels, tourism, and technical projects; two Britons (finance and marketing); two Germans (one engineer, one economist). Italian, French, and other experts are coopted as the need arises. Toward the end of 1968 they were joined by the Aga Khan's younger brother, Prince Amyn (Harvard 1964, now at the United Nations), whose first assignments were to deal with the big new tourist projects in East Africa and to arrange for an investigation into agricultural opportunities for Ismailis. As a member of the family, Prince Amyn is an invaluable link between the Imam and Ismaili leaders.

Because of his many industrial interests and his preoccupation with the education, housing, and health of the community involving major projects that depend on organization, technology, and finance, the Aga Khan sometimes seems more like a business tycoon than a religious leader. He is aware of this, but explains that Islam is concerned with the whole life of the faithful, not only their religion. The Prophet, too, was a businessman.

"Skiing," says the Aga Khan, "is ideal for taking one's mind off affairs." Total concentration on the sport is what attracts him. A winter sports enthusiast with Olympic standards, he spends the winter months in the Swiss Alps. He used to own a house in Gstaad (where he went to school at the famous Collège Le Rosay) but sold it in 1968 and rented a chalet in St. Moritz from the Greek shipowner Stavros Niarchos while making up his mind to build a house of his own. His staff stays with him and associates come for meetings, but Ismaili leaders by silent agreement try not to burden their Imam with community affairs during the month of February, which gives him a respite but doubles his work in the following month.

Last winter he rose early every morning and was out on the stiffest ski runs between eight and eleven, and when his half-sister, Yasmin (daughter of Aly Khan and Rita Hayworth), came on a visit, he took her out skiing for an hour or so in the afternoon whenever the weather permitted. Back in Paris for a few days, he made one of his rare visits to a night club, taking Yasmin and a small party of friends dining and dancing. Work and sport add up to a very full life. The Aga Khan recalled what his grandfather once told him: "Life is a wonderful mission which you should not shy away from. Do not refuse to accept the joys or the responsibilities!" Prince Karim said he tried to apply this philosophy with a certain integrity, but on closer acquaintance it seems that he inclines more toward the responsibilities than the joys.

In or out of season the Aga Khan is liable to make flying visits to Sardinia almost any time of the year. It is no secret that he is associated with the development of the Costa Smeralda as an elite holiday resort comparable to the Côte d'Azur and that he is manifestly succeeding. Until 1969 there were no landing facilities for his Mystère on the Costa Smeralda, and he had to break the journey in Corsica, where he transferred to his helicopter for the last stage of the trip. Now Olbia airport has been extended to take the biggest aircraft, a new airport is being built, and he can fly straight to his own strip of coast.

While he is there his white villa overlooking the sea at Porto

Cervo becomes the center of a great deal of activity. A suite in the Hotel Cervo serves him as an office and the secretaries with their bundles of correspondence are never far away. But he is more relaxed in Sardinia than in almost any other place and in the summer months entertains friends, Britain's Princess Margaret and Lord Snowdon among them. Others have bought villas there, forming the nucleus of an international Aga Khan set.

The Aga Khan made a typical preseason visit in 1969 to attend a week's intensive conference of the Costa Smeralda Comitato Directivo, consisting of himself, Maître Ardoin, and Dr. Hengel. Ardoin and Hengel also own villas on the Costa Smeralda. About nine each morning the Aga Khan, in slacks and short-sleeved shirt, walked from his villa across the piazza to the conference room in one of the new buildings. (Over longer distances he often drives himself in his small red Volkswagen.) After listening to the reports of his fellow directors—his symmetric, harmonious doodles reflecting his orderly mind—he asked questions and checked and counterchecked facts and figures. As usual, he was thorough, interested in details, persistent and difficult to convince, but quick to approve once he saw the merits of a scheme. With a short break for lunch, the committee usually worked till 7 P.M. It reviewed an urban master-plan for the Costa Smeralda prepared by an American expert, examined a new Mediterranean villa design with twenty-six variations, and checked the budget of the Port of Porto Cervo Corporation and the records of their tile factory in Olbia.

More diverting was their inspection of the new eighteen-hole golf course designed by American golf architect Robert Trent Jones that stretches from sea to sea across the neck of Sardinia. Back in their conference room, the Aga Khan and his two fellow directors dealt with the inquiries in response to their international advertising campaign for the sale of plots, which promised flourishing business. They were talking about structural changes in the hotels and a new heated swimming pool when a Telex message from East Africa required their immediate attention. Their Sardinian business was once more interrupted when a high executive of the International Finance Corporation was flown in from Milan for discussions on another proposition.

As he crossed the square at Porto Cervo, returning to his villa, the Aga Khan was recognized by tourists, who take a possessive interest in his activities. They remarked how well he looked and what a wonderful rest he must be having.

Because of his extreme reticence few people are aware of the Aga Khan's worldwide activities. He is on friendly terms with many royal rulers and heads of state, particularly the Shah of Iran, who is a Shia Muslim like him. He has been received by United States Presidents and frequently meets leaders of the British Commonwealth. He enjoys the fatherly friendship and respect of Kenya's President Jomo Kenyatta, to whom he gave the fine Aga Khan Bungalow in Nairobi in which he had spent his childhood during the Second World War.

Unobtrusively and almost unnoticed, he flew into London in mid-January, 1969, while the Commonwealth Conference was in session to discuss with the African delegates the difficulties of Asians living in East Africa. As the Aga Khan had instructed Ismailis of Asian origin in Kenya, Tanzania, and Uganda—in fact, in all emergent states—to adopt the nationality of the country in which they lived (a policy inaugurated by his grandfather), his followers were the least affected by xenophobic measures in East Africa, whereas Asians with British passports were deprived of their livelihood and then refused admission to Britain.

A few months before attending the Mahatma Gandhi centenary celebrations in India in March of the same year, the Aga Khan presented Yarovda Palace in Poona, jointly owned by him, his brother, and his half-sister, to the Indian nation as a gesture of goodwill. Said to be worth about £1 million ($2.4 million), it was built by his grandfather in 1897 to provide work for starving Indians during the famine and to relieve distress caused by the plague. In 1942 it was put at the disposal of Mahatma Gandhi when the British authorities decided to detain him, his wife, his secretary, and his goats. They were held there instead of being sent to the nearby Yarovda prison. Mrs. Gandhi died while under detention in the palace, and to avoid a public funeral which might have sparked serious unrest, she was committed to the pyre, and the ashes were buried on the grounds. "The Yarovda Palace," the Aga Khan said, "is now, as it should be, a national monument in memory of one of the great citizens of the world."

The crisis in Pakistan, aggravated by the dissatisfaction in the east with a government rooted in the wealthier but less populous western part of the country, created problems for the Aga Khan's followers who are prominent in the business community, but Pakistan, too, was a good example of his astonishingly farsighted policies. From the beginning he had supported industrial development in East Pakistan and backed it with considerable personal funds.

In 1970 it was difficult to keep track of his movements. Apart from commuting between Paris, Geneva, St. Moritz, and Sardinia (with a wary eye on the repercussions of recurrent financial crises in Europe), the Aga Khan visited the United States twice and came to London several times to attend business conferences —and the Derby. In London, until recently, he occupied an apartment in his mother's residence where his line drawings on the wall and a head sculpted by him testify to an unsuspected talent. He also maintains homes in St. Créspin and in the south of France, on his Irish stud farms and in Karachi. The houses of wealthy followers in Nairobi, Dar-es-Salaam, and Kampala, in Egypt and Iran, wherever they are, are available to him at any time. His legal residence is Switzerland.

Not many years before his death the grandfather of the present Aga Khan seriously considered the possibility of acquiring enough land to restore territorial autonomy to his family. Although eventually abandoned, the idea serves as a dramatic

flashback to the amazing history of his ancestors over the past
thirteen centuries, from the very beginning of Islam, when his
forebear, the Prophet Mohammed, conquered the minds of men
with his teaching and laid the foundation of a state based on the
religion of Islam, followed by the rise and fall of the illustrious
Fatimid caliphs who founded Cairo and ruled over a powerful
empire stretching from the River Oxus in the East across North
Africa and Morocco in the West.

Visions of the legendary "Old Man of the Mountain" and his
"Assassins" who struck terror—and daggers—into the hearts of
their foes are succeeded by glimpses of the period when Imams
and their followers lived behind the mask of *taqiya*, denying or
disguising their true religious beliefs. Presently, they emerge as
Persian noblemen, and then, quite recently in history, the first Aga
Khan appears in close liaison with the ruling house of Persia.
Through triumph and tribulation, in victory and defeat, millions
of Ismailis remained loyal to the Imam of the time, paying *zakat*,
their voluntary offering. According to one account, members of
an Ismaili community out of touch with their Imam still wrap
their offerings in handkerchiefs every month and throw them into
the Oxus) but the Aga Khan says the story is not true.

This great line is rich in eminent men who have left their mark
on the history of their time, but when I asked the Aga Khan, the
forty-ninth Imam, with which of his ancestors he felt in strongest
communion, his answer was prompt. "The life of the Prophet,"
he said, "is my main inspiration. One can study it all one's life
and never grasp the full extent, even though the guidelines of
his life are fundamental. The same applies to Hazrat Ali, cousin
and son-in-law of the Prophet and founder of the Shia
branch. . . ." And what did he have in common with Ali? "It is
the personal approach to the practice of Islam, the degree of
personal involvement, which is of fundamental significance for
Shia Islam. The Prophet and Hazrat Ali gave a spiritual approach
to Islam which tends to involve the Shia more intimately."

Thus in the setting of the elegant drawing room of his house on the Île de la Cité in Paris, His Highness Prince Aga Khan IV Shah Karim al-Huseini, Hazar Imam and highest religious authority of twenty million Muslims of the Shia Ismaili community, went back to the origins of the faith of which he is the living symbol. With an intensity that usually remains below the surface and is hardly suspected by his Western associates, he conjured up the world of the Prophet Mohammed and Hazrat Ali, the two great historic figures whose blood flows in his veins.

CHAPTER II

"Everything connected with Ismailism seems to be enveloped in a cloud of mystery and secrecy."

—Asaf A. A. Fyzee

THE STORY OF THE Aga Khan and his Ismailis starts in the sixth century of the Christian era in the desolate Bedouin country of al-Hijaz (the Hedjaz) by the Red Sea, which was sparsely inhabited by Yemenite and Jewish tribes and a few Christians. Trading caravans trundling through the desert along the "spice route" to Syria left seeds of Byzantine, Aramaic, and Persian influences in this lonely land whose main population centers were the cities of Makkah (Mecca), where Mohammed was born around A.D. 571, and Yathrib, which, when he moved there, became al-Madinah (Medina), the City of the Prophet.

The early history of Islam is a family affair, though not a happy one—a power struggle of closely related rivals. The Quraysh, Mecca's leading family, were the guardians of the Ka'bah, shrine of the pagan idols; Mohammed's father, Abdullah, belonged to the Hashim, a minor branch of the tribe. The Umayyads and Abbasids, who eventually emerged as temporal rulers of the Muslim empire, all spring from this source. Mohammed lost his father and mother when still very young and was brought up by his grandfather and later by his uncle abu-Talib, whose son Ali became his closest companion and earliest follower. Ali is the hero of the Aga

20

Khan's Muslim sect. Young Mohammed accompanied his uncle's caravans to Syria, then went to work for Khadija, a wealthy Quraysh widow. He looked after her business and caravans so well that she offered him her hand in marriage. She was forty and he was twenty-five, but their married life was happy, and while she lived, Mohammed looked at no other woman. They had three sons, who died in infancy, and four daughters, one of whom, Fatima, survived, married cousin Ali, and entered the pages of history. It is through Fatima that the Aga Khan traces his descent from the Prophet of Islam.

While continuing to trade, Mohammed spent many hours in meditation in a cave on a hill near Mecca where, in A.D. 610, he had the first of the revelations of "God's scriptures dictated by Archangel Gabriel as guidance to men." This was the "Night of Power," the birth of Islam, and from then on, Muslims believe, the voice of Allah continued to speak through the Prophet. The result was the Koran, which did for Mohammed what the New Testament did for Christ, but it is entirely in Mohammed's own words. The Koran is supplemented by *hadith*, tradition handed down by word of mouth.

Like Jesus Christ in his time, the Prophet inveighed against false pagan idols and preached belief in one God, in the Resurrection, in the Last Judgment, and in paradise, but the essence of his teaching was surrender to the will of God—the word "Islam" derives from *aslama*, which means "to submit." Like Jesus Christ, he was violently attacked by the establishment. The Quraysh, who saw in him a threat to their vested interests in Mecca as a center of pagan worship, persecuted his followers and drove many of them into exile.

Mohammed's closest associates rallied around him, foremost among them Ali, his son-in-law; abu-Bakr, a prosperous merchant; Umar, a late convert who became known as the St. Paul of Islam; and Uthman, a member of the Umayyad family. For a time the Prophet weathered the storm, but soon after his wife, Khadija, died, he left the city of his birth and took the road

to Medina. The date of the celebrated *Hijrah* (Hegira), which
has been translated as "flight" but which was in reality a well-
prepared migration, was September 24, 622. The "Year of the
Farewell," Anno Hijrah (A.H.), was later adopted as the beginning of the Muslim era.

For Mohammed and his Muslims it was a watershed because
Medina acknowledged him not only as a religious leader but as
head of their community. As a statesman, the prophet earned a
reputation for his wisdom, humanity, and kindness, but he and his
Muslims entered upon a period in which Mecca and Medina,
Muslims and pagan Arabs, Muslims and Jews, were locked in
one unending battle. Reports of the Prophet's bloody wars and
victories alternate with accounts of his inspired preaching and
the new morality he laid down for his followers.

He built mosques and homes for the Muslims who joined him
in Medina, and his own house was surrounded by quarters for his
wives, who numbered ten or twelve. His favorite wife was
abu-Bakr's daughter A'isha, who was only eight or nine years
old at the time of their marriage and who took her dolls with
her to the marital home.

In the many clashes with the Meccans and pagan tribes, Ali
fought by the side of the Prophet with great courage; he is said to
have killed 523 men in one day and on another occasion to have
put 37 to death with his saber. He was capable of severing a
horseman's body with one stroke of the sword, the lower part
remaining on the horse. Victory in one battle ("with the help of
Allah") was followed by defeat in another in which the Prophet
was wounded.

While the Muslim warriors battled in the field, their women
fought among themselves. A'isha supported her father's claim to
be first among the Prophet's Companions, as the Mecca emigrants
and their Medinese supporters were called. Fatima championed
the cause of her husband. The two factions were on bad terms,
and when Ali accused A'isha of having deceived the Prophet
with another man, the rift deepened. A'isha retaliated and

missed no opportunity to denigrate Ali and Fatima. Talking about these early conflicts, the Aga Khan said simply, "The quarrel between Fatima and A'isha is a historical fact." In effect it gave rise to the branch of Islam of which he is the head.

Mohammed extended the frontiers of Islam and subjugated many tribes, converting them or forcing them to pay tribute. Others sent delegations to swear allegiance to the great leader who changed the tribal society into which he was born into a state built on religion. Returning to Mecca, he smashed the pagan idols and preached the famous sermon: "Know ye that every Muslim is a brother unto every Muslim, and that ye are now one brotherhood." (The Muslim brotherhood is still a political force in the Middle East.) He put the Ka'bah out of bounds to unbelievers, and in the thirteen centuries that have passed, only a very few non-Muslims have visited it—and lived.

"I shall soon be called back to heaven," the Prophet told his followers, adding, "I leave amongst you two important things . . . the Qu'ran [Koran] and my family." The Muslims had heard him say, "He, whose master I am, has also Ali for his master," which Ismailis take to mean that he wanted Ali to become his successor. But when he fell ill and was too weak to lead the *salat* (prayers), he delegated the honor to abu-Bakr, which was interpreted as a sign that abu-Bakr was his choice as deputy (*khalifa*) and successor. On June 8, A.D. 632 (A.H. 10), the Prophet of Allah reached the end of his road on earth and died, leaving the succession in doubt.

It was at once fiercely contested by two factions, one favoring the staid, conservative abu-Bakr—and a caliphate based on the elective principle—the other opting for Ali as the legitimate heir, entitled to the succession as a member of the "House of the Prophet"—Mohammed, Fatima and Ali, and their two sons, Hasan and Huseyn. The Companions chose abu-Bakr, who became the first of the "orthodox Caliphs," whose followers are described as Sunnis (for "custom," "dogma"). Ali's partisans, the Legitimists, opposed the choice and formed the Shi'atu-Ali (Ali's Party), shortened to Shia, which developed into a political pressure group for the "great society" envisaged by the Prophet and against the Muslim establishment.

From this first split in Islam, Ali emerged as the leader of the Shias and the champion of the underprivileged. Today some 20 percent of all Muslims are Shias. "Sunnis and Shias do not differ about the basic tenets of Islam," the Aga Khan explained when I mentioned the split, but early Muslim history is complicated by dissensions among the Shias, from the first of which the Aga Khan's followers emerged as a separate sect.

Caliph abu-Bakr continued in the Prophet's footsteps and brought the whole of Arabia under the rule of Islam. His reign was brief. He was poisoned and died in the year 634. His successor, Caliph Umar, extended the Muslim dominion over Syria, Iraq, and Persia in the north and Egypt and Tripoli in the west. He was fifty-three when he fell to the dagger of a Christian.

Ali's followers then pressed his claim to the succession, but a committee chose Uthman, the Umayyad, who made further conquests but could not control the provinces under his rule. He was accused of nepotism and of feathering his family's nest, and in a general uprising angry opponents stormed his house and demanded his resignation. He was slain, it is said, by a son of abu-Bakr.

Uthman's murder marked the beginning of internecine struggles that rent Islam for centuries, but it finally opened the way for Ali. The Prophet's own family, the Aga Khan's ancestors, came into their own. In Sunni history Ali ranks as the fourth Caliph. Shias hail him as the first legitimate successor of the Prophet. The Caliph for whom the young Aga Khan feels such a strong affinity was a deeply pious and saintly man who frequently inflicted mortifications on himself. He was corpulent, short, and bald, with a long white beard that he sometimes dyed red, but he had a handsome face, a dark complexion, and prominent eyes that looked disdainfully at the world. "Whoever wants any part of it," he said, "must be satisfied to live with dogs!" His thoughts were on paradise, which awaits the devout Muslim. "Blessed are those who have renounced this world and only aspire to the world to come."

Ali's dynamic, progressive view of Islam, his support for the underdog, and his unswerving loyalty to the ideas of the Prophet were challenged by rivals who set out to destroy him. At Basra, they fought the "Battle of the Camel," A'isha making common cause with Ali's enemies and riding into battle with them on a camel. Ali won, captured A'isha, and sent her back to Medina with an escort of forty noblewomen. His defeated enemies were killed but buried with military honors.

The victorious Caliph never returned to the City of the Prophet but made al-Kufa, by the Euphrates, his capital city. Later the Umayyads accused him of complicity in the murder of Uthman, went to war against him, and defeated him by a trick. He was deserted by many of his followers but might have prevailed had he not been attacked by a rebel with a poisoned sword that penetrated his brain. The Wali Allah (Friend of God) died on January 24, 661. Imam, warrior, and saint, he lives in Shia memory as the godlike, ideal Muslim. A Yemenite Jew is thought to have been the first to acclaim him with the words: "Thou art God." Ali was buried at Kufa, which became the Holy City of the Shias, who still flock to it on the anniversary of his death.

After Ali's death his empire crumbled. Egypt was lost, but Iraq remained loyal and proclaimed his son Hasan, elder of the Prophet's beloved grandsons, as Caliph. Ali's son preferred the pleasures of the harem to the rigors of battle, made and unmade a hundred marriages, and earned himself the epithet of "the Great Divorcer." He abdicated and died in Medina. He remains under a historical cloud, and Ismaili records of the forty-nine Imams from Ali to Karim do not include his name. His younger brother, Huseyn, succeeded him as Imam and Caliph of Iraq.

The battle with the Umayyads flared up again. Hoping for popular support, Huseyn crossed the desert with a small band

but was cut off without access to the Euphrates. At Kerbela Imam
Huseyn and his men were massacred. The date of this tragedy,
10th Muharram in the sixtieth year of the Hijrah, is a day of
deep mourning for all Shias. They lost more than their Imam.
With him gone, they forfeited their political power and did not
regain it for centuries.

Imam Huseyn's son, Ali Zayn al-Abedin, who escaped un-
harmed from the death trap of Kerbela, went to live in Medina,
where he became greatly respected as a religious leader. He and
his successor were popular with the growing number of Muslims
who opposed the ruling Umayyads. In 732 the rule of the Umayyads came to an end and a new dynasty assumed power. The
Abbasids (descendants of al-Abbas, a brother of both Mohammed's and Ali's fathers) were, alas, no less hostile to Ali's heirs.
Shias were cruelly persecuted and the Imam's life was in constant danger.

To protect his eldest son and heir, Ismail, the Imam Jafar Sadiq
smuggled him out of the country, spreading a rumor that Ismail
had died and even staging a mock funeral. It caused a lot of confusion, and when Jafar Sadiq was killed, there was a new
succession tangle. Ismail's younger brother Musa Kazim claimed
to be the new Imam. Two opinions existed among the Shias:
Some argued that Ismail was the rightful successor and swore
allegiance to him; others accepted Musa Kazim as their new
Imam.

The Shia community was split. Musa Kazim functioned as
Imam, and his Imamate passed to his son, grandson, and so on in
succession until the twelfth in line, Mohammed Mahdi, who is
said to have gone into concealment. This branch of the faith,
that of the Ithna Ashari ("Twelver Shias"), became the official
religion of Persia (Iran), where the Shah is revered as the deputy of the Mahdi, whose return is still awaited.

Those who remained loyal to Ismail—"Ismailis"—were persecuted from all sides. Driven underground, they practiced their
faith in secret, starting a tradition that became second nature

to all Ismailis and has survived to this day. Hiding their religious conviction (*taqiya*) became a matter of life and death and permissible as a perfectly honorable expedient. They even pretended to be orthodox Sunni Muslims. Imams themselves sometimes adopted the coloring of their mortal foes. Ismaili manuscripts were hidden away; when discovered, they were seized and destroyed by their opponents.

It was a long time before evidence in support of Ismaili claims came to the surface. As new sources were uncovered, references to Ismail in old manuscripts proved that he survived his father by at least twenty years. He turned up in Basra, where he was noticed because of his extraordinary powers to cure the sick. Hotly pursued by the Abbasid Caliph, he fled to Syria and escaped death only because the Governor of Damascus refused to arrest him and became his loyal follower.

The split has not been healed, but the two main Shia branches are no longer hostile, and their leaders—the Aga Khan, heir to Ismail's Imamate, and the Shah of Iran, whose subjects are "Twelvers"—are on the friendliest terms.

Ismail himself remained in hiding throughout his Imamate (765–775), and neither he nor his successors could defend themselves against false accusations, some of which are still in currency. According to Professor W. Ivanow, greatest Western authority on Ismaili history, Sunni scholars have recounted only what was derogatory about the hated Ismaili "heretics."

Ismailis themselves believe that they are on the highest level of religious comprehension, which is called *haqiqat*. Professor Bernard Lewis praises their unity and discipline, which resulted from Sunni oppression and their secret work. Ismaili loyalty to the tradition and law of Islam, he says, was from the beginning allied to a philosophical interpretation of the faith and a strong, highly emotional approach.

The Ismailis met in secret lodges. Novices were obliged to swear an oath of secrecy, and initiation was by seven stages (the number seven acquired sacred importance). They believed that the esoteric truth that reposed in the living Imam, descendant of the Prophet and God-inspired leader, was inaccessible to the ordinary man. When the Crusaders came into contact with Ismailis, they adopted the idea of secretiveness, which gave birth to many religious and secular secret societies in Europe. The Knights Templars' system of Grand Masters, religious devotees, and degrees of initiation is reminiscent of Ismaili practices. Ismaili historians find analogies with the Society of Jesus and its unsurpassed spirit of sacrifice and devotion. The Freemasons copied Ismaili lodges and initiation.

From Salamiyya in Syria, where they settled, Ismaili Imams sent their *dais* (clerics) and missionaries to spread propaganda in distant lands. They became known as Fatimids, after the Prophet's daughter Fatima. Without revealing themselves as Imams, Ismail's successors secretly organized rebellions and struck at the Abbasids wherever they could. These were the times of Harun al-Raschid, the Abbasid Caliph of the Arabian Nights, but romance and glamor took second place to bloody wars. The Abbasids harassed Jews, Christians, and Shias alike and razed Huseyn's mausoleum at Kerbela to the ground, but the Ismaili flame continued to burn and Fatimid propaganda made tremendous headway in North Africa. When Ubaydullah, eleventh Imam of the Ismailis, followed his missionaries there, he was received as the long-awaited Mahdi, adopted the name of Mahdi Mohammed, and was proclaimed Caliph at Qayrawan in Tunisia. The descendants of Ali and Fatima, the forebears of the Aga Khan, were out of the shadows and in power, entering the most glorious period in their history.

The enemies of the Ismailis were not inactive, and to undermine the Caliph's authority they spread rumors. It was suggested that Ubaydullah was descended from a Jew and was not the real Imam at all, but responsible historians acknowledge him as the founder of the Fatimid empire, biggest of all Islamic kingdoms, which eventually included Morocco, Algeria, the whole of northern Africa, and the greater part of Somaliland. It stretched to

Asia Minor, Mesopotamia, and Sind in India. Fatimids ruled Sicily and Calabria and gained a foothold in Sardinia, to which the young Aga Khan has recently returned as head of a tourist consortium.

Mahdi Mohammed's successors had their eyes on Egypt and built a formidable fleet. In 969 the Fatimid Caliph and Imam Moizz sent the commander of his forces, General Ghazi Jawarhar al-Siquilli (the Sicilian), to launch an attack on Egypt by land and by sea. Alexandria surrendered quickly, but Fustat, the capital, refused to yield, and the Caliph instructed his General to build a new capital. Jawarhar ordered a square of 1,200 yards to be pegged off with ropes to which bells were attached, and kept men with spades in readiness to begin work as soon as the signs were favorable. A raven settling on one of the ropes set the bells ringing, which was the signal to begin, and work on the city was started just when Mars (Al-Kahir) was in the ascendant. The city that rose was named Al-Kahira, city of Mars, which later became Cairo.

Caliph Moizz, one of the Aga Khan's most imposing ancestors, entered his new capital in state and took up residence in a palace that accommodated all members of his family and his slaves, eunuchs, and servants, numbering over twenty thousand. Moizz studied the world with the help of a map made of solid gold. One of his daughters was said to own twelve thousand dresses, and another five sacks of emeralds, vast quantities of other precious stones, and many works of art. But amid all this splendor he ruled justly and introduced reforms such as a system of land administration that curbed the powers and profits of the collectors. His right-hand man, Yakub ben Killis, a Jewish convert to the Ismaili faith, survived him and founded the University of Al-Azhar, which is still the greatest seat of Islamic learning. Al-Azhar, meaning "the luminous," is the masculine version of the name by which Fatima was known.

Controversy blurs the history of Moizz's successors. There were many disputes and schisms, but Cairo with its university continued to be a center of civilization throughout the Dark Ages in Europe.

At this time lived Hasan-i-Sabbah, one of the most fascinating figures of the epoch. Son of a Twelver Shi'ite from Kufa, Hasan was born around 1050, brought up at Rayy (Teheran), and became a convert to Ismailism. Approximately when William the Conqueror was fighting the Battle of Hastings, Hasan swore allegiance to the Imam of the Ismailis and decided to go to Cairo to discover the Koran's innermost meaning at the fountain-head of Ismaili knowledge.

One of his fellow students was Omar Khayyám, who fell out with him and produced a malicious account of his life and activities, which Edward FitzGerald quotes in the preface of his translation of the *Rubáiyát*. Hasan was supposed to have become "the head of the Persian sect of Ismailians, a party of fanatics who had long murmured in obscurity but rose to an evil eminence under the guidance of his strong and evil will." They seized the castle of Alamut in the province of Rudbar south of the Caspian Sea. Known to the Crusaders as the Old Man of the Mountain, Hasan was said to have spread terror through the Moham-medan world and left behind the word "assassin" as his dark memorial—it is supposed to be derived either from *hashish* (opiate of hemp leaf, the Indian *bhang*), with which his fol-lowers maddened themselves to a sullen pitch of oriental des-peration, or from Hasan's name.

No Ismaili accepts this story. Hasan-i-Sabbah was neither the head of the Ismailis nor an Imam. After completing his studies, he went out to spread a version of Fatimid philosophy in Persia and Syria, recruiting many followers. He finally chose the moun-taintop fortress of Alamut ("Eagle's Nest") as a base, and in the thirty-five years that remained of his life he never set foot out-side it. Much of his time was devoted to study in his library, a treasure house of contemporary knowledge. He was not only one of the most erudite men of his time, but also a forceful guardian of Ismaili security and a stern upholder of the religious laws. Sunni caliphs and Seljuk sultans tried to break his hold in a protracted struggle in which so many of his men were imprisoned and executed, mutilated and massacred, that towers were built of Ismaili skulls. The Grand Master of Alamut retaliated no less ferociously, earning a reputation for severity and stealth that descended to his successors and rubbed off on all Ismailis. Because he could not match his enemies in numbers, Hasan did employ the dagger against the sword, relying on a small force of self-sacrificing, death-defying *fida'is* (devotees). Although Muslims were not permitted to take alcohol, his enemies said that Hasan recruited his devotees with the help of intoxicating liquor and drugs. He is supposed to have promised them that if they lost their lives in his service, the pleasures of paradise would be theirs forever. They became known as *hashish-iyyum*, hashish-takers, or Assassins, and the evil association still clings to Ismailis.

Assassination developed into a highly effective instrument of guerrilla war, and the harvest of lives Hasan's men gathered was rich in quality and quantity. His successors continued the practice. It was into this siege atmosphere of fanatical Ismaili devotees that the new Imam Hadi was said to have been taken. Records are confused, and it is uncertain whether Hadi, whom Ismailis regard as Imam Nizar's successor, was his son or his grandson.

Controversy over this incident has never quite died down. According to one theory, the direct line of succession from the Prophet and Hazrat Ali was broken at this stage, and Hasan i-Sabbah became the new Imam of the Ismailis, which would make the current Aga Khan his descendant.

Hasan, when he died at the age of ninety, left no natural heir and was succeeded by Buzurg, one of his military commanders. Eventually his heir, Mohammed, became the Grand Master of Alamut, while Hadi, Nizar's successor as Ismaili Imam, was succeeded by his son, who in turn handed down the Imamate to his son, Hasan Zakaresalam, who became Imam number twenty-three and the central figure in a new argument about the Aga Khan's genealogy.

Professor Bernard Lewis quotes this Hasan as saying that he

was outwardly known as the grandson of Buzurg, but in esoteric reality he was the Imam, the son of the previous Imam of the line of Nizar. "It is possible," says Professor Lewis, "that, as some have argued, Hasan was not claiming physical descent from Nizar . . . but a kind of spiritual filiation."

The issue was publicly ventilated in 1866 in the High Court of Bombay in the famous Khoja Case in which the descent of the then Aga Khan was the central issue. In his summing up, the judge, Sir Joseph Arnould, said he would not attempt to clear up the obscurity of an Asiatic pedigree, a task that even Gibbon renounced as hopeless. However, Ismailis have no doubt that the Aga Khan's family tree remained intact.

The line later becomes easier to follow, although allegiances and policies continued to change frequently. Alamut, like Cairo under the Fatimids, became a center of learning and attracted many foreign scholars. But the time was fast approaching when neither dagger nor learning could save the "Eagle's Nest" from disaster. One Imam was poisoned by his chief adviser in 1255 and his son became the last Ismaili Imam to wield territorial as well as spiritual power in his own right. The Mongols under Genghis Khan's grandson Hulegu attacked the Ismaili strongholds, and though the Imam tried to rally all Muslims and come to terms with the enemy, Alamut was occupied by the Mongols who burned the castle and razed the ruins to the ground.

The temporal power of the Ismailis was broken, but sustained by their faith in God's guidance through their Imam, they managed to survive as a religious community. Alamut has been a heap of ruins ever since. "Yet," said the judge in the Khoja Case, "the race of the Ismailis still survives in Persia and the hereditary succession of their unrevealed Imams is traced in unbroken line down to the Aga Khan."

In a fiercely hostile world *taqiya* disguised Ismaili activities and hid the identity of the Imams, although in the sixteenth century the Shia faith became Persia's official religion and persecution of the Ismailis ceased. Without revealing their position as spiritual leaders of the Ismailis, Imams became prominent in Persian affairs. Ismaili records lift a little of the secrecy. Against all odds and even while practicing dissimulation, they continued to proselytize and send out *dais* to spread the faith.

The missionaries' technique was to "accept" the creed of the people they wanted to convert and to master their languages (some of the finest Ismaili poetry was written by missionaries in their adopted tongues) before proceeding to break down rival beliefs and to substitute, step by step, their own credo. Considering the circumstances, they were amazingly successful. Under Imam Shah Islam Shah (1370–1424)—eighteen generations ahead of Karim Aga Khan—the great *dais* Pir Sadruddin went to India, where he converted several Hindu tribes to the Ismaili faith. The new Ismailis called themselves Khojas, or "honorable converts."

In the meantime the Shia faith was gaining ground in Persia, and in the eighteenth century we find the Aga Khan's ancestors once more without disguise or camouflage on the stage of history.

CHAPTER III

Taqiya played havoc with the recorded history of the Ismaili Imams and their followers, and outsiders seldom knew who was who. One of the Aga Khan's ancestors, Imam Nizar Ali Shah (1585–1629), seems to have carried the practice further than most when he joined forces with Nadir, Shah of Persia, who was Turkish by race, a Sunni, and hostile to the "Shia heresy." They fought side by side in many campaigns. By 1730 Ismaili Imams were firmly established as members of the Persian hierarchy. One, Abul Hasan Ali, was Viceroy of Kirman Province and later retired to his huge estates at Mahallat from which he and his descendants took the title "Lords of Mahallat." The Shah of Persia gave his grandson the hand of his daughter in marriage. The house of the Prophet of Islam was thus joined with the Persian dynasty that went on to rule until 1925.

A wealthy, charming, and impressive young man, his handsome face framed in a full black beard, this Imam became his royal father-in-law's favorite but aroused a good deal of jealousy at court. He was known by the pet name of Aga Khan (Great Chief), which he adopted as his hereditary title. But he remained very much the Imam of the Ismailis.

34

For the privilege of setting eyes on him or kissing his hands no sacrifice was too great for loyal followers who traveled thousands of miles by sea and land to his *darkhana*. In 1829 a hundred or more Khojas from India spent £500 a head—a fantastic sum at the time—on the trip, but had the satisfaction of seeing the Imam twelve times in a few weeks while they camped on the grounds of his palace. He conferred titles on deserving Ismailis, and his successors have continued the practice and created a religious hierarchy of *kamarias* (treasurers) and *mukhis* (clerics), *aitmadis* and *wazirs* (in East Africa, *vazir*, count).

Little was then heard of him until the year 1838, when an officer of lowly origin, encouraged by the Shah's Prime Minister, demanded his daughter as wife for his son. It was a preposterous idea and a wounding personal insult. Since the Prime Minister had also refused to pay money owing for the Aga Khan's military services, the Aga Khan decided to avenge the insult and get his money at the same time. According to a contemporary account, he "raised the standard of revolt," proclaimed an independent government at Kirman, and marched his men against the capital.

Before he could get very far, he was captured and taken to Teheran, where he might have languished in prison for life had his wife not sent their young son—the great-grandfather of Karim Aga Khan—to court to recite poems in praise of forgiveness before the Shah, who was so moved that he set the Aga Khan free. But the Prime Minister soon provoked him into another open rebellion and sent another army against him. Narrowly escaping capture for a second time, a rearguard action took the Aga Khan across the border into Afghanistan, which was still at war with Britain.

He offered his services to the British, who accepted and promised to help him regain his Persian possessions. The records speak highly of the heroism and diplomatic skill of the "Persian Prince." A mutiny of native troops—the Aga Khan dealt with the situation. British officers held prisoner—the Aga Khan's men smuggled letters in and out of prison. The city of Herat in danger —the Aga Khan to the rescue. The Mirs suspicious—the Aga Khan established contact with the British.

The British General Sir Charles Napier was fulsome in his praise. "I have sent the Persian Prince Aga Khan to Jarrack, on the right bank of the Indus," he wrote on one occasion. Jarrack was the Aga Khan's first *darkhana* on the subcontinent and the scene of his first encounter with the Baluchis. "His influence is great," Napier continued, "and he will with his own followers secure our communications with Karachi." In a private letter sometime later he explained, "The old Persian Prince is my great crony here, living not under my care but paid by me £2,000 a year. He is a God . . . I speak truly when saying that his followers do not and dare not refuse him any favour . . . he could kill me if he pleased, has only to say the word, and one of his people can do the job in a twinkling and go straight to heaven for the same. He is too shrewd a man for that, however."

The Aga Khan was gratified when his help in the Afghan war was recognized. "As a reward for my services," he wrote, "the General gave me presents. He further assigned to me the territory of Moola Rusheed, yielding an income of forty thousand rupees." When the British attacked Sind, the Aga Khan led his own cavalry regiment in the field by their side. The campaign ended with the conquest of Sind, and the Viceroy, Lord Ellenborough, sent his famous punning Latin telegram to Whitehall: "Peccavi" ("I have sinned [Sind]").

Fighting Britain's battles, however gallantly, did not bring the Aga Khan any closer to recovering his Persian rights and properties. On the contrary, the wheels of history turned, Persia and Britain resolved their quarrel, and the Aga Khan was left in the lurch. The Persians promptly reminded London of an agreement dating back to 1814 that provided for the extradition of Persians hostile to the Persian government, which looked like a ready-made noose for the Aga Khan's neck. London seemed indifferent to the fate of this loyal ally.

For the Aga Khan the problem now was how to escape

extradition. Calcutta was suggested as a safe place of exile, but he protested that he would be alone and without friends and followers. When the British government threatened to stop his pension if he refused to go, he made his way to Bombay, where he arrived in 1845 at the head of an imposing regiment of some eight hundred fiery horsemen. Rumor, which was probably not far wrong, had it that all eight hundred were the Aga Khan's natural sons. Though a refugee in a foreign land, he was received with the homage due to the spiritual head of the strong Khoja community.

His enemies were not happy to see him residing at a port from which he could easily return to Persia and persuaded the British authorities to force him to go to Calcutta. The Superintendent of Mysore Princes was instructed to take him under his care. "Aga Khan Mahallati is a nobleman of high rank and allied to the royal family of Persia. He is in receipt of a British allowance of 3,000 rupees. . . . The President in Council requests that you engage provisionally a suitable house for his use. . . . His position as regards the Persian government makes it inexpedient to show him any marked distinction but . . . he should be treated with the utmost courtesy and consideration."

The Aga Khan spent an unhappy time in Calcutta, but in 1848 Muhammed Ali Shah died, and though even Lord Palmerston's intervention failed to secure his admission to Persia, he was permitted to return to Bombay, which became his main base. With a taste for oriental splendor, he established an imposing residence on Malabar Hill overlooking the sea and installed his family in equally sumptuous and costly houses around him. The affairs of the Khoja community were conducted from Aga Hall, a magnificent palace with separate library and staff quarters, set in fine parkland and enclosed by a high wall. The Aga Khan's Bombay realm occupied an area about half the size of London's Mayfair or roughly the slice of Paris between the Madeleine, the Opéra, and Pont d'Iéna. A similar complex came into being in Poona, where the family spent part of the year, and in Bangalore.

Apart from his three wives, three sons, and three daughters, the Aga Khan also looked after a thousand or more relatives and retainers who had come with him from Persia. He also married Indian wives and produced children by them. These family responsibilities devoured a tremendous amount of money, but although he complained bitterly about the loss of his Persian estates, he was by no means short of funds. As their fathers and fathers' fathers before them, his followers paid *zakat*, which was collected by the *mukhi* and the *kamaria*. A few years later, the amount he received in this way was stated to be approximately £10,000 a year.

The Aga Khan took his religious duties very seriously, visited the *jamatkhana*, the Ismaili religious center, on all holy days and led the community in prayer on the anniversary of Hazrat Huseyn's martyrdom, presiding over the ritual distribution of water mixed with the holy dust of Kerbela. On Saturdays the community came to kiss hands—it was a united community of small traders with some very rich men among them.

They could also be troublesome. About this time one group of Khojas, some three hundred families, refused to pay *zakat*, an outrageous offence among Ismailis, who usually insisted on pressing their contributions on the Imam in the hope of reward in paradise. The recalcitrant Khojas were expelled from the community. They applied for readmission and promised to pay up but defaulted a second time and were again expelled. In the meantime an English court confirmed that the Aga Khan was entitled to *zakat* by precedent and by Muslim law. The conflict caused a lot of bitterness. In the *jamatkhana* of Mahim in 1850 the rival factions clashed and four Khojas died. Nineteen were tried for murder and four of them were sentenced to death and hanged.

Such violent interludes cast a rare shadow over the Imam's illustrious establishment. His family traveled widely and his eldest son, Aga Ali Shah, spent much time in Baghdad and Kerbela trying to make up the old family quarrel with the Persian ruling house. A highly intelligent young man, the Aga Khan's heir diligently prepared himself for his future as Imam. Persian and Arab *mullahs* taught him oriental languages, literature, and metaphysics, and instructed him in the esoteric secrets of the Ismaili faith. He passed on much of his knowledge to the community and pioneered in establishing educational institutions. A commission on which he worked brought the sect's confusing religious laws up to date.

An intrepid horseman and hunter, Aga Ali Shah was a legend in his own lifetime, the only prince in India who pursued tigers on foot. He was such a deadly shot that he bagged at least forty in this unorthodox fashion. When the Prince of Wales, the future Edward VII, came to Aga Hall during his visit to India, he could not hear enough about this sensational hunting technique. Pointing to his considerable embonpoint, Aga Ali Shah confessed that it was difficult for him to climb onto a high platform. The Prince of Wales, who was not much slimmer, readily understood. He admired Aga Ali Shah's hunting trophies and the Aga Khan's many cups won on the Indian turf.

It was in Bombay that the first Aga Khan started the tradition of racing and breeding that made his grandson, the third Aga Khan, a household word everywhere—a tradition carried on by Prince Karim today. The earlier Aga Khan's stables housed the world's finest Arabian blood, and the stud in the valley of Nejd produced superb animals. No expense was too great to improve the bloodstock; leading trainers and jockeys, mostly English, were engaged. Bombay race course was one of the few public places where the Aga Khan showed himself—the stand from which he watched his horses was preserved by Bombay's leading club.

Once more the tranquillity of the community was disturbed by Khojas who claimed to be Sunnis and refused to pay the *zakat*. The community was so widely dispersed that it was difficult to ascertain who acknowledged the Aga Khan as spiritual leader and who did not, who was paying *zakat* and who was not. In predominantly Sunni areas Ismailis still practiced *taqiya* and it was well-nigh impossible to tell Sunni from Shia. To clear the air the Aga Khan ordered his followers everywhere to reveal themselves openly as Shia Imami Ismailis. Officially this was the end of *taqiya*. He sent open lists to all communities and asked members to sign their names "so that I may know them."

The overwhelming majority signed and declared unswerving support for the Imam, but the so-called Khoja Reform Party challenged the Aga Khan's claim to religious leadership and took their case to court. In February, 1866, Sir Joseph Arnould, an English judge sitting in the High Court in Bombay, began to hear the *cause célèbre* that became known as the Khoja Case. High principles and big amounts were at stake. The Aga Khan's religious empire was on trial. If he did not cherish washing the community's dirty linen in public, he welcomed the opportunity to put an end to the whispers that caused dissent.

The Khojas asked the court to order the chief defendant, Mohammed Huseyn Husseini, otherwise called Aga Khan, and his two principal fellow defendants (chief *mukhi* and chief *kamaria*) to hand over the property of the Khoja community and vacate their offices. They wanted the Aga Khan to be restrained from interfering in the management of the community and also hoped for a declaration that he was not entitled to excommunicate them. Their argument was that they were Sunnis and thus rejected the Aga Khan's right to *zakat*. Many side issues were raised and many historical and religious assumptions paraded.

The proceedings lasted twenty-five days, after which the judge settled down to study the mountain of evidence and seek enlightenment in history—in the history of the Aga Khan and the Khojas. When giving his verdict in November, 1866, he started out by saying that the crucial points in the case were the Khojas' spiritual and temporal relations with the ancestors of the Aga Khan and the Aga Khan's claim that they had, in the long line of hereditary descent, successively been the spiritual chiefs of the Shia Imami Ismailis. The cardinal question was whether the Khojas in their origin as a separate religious community were Sunnis or non-Sunnis, that is Shia Imami Ismailis.

The verdict unequivocally confirmed the Aga Khan as the spiritual head of the Khoja community. Sir Joseph Arnould took the view that their ancestors had been converted to the Ismaili faith, had throughout abided by it, had always been and still were bound by ties of spiritual allegiance to the hereditary Imam of the Ismailis. "Mohammed Huseyn Husseini," the judge said, "otherwise Aga Khan, or, as he is more formally styled in official documents, His Highness Aga Khan Mahallati, is the hereditary chief and unrevealed Imam of the Ismailis, the present or living holder of the Imamate, claiming descent in direct line from Ali, the Vicar of God, through the seventh and (according to the Ismaili creed) the last of the Revealed Imams, Ismail, the son of Jafar Sadiq." He was fully entitled to the customary dues and "rightfully wielded his formidable powers of mediating sentences of excommunication." The Ismaili version of the Aga Khan's family history received the court's seal of authenticity, but descendants of the Khoja rebels of 1866 have on several occasions, albeit unsuccessfully, tried to revive the old feud and to reverse the Bombay verdict.

The old Aga Khan, well into his seventies, delegated many functions to his son Aga Ali Shah, whose third marriage was an exceptionally happy one. Lady Ali Shah was a well-rounded woman with soft good looks and luminous dark eyes hidden behind her *yashmak*. For an oriental princess she was open-minded, practical, shrewd, and interested in public affairs. The couple started their married life in a hilltop palace in Karachi bought from the Maharajah of Kolhapur and renamed Honeymoon Lodge. They had two sons in quick succession, both of whom died in infancy. On November 2, 1877, at Honeymoon Lodge, Lady Ali Shah gave birth to a third baby, a delicate but lively boy who was named Sultan Mohammed. Karachi took the baby to its heart; his birthplace became known as Sultan Tekri (Sultan Hill) or Tekri for short.

Prince Sultan Mohammed was still a small boy when his father first took him on visits to Ismaili communities and to *jamatkhanas* for prayers and religious ceremonies. One of his earliest memories was of his grandfather, "an old man, almost blind, seated on a grey horse, peering to watch a line of other horses galloping in training."

Supported by servants, the baby Prince was on a pony by the old man's side. For his grandfather, the fine old Persian aristocrat, it was almost the end of the road. His Highness Prince Hasan Shah Mahallati, Aga Khan I, died in April, 1881, and was survived by three sons: Aga Ali Shah, Aga Jangi Shah, and Aga Akber Shah. After an impressive funeral, he was laid to rest in Hassanabad, a mausoleum on the grounds of his palace. The Shah of Persia sent a warm message of condolence, and following an old Persian tradition, gave the new Imam, Aga Ali Shah, Aga Khan II, a precious robe and the emblem of the Persian crown studded with diamonds, which has been handed down to Karim Aga Khan as a treasured family heirloom.

The health of little Prince Sultan Mohammed was at first so precarious that doctors feared he might not live. He was fussed over by his mother and her servants, and the thought that he would one day inherit the Imamate was never far from the minds of the people around him. The day came sooner than expected. Aga Ali Shah had been Imam for only four years when he caught a chill hunting and developed pneumonia. He died in Poona in August, 1885, and his body was embalmed and taken to Kufa, the Shias' holy place, where he was buried in the same spot as his saintly ancestor Hazrat Ali, the first Imam.

To the boy of eight who now became the forty-eighth Imam and Aga Khan III—*the* Aga Khan—the death of his father was "the first big emotional and spiritual crisis of my life." A historic photograph shows him at his installation on the Gadi of Imams, a divanlike throne, surrounded by the bearded, turbaned Ismaili nobles. In his smart *sherwani* and Astrakhan hat he looked solemn but completely self-assured among the figures of a passing age. Like other Imams before him, he mourned the end of a carefree childhood. As so often in earlier Ismaili history, but even now in a more enlightened period, a little boy was suddenly credited with mystical powers and unusual wisdom and became the subject of deep veneration.

His early contacts with the English in India served as useful checks and balances. Lady Dufferin, the Viceroy's wife, took an interest in him, and Lord Reay, Governor of Bombay, and his wife asked him to tea. An English tutor, Mr. Kenny, stimulated his interest in "Eng. Lit." (Shakespeare, Milton, Macaulay, Scott), and other mentors, religious instructors, and governesses belabored him with French, Arabic, Urdu, Gujerati, Persian literature (Hafiz and Omar Khayyám became his favorites), history, and the philosophy of the faith of which he was now the supreme arbiter. He was constantly exhorted to think good thoughts, do good deeds, speak good words—and he tried hard to oblige.

Although acutely nearsighted, he was forced to practice calligraphy in a cruel daily discipline that was plain torture and would have broken a less indomitable spirit ("I cannot understand that I did not die"). Before he was much older, theology, science, mathematics, astronomy, chemistry, and mechanics were added to his curriculum, laying the foundations of his encyclopedic knowledge, which he constantly improved by asking questions of everybody about everything.

Sport was not his strong suit. Unlike other Indian princes, he never took up cricket, but liked hockey and eventually introduced the sport to India. In later years he went fox or jackal hunting in a desultory way. Spectator sports like horse racing were more to his taste. When his mother got rid of her late husband's hawks and hounds, he was not particularly concerned, but the family's racing establishment, though reduced from eighty to thirty horses, was still good enough for his colors—red and green, the colors of the Ismaili flag—to show up well on the Indian turf. He was, of course, very rich, but the British government made him an allowance of a thousand rupees a year, and when he was nine years old, Queen Victoria conferred on him the title "Highness"

as, some seventy years later, Queen Elizabeth II honored his
grandson Karim (who, however, did not receive the pension).

The Aga Khan's early life was dominated by the remarkable
Lady Ali Shah, who frequently ordered that his bottom be
spanked. "My mother," he said, "is the only woman of whom I
have ever been afraid." She made the oriental attitude toward
women look rather foolish, and it was with her in mind that he
campaigned for the emancipation of Indian women. Social ad-
vancement and happiness, he came to think, were greatest
where women were least constrained by artificial barriers and
narrow prejudices. He ordered Ismaili women to do away with
the veil and come out of *purdah*, "the imprisonment of half the
nation." Orthodox Muslims reproached him, but he was simply
ahead of his time.

In the manner of Indian princes, the family moved with the
seasons from Bombay to Poona to Mahabaleshwar and back to
Bombay. Lady Ali Shah managed the boy's fortune and made
excellent investments. She bought properties in Ismaili centers
in India and Africa at favorable prices, which later enabled the
Aga Khan to stay at his own palaces whenever he visited his
communities. Although he was under no legal obligation to support them, his relatives not only lived in houses he owned, but
also received allowances from him that were taken so much for
granted that an angry family wrangle in the courts came about as
a result. People living on his estates were fed at his expense, a
practice dating back to the first Aga Khan.

At the age of sixteen the Imam took charge of his own affairs,
but Mother continued to keep an eye on his extensive properties
and to look after the community. The management of his racing
establishment he shared with Aga Shamsuddin, his cousin and
closest friend, and some of their horses did extremely well,
winning the Nizam's Gold Cup, the most important race in
western India, four times in succession. In spite of his youth,
western India's Muslims chose him to present their address on the
occasion of Queen Victoria's Diamond Jubilee. At the same time

he handed over his own and the community's homage in a solid gold casket in the shape of an elephant. His address assured the Queen that he was as loyal to the English throne as his grandfather who had fought on the battlefields of Afghanistan and Sind.

The young Imam had his own battles to fight. While on a pilgrimage to Jeddah, Uncle Aga Jangi Shah and his son were murdered and word was put out that the culprits were *fida'is*, as fanatically devoted to the Aga Khan as those of Alamut had been to the Old Man of the Mountain. Lady Ali Shah was said to be at the head of Moto Punth, a secret Ismaili society not unlike Hasan-i-Sabbah's Assassins. Aga Jangi Shah's murderers were arrested, but when they were found poisoned in their cells before they could be brought to trial, it was announced that they had committed suicide. Speculation was rife. Some said they had been murdered on the Aga Khan's orders so they could not incriminate him.

The Aga Khan's health suffered as a result of the tragedy, but as soon as he was fit to travel, he went on a tour of Muslim centers in the course of which he visited the Anglo-Muslim College of Aligarh and was deeply impressed by its founder, Sir Sayed Ahmed Khan, and the students, who shared his deep sense of Muslim tradition and destiny. How wonderful if Aligarh could become a full university for training a generation of young leaders and advancing the cause of Islam. Here was a chance to follow in the footsteps of his ancestor who had founded Al-Azhar, the first Muslim university. The idea greatly appealed to the young Aga Khan. He decided to put up money for the cause and persuaded wealthy friends to contribute. It was a long struggle, but he missed no opportunity to plead for this cause, and when Aligarh finally became a university two dozen years later, it was more to Muslims than a seat of learning. In retrospect, it was recognized as the intellectual cradle of independent Pakistan, and the Aga Khan's enthusiasm and support, which had made it possible, earned him a place among Pakistan's founding fathers.

When he returned to Bombay, he found a bride. Gallantly, the Aga Khan always insisted that he had been deeply in love with his cousin Shahzadi, daughter of the murdered Aga Jangi Shah and sister of Aga Shamsuddin. But in spite of his protestations, it looked suspiciously as if Lady Ali Shah had arranged her son's marriage so as to silence the rumor that either she or he was responsible for the death of the bride's father. As Aga Shamsuddin was also taking a wife, a spectacular double marriage was arranged.

The nuptials were celebrated with customary ritual and extravagant hospitality. Surrounded by friends and relatives and dressed in precious robes, the two bridegrooms and their brides sat side by side on a platform on the grounds of the palace. Thousands of guests looked on as the *mukhi* chanted his prayers, and the religious formalities completed, an unending line of Indian princes, British dignitaries, and Ismaili delegations offered congratulations. For sixteen days running, guests were treated to delicacies and (nonalcoholic) drinks, and in the atmosphere of a joyous elite fairground, entertained with music, swordsmen's dances, and performances by acrobats and tumblers. The cost of the double wedding was more than £50,000—in those days a gigantic sum.

But life in Bombay was not all glitter and gold. When violent rioting broke out, the Aga Khan ordered his followers not to join in attacks on Hindus and even offered Hindus refuge on his estate. When India was hit by famine and thousands of his followers became destitute, he supplied them with seeds, cattle, and tools, enabling many to start a new life. They camped at Hassanabad and were fed from his kitchens. From his own pocket he put up half a million rupees to build Yarovda Palace in Poona for no other purpose than to provide employment for his followers.

After the famine came the bubonic plague. Khojas living in the affected parts of Bombay refused to be inoculated. To break down their prejudice, the Aga Khan gave his bungalow to the medical authorities as a laboratory and allowed himself to be inoculated not once but several times to set an example. (Similarly, he took a sympathetic interest in the Untouchables, many of whom were converted to the Ismaili faith, educated at his expense, and given employment—long before Mahatma Gandhi took up their cause.)

The young Ismaili leader had little time to attend to his own problems. Although he was reluctant to admit it to himself, his marriage was not a success. The wedding bells—and the Reform Party's campaign—had hardly died down when he exchanged his oriental silk robes for a well-cut lounge suit and went on a visit to Europe without Shahzadi. The change of clothes and the change of climate were meaningful. His first trip overseas turned out to be more than a voyage of discovery. It was a giant stride from the nineteenth toward the twentieth century, from the battlefields of the East to the parquet floors of the West, a plunge into another world which he would soon make his own.

Accompanied by a retinue of servants, he sailed from Bombay to Marseilles. The Côte d'Azur was the destination of this very presentable, round-faced young man with a dark, drooping mustache and nearsighted eyes that deceptively disguised a quick mind. Not very tall and with an early hint of corpulence, he did not look too prepossessing but already had a quality best described as "personality." In these strange surroundings he seemed at first shy and reticent, but the tails and frock coat, patent leather shoes and spats, sashes and decorations in his luggage suggested the social landscape for which he was heading.

In the high season of 1898 the man who later came to own some of the Riviera's finest villas found it difficult to get a place to stay. Queen Victoria was at Cimiez, Austria's Emperor Franz Josef at Cap Martin. There were so many Balkan kings, Russian grand dukes, and German princes about, the newcomer was "dazzled and awed." But people were not unmindful of his status in his own world. Apartments were found for him at Queen

Victoria's hotel and he was thrilled to watch her come and go and noticed the Indian servants in attendance.

From the Riviera he went to Paris, where he saw Sarah Bernhardt at the Comédie Française, visited the Opéra, and lunched at the Jockey Club. He was incognito, and discretion governed the mundane pleasures of a young man on his first visit to Paris. But when he moved on to London it was as "His Highness, the Aga Khan." The Duke of Connaught welcomed him on behalf of the Queen and presented an invitation to meet her and spend the night at Windsor Castle. At the dinner in his honor he was seated on the Queen's right and noticed that she had the German habit of frequently inserting "so" (pronounced "tzo") in her conversation. He thought her Indian servants inferior to his own. The Prince of Wales nominated him for the Marlborough Club (fifty years later, he was fond of saying that he and the hall porter were the club's oldest inhabitants).

His successes as an owner and breeder of race horses in India were, of course, well known. Queen Victoria gave him a Royal Household badge for the enclosure at Ascot race course, and all her successors bestowed the same privilege on him as "a friend of the family." When he went to register his colors, he found that this had already been done as a courtesy by one of his English racing friends. The colors turned out to be not green and red (the Fatimid colors), which were not available, but green and chocolate instead. They became so successful that he never changed them at Ascot, although elsewhere his horses raced under green and red colors, which his son adopted when they became free.

The lure of racing was strong, and the Aga Khan attended the exciting Derby that was won by the 100-to-1 outsider Jeddah; he was a winner but had managed to get only 66 to 1. He told the Duke of Connaught that he hoped to win the Derby one day but could not have expected in his wildest dreams that he would win the world's greatest classic race five times. The London season over, he visited Paris, Geneva, Lausanne,

Florence, and Vienna. It would have been a perfect summer had there not been news from India with an ominously familiar ring —Hashim Shah, a cousin, had been killed by a steward in his own house in Poona. The murder was prompted by a personal grudge and had no religious significance.

Lawlessness and violence in his own back yard would have to be dealt with firmly, he decided, as he traveled back to India and Malabar Hill—but not to his wife. Only the splendid oriental isolation in which they lived disguised the failure of his marriage. Though living under the same roof and maintaining appearances, he and Begum Shahzadi drifted apart, she—according to him—"to a private purgatory of resentment and reproach," he to the social round and his duties as a religious leader. He played a little golf and went racing. The English in India liked him; East and West met in perfect harmony. His working day at his main office at Aga Hall was occupied with the affairs of the Khoja community.

The feudal establishment he had inherited was becoming quite insupportable. The number of descendants of his grandfather's horsemen and of Ismaili pilgrims who had stayed as retainers had vastly increased and included whole families from Central Asia, Turkistan, Sinkiang, Bokhara, Afghanistan, and Africa. The bigger they grew, the smaller were their allowances from the Aga Khan, whose money had to be split so many ways that each received only a pittance. Some of them made a little money on the side as hawkers, racing tipsters, and odd-job men, but the majority just idled. They were well fed (by the Aga Khan) but unruly and mischievous, and though he was anxious to get rid of them, once let loose on Bombay as vagrants, they were liable to become a public danger.

It took many months to liquidate this embarrassing heritage of a turbulent phase in Ismaili history. In the end the Aga Khan paid lump sums to some and sent them packing. Others were helped to start new careers away from Bombay, and some who were not Indian citizens were deported. He provided funds to set up

schools for children who stayed behind and many of them went
on to universities and became lawyers, doctors, and civil servants.
The purge did not completely deprive the Aga Khan of servants. When it was over, he still employed about a thousand at
his various residences.

His next trip was to Africa, where Indians worked and traded
much as the Irish in England and the United States. Many were
Hindus—Gandhi was practicing law in South Africa in the 1890s
—but thousands who had settled in East Africa were Muslims
and Ismailis, many of them rich and prominent in public life and
politics. Without help from Indians, explorers could not have
mounted some of their expeditions—Tharia Topan, who became
the leader of Ismailis in East Africa, saved the life of the famous
H. M. Stanley who, in November, 1871, found Dr. David Livingstone ("Dr. Livingstone, I presume?") at Ujiji, Lake Tanganyika.
"One of the honestest among men, white or black, red or yellow,"
Stanley wrote, "is a Mohammedan Hindi called Topan. . . . Among
the Europeans at Zanzibar he has become a proverb for honesty
and strict business integrity. He is enormously wealthy, owns
several ships and dhows, and is a prominent man in the councils
of the Ruler of Zanzibar." Zanzibar was the Ismaili headquarters
in Africa.

Sir Tharia—he was knighted by Queen Victoria—received the
young Aga Khan on his arrival and introduced him to the community. (Sir Tharia, incidentally, was typical of the cross-
fertilization of Ismaili talent between India and Africa. When
Pakistan became independent in 1947, descendants of many
East African Indians returned to the subcontinent, and Sir
Tharia's great-grandson, Dr. Habib Patel, a leading member of
Pakistan's medical profession, now heads the extensive Ismaili
health organization in Karachi.) For Ismailis, it was a tremendous
occasion. Because they had not yet built their big *jamatkhanas*,
in most of their homes one room, or at least a corner, was set
aside for worship. Now their veneration concentrated on the
supreme pontiff to whom they looked for guidance.

"I was staying in Bagamoyo in August of 1899," wrote Otto

Mahnke, a former German colonial official, "when His Highness the Aga Khan set foot on the African continent for the first time. His Highness arrived in his own yacht which was anchored about four miles from the shore. Thousands of Indians, natives and also Europeans were waiting on the beach to see His Highness and welcome him. . . . The enthusiasm and the veneration for His Highness on his arrival as well as during his whole stay was tremendous. . . . Europeans, too, received him with great honour and an Indian from Zanzibar sent a cab with a white horse so that His Highness might move about with great speed. Ovations of the highest veneration took place everywhere but as soon as His Highness gave an almost imperceptible sign to say a few words absolute silence reigned."

Followers crowded around him to catch his *didar* (glance), feel the touch of his hand, get his blessing, and listen to his every word. They told him their personal and business problems and firmly believed that a wave of his hand could make their difficulties disappear. The Ismailis in Zanzibar were then involved in an angry dispute over valuable real estate which the natives claimed. The Aga Khan ordered his people to compromise—all his life he believed in compromise. At Dar-es-Salaam there was ill feeling between Ismailis and Germans who suspected them of hostile activities. The young Aga Khan managed to smooth out the differences, but his first official contact with the Germans did not endear them to him and prejudiced him for decades to come. Non-Ismaili Indians were impressed and he made his first converts then, whose descendants became Prince Karim's most loyal followers.

On his first visit to Cairo he was struck by the all-pervading presence of the English, who were as powerful as his Fatimid ancestors of yore. The city seemed like another Poona or Simla, and Egypt as much a citadel of British supremacy as India. British colonial snobbery was such that Egyptians were barred from the Gezira Club and similar social centers. A more leisurely precursor of the jet set of which his grandson was a prominent member two generations later, the Aga Khan returned to Bombay,

but a week later was already on his way to Burma to visit his
followers there. Soon he was back in Europe once more.

In Paris he spent some time with his kinsman, Persia's Shah
Muzaffir ud-Din, but there was little love lost between them.
The Aga Khan was shocked by the Shah's behavior: "Grossly
ignorant, capricious, extravagant," he called him. The Shah took
fright when M. and Mme. Curie showed him a glowing
piece of radium in a dark cellar. "He began to scream and shout
and run about the room," the Aga Khan recalled. "He raved and
ranted and accused the Curies of trying to murder him."

In Berlin the Kaiser gripped the young Indian leader's hand
firmly with his powerful right, which compensated for a withered
left arm. The Aga Khan's next stop was Turkey, where he was received by Sultan Abdul Hamid the Terrible. An amicable discussion between a Sunni and a Shia was an unusual ecumenical
occasion. To see the Sultan heavily made up, lips rouged, beard
died black, surprised the visitor, who knew Hamid to be a virile
man and father of many children. He also knew of Abdul Hamid's pathological fear of assassination, which accounted for the
heavy armor under his enormous greatcoat. This "Terrible Turk"
smoked incessantly, which did not endear him to the nonsmoking
Aga. The meeting was not a success—the Aga Khan later blamed
the Sultan's "disastrous reign" for Turkey's joining the wrong side
in World War I.

Czar Nicholas of Russia and the Emperor of Japan were the
next additions to his growing collection of crowned heads. But
in the following year he lost the dearest of them, Queen Victoria,
who had launched him on his progress through the corridors of
royal power. Yet though the Queen was dead, long live the King!
In spite of the big difference in their ages, King Edward VII and
the Aga Khan were very much birds of a feather, with similar
interests and many mutual friends. Mayfair gossip obscured
the Aga Khan's real interests. The Aga Khan and a beautiful
woman was news, the Aga Khan at the races a social event, and
the Aga Khan at a party a rewarding experience. But his quest-

ing mind was largely stimulated by artists, lawyers, surgeons, and politicians—mainly politicians. His friendships with kings and statesmen gave him a healthy appetite for politics. Unlike his ancestors, he had no territorial power, but he had a vested interest in India, in an India where Muslim and Hindu could live in communal peace. Although the trend was against him, he worked hard to ward off the gathering storm.

The Viceroy, Lord Curzon, offered him a seat on the Legislative Council in Bombay, which gave him the opportunity he had been looking for. By far the youngest member, he quickly made friends with two outstanding colleagues, Lord Kitchener (whom he helped with his recruiting campaign) and G. K. Gokhale, the biggest political figure among pre-Gandhi Hindus. With Muslim-Hindu relations under constant discussion, the Aga Khan, an ardent advocate of Muslim rights, was scathing about the Indian Congress Party, which he thought to be blind to Muslim claims. For him the basic issue was education, education, education. Education, he told all who would listen, was the key to a rewarding life; illiteracy, the root cause of poverty and disease. If he could not carry all Muslims with him, among Ismailis his word was law. He made education the main plank of Ismaili development and it became the pillar of Ismaili success.

In England the following summer the King consulted him about the Prince of Wales' forthcoming Indian tour. On this visit he went to see the aged and ailing Florence Nightingale and was annoyed when Lytton Strachey's account of their conversation made it look as if they had talked at cross purposes—he about God and Florence Nightingale about sanitation. Strachey quoted Miss Nightingale as saying of the Aga Khan, "A most interesting man but you could never teach him sanitation." Actually the Aga Khan had asked her serious questions about the human condition, and they had discussed the topic, he said, "with the gravity with which I had expounded it."

Around that time he first met "Whimsical Walker"—Colonel

Hall Walker (later Lord Wavertree)—owner of a big stud in Ireland, on whose help and advice on racing he came to rely. Their meeting foreshadowed the time, still some fifteen years distant, when the Aga Khan came to dominate the English turf. One of the first Aga Khan anecdotes that began to circulate (some were true, some invented; all reflected his wit and humanity) was about a man who asked how someone regarded by his followers as God could spend so much time at the races. "And why should not God go racing?" was the Aga Khan's retort. He was seen drinking wine and was asked whether this was not a sin for a Muslim and was credited with the classic answer, "I am so holy that when I touch wine it turns to water."

By this time the Côte d'Azur was home away from home for him. His interest in pretty women was apparent and he was seen enjoying life to the full. But his mind was on more weighty matters. Africa, and his duties as a religious leader, claimed much of his time.

CHAPTER IV

"WHEREAS *the Holy Prophet (May Peace be upon Him) is the last Prophet of Allah,*

"AND WHEREAS *Hazrat Mowlana Ali (May Peace be upon Him) is the first Imam of the Shia Imami Ismailis,*

"AND WHEREAS *Hazrat Mowlana Shah Karim Al-Husseini Hazar Imam is the forty-ninth Imam in whom is vested absolute and unfettered Power and Authority over and and in respect of all religious and social matters of the Shia Imami Ismailis, . . . His Highness Hazrat Mowlana Shah Karim Al-Husseini Aga Khan is graciously pleased to ordain . . .*

"*Mowlana Hazar Imam has absolute and final authority and discretion to abrogate, suspend, rescind, amend, delete, alter, add to, vary or modify the Constitution.*"

—*The Constitution of the Shia Imami Ismailis in Africa* and *The Constitution of the Councils and Jamats of Shia Imami Ismaili Muslims of Pakistan,* 1962

CONDITIONS IN INDIA had deteriorated and the Aga Khan worked out a plan to settle large numbers of Indians in Africa. He put it to the Viceroy's Council and it was still being considered when, in 1905, he decided to pay his second visit to East Africa. He was twenty-eight, well informed on political and social conditions in the West, and anxious to bring the benefits of Western civilization to his people.

In Zanzibar he found his followers' state of health left much
to be desired. Although they were well off, he was shocked by
their poor physique and by the high incidence of tuberculosis
among them. Many were listless and apathetic, but when they
blamed the climate, he called the community leaders together
and told them that the climate was no different in India and yet
his Khojas were certainly not apathetic. He converted one of his
palaces into a sports center, offered prizes for athletics, football,
and cycling competitions, and laid down a program for systematic
health care.

He had even bigger plans. What his followers needed was a set
of firm rules to embrace their whole life, an administrative and
religious framework. He decided to give the Ismaili community
a written constitution. With the authority of his office, he told
local leaders what he had in mind, and in a series of consultations
with them he laid the groundwork of the Worldwide Ismaili
Organization of Territorial, Provincial, and Local Councils, the
leaders to be chosen by the Imam from panels of local candidates.
He instituted a "Pledge of Office" by which officials would swear,
in the name of Allah, to discharge their duties without fear,
favor, affection, or ill will, to bear allegiance to Mowlana Hazar
Imam and the Ismaili faith, not to disclose matters discussed *in
camera,* and to preserve, protect, and defend the Constitution.

The rights and duties of *mukhis* and *kamarias* were clearly
defined, and organization was brought into social and cultural
activities. Health and education, the twin pillars of Ismaili
strength, and economic welfare were regulated. One set of rules
was devoted to *jamatkhanas,* where Ismailis meet not only for
prayers but also for group activities, children's exercise, and religious instruction (*jamat* means "community"). A cornerstone of
the Constitution was a personal law to govern the lives of Ismailis
from cradle to grave. Antiquated Muslim practices were discarded, contamination with tribal customs shunned. Polygamy
was out, as were child marriages. Engagements would be registered and could not be lightly broken off. Divorces were a

matter for the *mukhi*, perhaps even the Council; among grounds for divorce were a partner's renunciation of the Ismaili faith, a husband's impotence, or a disease that made married life dangerous for the other partner. Disputes about dowries and alimonies were to be submitted for decision to the *mukhi* and *kamaria*.

The Constitution eventually laid down the details of engagement and wedding ceremonies: Avoid ostentation, limit the number of guests (to two hundred in Africa), no extravagant wedding gowns, no alcoholic drinks. As for children, strict rules on legitimacy, guardianship, and adoption were laid down. At the other end of the line were the rules for burials. The Imam's judicial powers were not limited except by his sense of duty and fairness, but Councils were given wide authority to admonish or punish offenders. The severest punishment was and is excommunication, which completely divorces the offender from his fellow Ismailis and can be ruinous. (Paragraph 220 of the African Constitution says, "No Ismaili other than the immediate family members of a person who has been 'excommunicated' shall have any social or other association with him.") Apostates were regarded as enemies and no Ismaili was to marry a defector from the faith.

The first Ismaili Constitution was issued in Zanzibar on September 9, 1905, but was not published in printed form until 1922, when it appeared in English and Gujerati (more recently it has also been translated into German). Although it has since been revised several times, the basic laws remain the same as those first laid down by Aga Khan III. Designed for a society that was still largely primitive, the original 1905 draft was a splendid testimonial to his scholarly and modern mind. He issued a holy *firman* ordering Ismailis to abide by it and instructed local leaders to send him regular reports about every aspect of their community's life. The practice is still followed and his young successor is often snowed under with communications from Ismailis all over the world.

Back in Bombay the Aga Khan found India's Muslims in need

of political attention. Lord Minto, the new Viceroy, and John
Morley, Secretary of State for India in Campbell-Bannerman's
Liberal government, were working on a reform of the Indian
administration and Muslims were concerned about their place in
the new scheme. The Aga Khan no longer saw them as merely a
religious community; they were developing into a national entity
with the right to be represented by their own leaders. Chosen to
lead a Muslim delegation, he put the Muslim case to the
Viceroy and obtained a promise that their rights and interests
would be safeguarded. This established the principle of "separate
electorates" for Muslims and Hindus and was the first step
toward an independent Muslim state.

Only a strong central Muslim organization could maintain the
impetus. The Aga Khan and his friends founded the Muslim
League and turned it into a political force. He became the first
President and pressed the Muslim case wherever he could until
Morley warned him, "You mustn't get too much power, you
know!" Indeed, when the reforms came into force as the Indian
Councils Act of 1907, they did not take Hindus or Muslims very
far toward self-government.

Defying the leisurely pace of the period, the Aga Khan com-
muted between India and Europe. One day he was in Bombay
crossing swords with Mohammed Ali Jinnah, a young lawyer
and (nonpracticing) fellow Ismaili who thought separate electorates would divide the nation; the next he was in London
arguing with Winston Churchill. He could not foresee that
Churchill would one day "refuse to preside over the liquidation
of the British Empire," while Qaid-i-Azam (Great Leader) Jinnah would be hailed as the founder of Pakistan.

The strain of this active life was beginning to tell. The Aga
Khan's eyesight was poor and his heart weak, but he would not
spare himself. While visiting the Viceroy in Simla, he collapsed
and was ordered to take a rest, which to him meant only one
thing—travel. Accompanied by a French friend, he headed east
and visited Malaya and Singapore. He went on to China, a

"crumbling empire." In Shanghai he was entertained at a splendid meal prepared by a Chinese Muslim. (Several Ismaili groups were living in China at the time, and some of them are still there, but like those in Russia, cannot communicate with their Imam.)

After a brief visit to Japan he reached Honolulu, which, at a time when it was neither a tourist center nor a great naval base, struck him as a haven of absolute peace and happiness. His next stop was San Francisco, still in ruins after the catastrophic earthquake of 1906, and he was glad to move on to New York, where he was a great social hit, went to scores of parties, and visited museums, theaters, and the Metropolitan Opera (music and ballet were his favorite aesthetic pleasures).

Most mornings he could be seen in the criminal court, watching the sensational trial of Harry K. Thaw, the millionaire husband of the beautiful Evelyn Nesbit. Until he himself told the story, few people were aware that he knew Evelyn. He had met her in London at a dinner party some years earlier and was talking to her when a friend took him aside and warned him that her husband was violently jealous and that it was perhaps not prudent to pay her too much attention.

The incident came back to his mind as he listened to the proceedings. Evelyn, it appeared, had confessed to her husband that before their marriage she had been drugged and seduced by the well-known architect Stanford White. Coming face to face with White in Madison Square Roof Garden, Thaw had pulled out a revolver and killed him. Observing the courtroom drama, the Aga Khan could not help thinking that something like that might easily have happened to him in London.

Restored to health, he returned to the south of France, where he made friends with some of the finest contemporary musical talents—the young Stravinsky, Puccini, and Massenet among them. Massenet once received him at his hotel while sitting stark naked in his bath dictating music to a woman secretary. Diaghilev allowed the young balletomane to attend his rehearsals, which was bliss. He made Cannes his headquarters and sallied forth to cultural events all along the Côte d'Azur. What drew him to the Casino of Monte Carlo in the year 1907 was not the gaming rooms but the theater under the same roof where the ballet and opera of Monte Carlo performed.

He became the ballet's most enthusiastic supporter, and it was not difficult to guess why. He never missed a performance when the cast included the handsome *première danseuse* whose name appeared in the program as Theresa Magliano. Personal and artistic interest coincided. The Aga Khan was anxious to meet her and it was not hard to find a mutual friend to introduce them. He soon learned that Ginetta, as Theresa called herself, came from an artistic Turin family. She was nineteen and at the beginning of her career. Her teachers predicted a great future for her—Monte Carlo was her first foreign engagement, a great opportunity to be noticed.

In the ten years since the Aga Khan's unhappy first marriage he had escorted some of Europe's most desirable women but none of his affairs had been serious. He was very serious now and Ginetta felt as strongly about him. "We fell deeply in love," he said simply. So sure was he about his feelings that he proposed only a few weeks after they first met. From the little *pension* where she shared rooms with two other girl dancers, he moved her to a suite in the Hôtel de Paris, then left for Bombay to tell his mother that he proposed to make his home in Europe and marry a European woman.

He could not have chosen a less opportune moment. For the Aga Khan to take another wife at this stage—or for some time to come—would have advertised his estrangement from Shahzadi just when a vicious family feud between her and his immediate relatives was coming to a head in the courts of Bombay. In essence, the challenge to the Aga Khan and his mother was almost identical with the old Khoja case. As in 1866, the dispute was largely about finances, and once more the history and background of the Imam's relations with the Ismaili community came under public scrutiny. The case arose from the purge of the hangers-on who, reluctant to give up their sinecures, constructed a claim out of arguments designed to embarrass the Aga Khan and damage him in the eyes of the community.

His principal adversary was Shahzadi's sister, Haji Bibi, daughter of Aga Jangi Shah, whose murder had shaken the community ten years earlier. The Haji Bibi Case was as difficult to follow as the Khoja Case. Although all claims against the Aga Khan had long been renounced on her behalf, she and other relatives demanded a share of the community's property and the Imam's income as of right. They were no more likely to succeed than the plaintiffs in the Khoja Case.

For outsiders the main interest centered on the public discussion of the Imam's financial relations with the community. For the first time the technicalities of *zakat* were revealed to the eyes of unbelievers. Witnesses recited a long list of rituals and ceremonies for which the Aga Khan was entitled to receive fees. It started with followers, twice or three times a day, bringing sweetmeats, fruit, and food for Hazar Imam that were put up for auction to the highest bidder, who paid up saying, "This is the property of Hazar Imam." Ismailis (Khojas) made payments when assembling for special prayers, and when the collecting box was handed around in the *jamatkhana,* paid the *dassoon*—two annas in the rupee.

Marriage fees went to the Imam; a percentage of the dowry or the cost of the dowry was (and still is) paid for the use of the *jamatkhana,* the *mukhi* often providing refreshments and even transport for the guests. Fees to mark the birth of a child, bigger for a boy than for a girl, went largely to cover similar expenses. The Imam was entitled to a fee for death ceremonies, but this might go toward the cost of the coffin, the burial place, the undertaker, and the religious service. In the spiritual sense, a family's payments made after a relative's burial were to insure that his soul rested in peace, a practice borrowed from the ancient

Greeks, who placed a coin in the mouth of their dead to pay their fare across the River Styx.

Payments were made when Hazar Imam came to the *jamatkhana;* on the seventh day of the month, when followers fasted from 6 to 10 A.M.; and when Hazar Imam named a child. At the ceremony of Sir Bundi (literal meaning: offering of the head) a faithful put his property at the disposal of the Imam, and the Elders magnanimously saved him from too great a sacrifice by fixing a price at which it could be bought back, the money going to the Imam.

The judge in the Haji Bibi Case went to see for himself and described the ceremony. "We sat on chairs in front of a raised seat or throne on which the Aga Khan sits when he attends the *jamatkhana.* The whole room was filled with Khojas seated or kneeling on the ground, in another room the women of the community . . . a most impressive sight owing to the reverence with which the whole proceedings were conducted."

As the trial went on, not much reverence was shown by the Aga Khan's opponents in court. Witnesses tried to spread as much dirt as possible, rouse religious feelings, repeat every damaging rumor, and injure the Aga Khan in every way. So outrageous was some of the testimony that Justice Russell cleared the court on more than one occasion. Some of the witnesses were not too particular about the truth either. "As regards the ladies," the judge said, "I could not see their faces as they were covered from head to foot in black dominoes with white pieces of muslin let in across the face. But one has only to read the evidence . . . to see how full of inconsistencies and untruths it is."

The main issue was almost completely submerged by the petty quibbles the other side raised. The history of every Aga Khan bungalow in Poona, Bangalore, and Bombay was traced back, mostly on the basis of hearsay, each piece of family jewelry was discussed, the amounts some relatives had received as allowances from the Aga Khan were analyzed. The acid atmosphere was reflected in attacks on the judge, who had to defend himself against the insinuation that he could not be expected to hand down a fair verdict because he was friendly with the Aga Khan, had been his guest at dinner, and had entertained him in his own house. "The same could probably be said about every judge in Bombay," the Aga Khan's counsel remarked.

At the end of the long proceedings the judge was left to decide 128 specific points. He answered the question whether the offerings and presents made to the first and second Aga Khans were their absolute property with a firm "Yes." Was Haji Bibi, or any member of the family, entitled to any interest in such property? The judge said equally firmly "No."

The key question was whether the offerings and presents the Aga Khan was receiving from his followers were given to him as "the Hazar Imam and in consequence of the veneration and devotion of the Shia Imami Ismailis to his person." The judge's answer was "Yes." In every one of the 128 points the verdict went in the Aga Khan's favor. His legal triumph was complete, and except for an occasional local difficulty, the Imam's right to *zakat* was never again challenged. It developed into a kind of church tax, most of which is invested in schools and health and community centers. As in the time of the Prophet and his *baitumal* (treasury), which was filled by contributions from his followers, Ismailis pay *zakat* (2.5 percent of their income) and *khums* (10 percent) voluntarily and directly to the Imam. The Haji Bibi Case anchored this arrangement in modern law.

Not wanting to rub the noses of the losers in the dust by a public announcement of his divorce and a spectacular second marriage, the Aga Khan bade farewell to the splendor of Malabar Hill and his palace in Poona with its the sweet mango trees (the fruit was sent to him wherever he went) and returned to Europe, the Côte d'Azur, and Ginetta, for whom he bought a house in the rue Bel Respiro in Monte Carlo, overlooking the Casino. He named it Villa Ginetta.

Writing about the events of 1908 and his great love for "Mlle.

Theresa Magliano," the Aga Khan recounted the next move: "In the spring of that year she accompanied me to Egypt and we were married in Cairo in accordance with Muslim law." His marriage brought him great happiness—he called it "spiritual and mental satisfaction"—and those who met him and Ginetta thought they made a splendid couple.

But in view of the situation in Bombay, it was all done so quietly, almost stealthily, that some of the Aga Khan's friends refused to believe that a marriage had actually taken place, and if they were thinking in terms of a European marriage, they were, of course, quite right. Almost sixty years later, Leonard Slater, an American writer investigating the life and death of Prince Aly Khan, quoted official documents in which Ginetta, long after 1908, was described as "Theresa Magliano" and as "nubile" (unmarried). But things were not that simple.

A Roman Catholic country abiding by the laws of the Vatican, Italy did not recognize the marriage of an Italian Roman Catholic which had not been solemnized in church. (Sophia Loren's marital tribulations show that nothing has changed in half a century.) A Muslim marriage contract concluded in Cairo had certainly little chance of finding favor in the eyes of Italian officials. That the intended husband had another wife or was divorced finally ruled legal marriage for an Italian subject out of court—in Italy the Aga Khan might even have laid himself open to an indictment for bigamy. The position in France in those days was not very different.

The reason why the owner of Villa Ginetta appeared in the local land register as "Theresa Magliano" was that the Aga Khan had put the house in his bride's name before they went to Cairo. This was also the case with regard to another villa he was building for her at Cimiez (Nice), where he had stayed on his first visit to Europe. It was a temple for their favorite muse and he called it Villa Terpsichore.

Untroubled by complications in Italy or India, Ginetta was expecting her first baby. For the Aga Khan the birth of a son in the following year was a joyful event. To have a male heir was no less important to an Imam in modern times than throughout Ismaili history. He named the boy Mohammed Mahdi, but his mother and her Italian relatives called him Giuseppe. Oriental husbands were not in the habit of attending on their wives for days and weeks on end. The Aga Khan was no exception. He continued to travel around the world and Ginetta was often lonely, although her brother Mario and her two sisters frequently stayed with her. She was devoted to the baby but missed her dancing and as an outlet for her artistic temperament took up sculpture. When her husband was with her, her happiness was complete, but his sojourns in Monte Carlo or Cimiez were brief.

The deteriorating political situation in Europe and the Near East kept him busier than ever. German influence in Turkey was on the increase and it worried him to see a Muslim country moving into the anti-British camp. Western statesmen were glad to know that he was pleading their cause, and although some Muslims frowned on his pro-British outlook, he went to Constantinople to do what he could to preserve peace. The Turks were as intransigent as the British, tempers in the Balkans were getting shorter, and a bloody conflict seemed inevitable.

One of his trips to England was in the line of a sad duty. "In May 1910," the Aga Khan wrote later, "my great and good friend King Edward VII died in London." The assembled crowned heads bickered about status and seniority; quizzically he watched the Kaiser and the Kings of Greece, Spain, and Bulgaria competing for places of honor in the funeral procession.

From Bombay came the sad news of the death of his old friend Aga Shamsuddin, one of the last links with his early youth. An even more grievous loss was imminent. Before reaching his second birthday, little Mohammed Mahdi died of meningitis. Father and mother were disconsolate, but at least Ginetta was expecting another baby. Desperately anxious to protect the new arrival against all risks, the Aga Khan sent his wife to her native

Turin, where she could be with her family and have the constant attention of a top-class gynecologist. He installed her in a big flat in the fashionable Corso Oporto where, on June 13, 1911, her second son was born.

The Aga Khan received the news while attending the coronation of King George V in London. Although he was not there to see the baby, his birth was, as he put it, a great solace and joy to his wife and himself. The mother had a difficult time and the baby was not strong, but he would not lack the fondest care and the best medical attention. There was a legal complication. Because no official evidence of a wedding was available —at least none that would have been accepted as legal in Italy— the baby's birth certificate embarrassingly described the mother as "Teresa Magliano, unmarried, twenty-two years old, living on independent means," and the father as "His Highness The Aga Khan, son of the late Aga Ali Shah, thirty-four years old, born at Karachi (British India), living at Monte Carlo." The boy was given the name of Aly Salomone Khan.

In later years ill wishers suggested surreptitiously that Prince Aly Khan was of illegitimate birth because his father and mother were not legally married when he was born. Friends countered helpfully that it was all above board because the Aga Khan had contracted a *mut'a* marriage. (*Mut'a* marriages were first practiced by Muslim warriors who, separated from their wives for long periods, were permitted to enter into temporary associations [*mut'a*] with one or more other women for a night or a week or even longer.)

Both the insinuation and the well-meaning defense were ill founded. As the highest religious and legal authority in his community, the Aga Khan could, if he so wished, legalize his own marriage whatever the circumstances. If his first marriage was an obstacle, he needed only to tell his wife, "I divorce thee," and that marriage would be ended, although there was no evidence that he had done so. He could take a second bride by telling her, "I take thee as my wife," and they would be legally married, which is what he had done in Cairo. Where Muslims are concerned, many countries recognize the law as it is practiced in the land of their origin. Although some Muslim writers (among them Asaf A. A. Fyzee, writing in the *Aga Khan Diamond Jubilee Souvenir Book,* 1945) have claimed that *mut'a* is, according to Ismaili Law, altogether unlawful, the Aga Khan himself, supreme arbiter of Ismaili religious practices, obviously did not concur, because he mentioned in his will that he had married his second wife "by mut'a marriage."

Even in the Aga Khan's frantically busy travel schedule, few periods were quite as crowded as the first year of Aly's life. The coronation in London gave him an opportunity to discuss the dangerous developments in the Balkans with several statesmen. More than anything, he wanted to prevent a conflict between Britain and a Muslim country and spare the Muslims of Turkey an unnecessary war. His support for the British Empire never wavered, and one of his hobbyhorses was the potential Indian manpower that could be summoned to defend the Empire in the event of war. "India could put troops into South Africa as quickly as they could be sent from England," he wrote prophetically in a 1911 issue of *National Review.* "She could land soldiers in Australia long before England could do so; and forces from India could reach western Canada almost as soon as from England." He wanted the myriads of India to be taught that they were guardians and supporters of the Crown just as the white citizens of the Empire. "India and the self-governing dominions stand and fall together!"

His range of interests was as wide as ever. He joined the Maharajah of Patiala in organizing the first all-India cricket eleven to visit England: They lost fifteen matches, won six, and started a tradition that is still going strong. His campaign for Aligarh University required a final big effort, and as chairman of the fund-raising committee, he went on a collecting tour through India's main Muslim areas. "As a mendicant," he announced, "I am now going out to beg from house to house and from street to street for the children of Indian Muslims." It was a triumphal tour. Wherever he went, people unharnessed the horses of his carriage and pulled it themselves for miles. He collected "rupees thirty lakhs"—three million rupees—of which 100,000 were contributed by him. For decades, whenever the university was in need of funds, he made new donations and persuaded others to give generously.

The year 1912 saw the historic Coronation Durbar, when the new King-Emperor George V met the people of India at their new capital at Delhi, the only British sovereign to visit India during the period of British rule. The ceremonies were the most colorful ever staged, but owing to some disaster in the kitchen, the great state banquet provided food only for the King and a handful of guests sitting near him; the rest went hungry. During the investiture in a brilliantly lit tent (to add to his titles of Knight and Grand Knight Commander of the Indian Empire, the Aga Khan was made a Knight Grand Commander of the Order of the Star of India) an electric bulb burst and others began to flicker. For an instant it was thought fire might break out and engulf the distinguished company. Whistles blew and fire engines started up, but panic was avoided and the lights and the excitement settled down.

Although not much in evidence himself in his family circle, the Aga Khan made sure that Ginetta and the baby were surrounded by comfort and luxury worthy of their status. He was concerned about his son's health and had a new idea for his welfare almost every week. Might the boy and his mother not benefit from the mountain air of the Italian Alps? Would the climate in Normandy be more conducive to the child's well-being? He took a summer house, Villa Gorizia, in Deauville, bought a Paris town house in the rue de Prony, and acquired yet another residence at Maisons-Lafitte, not far from the capital.

Almost before he could walk, Aly was taught to ride a horse; he learned to swim and was introduced to tennis as soon as his little hand could grip a racket. But he lacked the company of other children; instead his Uncle Mario spent much time with him and remained a close companion of Aly's in later life. Alfredo, the Italian chauffeur, was another of his "playmates." Ginetta was happiest in her studio; she exhibited some fine sculptures under the name of Yla, an anagram of her son's name, and received several important commissions, one of them for a fountain statue in Vienne. (Though he was born more than ten years after her death, her grandson Prince Karim has inherited her talent as a sculptor.) Her art was her life and she rarely accompanied her husband on his social and diplomatic rounds. But when she appeared in public, Princess Theresa's lively beauty, elegance, and magnificent jewels were the talk of Deauville and Paris.

Moving easily among the European elite, the Aga Khan was so much a part of the Western scene that his Eastern origins and connections tended to be overlooked. But he never forgot them for a moment. "My way of life," he wrote at one time, "has taken me from the slowly changing East to the West, which is ever-swiftly changing. The work I have to do keeps me, for the most time, in Europe and on the move. I am a pacifist and an internationalist. Yet I belong to no country in the West but only to many people in the East. My skin, my religion, my taste in food, my way of thinking—all these make me differ profoundly from the people among whom I move."

His health was precarious, but his love of golf triumphed. Whenever he was in London, he could be seen early in the morning emerging from the Ritz Hotel in his white sports outfit, bound for one golf course or another. His increasing weight worried the doctors, but his energetic travels were as much exercise as any man could be expected to take. He always carried a little instrument with him, a watch and compass combined, which told him the time in, and the direction of, Mecca. Every Friday, wherever he was, he turned toward the holy city of Islam and spent an hour in meditation and prayer. "That hour is my greatest hour!" he used to say.

But his prayers for peace in the Balkans remained unanswered. The strains and stresses of so many peoples—Greeks, Serbs, Bulgars, Turks—jostling each other in a narrow place portended the eruption of power politics and rival alliances at any moment. Behind the scenes the Aga Khan did what he could on behalf of his fellow Muslims in the old Ottoman Empire, which had become the "Sick Man of Europe." He traveled to Russia and in his memoirs, which he dictated to the late John Connell some forty years later, described his leisurely progress in St. Petersburg and Moscow. Reticent about the really important things—reticence remains a predominant Ismaili characteristic—he wrote about overheated palaces rather than the rising political temperatures on Russia's borders, dwelling on the former lovingly as if he sensed that they would be destroyed in the impending world conflagration together with much else.

In Moscow he was shocked by the poverty around him and described the gulf between rich and poor as "truly appalling." Unlike many other wealthy men, he had a strong sense of social justice and genuine compassion. His feeling was that such contrasts created pressures that could not be bottled up for long. Even so, his sense of humor did not desert him. In a Moscow public steam bath he saw women attendants looking after male visitors, passing the soap and towels and acting as masseuses. They were so elderly and ugly, he commented, that it was utterly impossible to imagine the slightest misbehavior with them.

While he was in Moscow, the situation in the Balkans came to a head. In October, 1912, Bulgaria, Serbia, and Greece went to war against Turkey. The Turks emerged severely mauled from a short, sharp burst of fighting and were unable to continue the war. Bulgaria and Serbia agreed to an armistice, but hostilities between Turkey and Greece continued. The Aga Khan returned hurriedly to India, where tempers were on edge and Muslims wanted to go to the aid of the Turks. He and his friends protested against Britain's "delicate but chilly policy of non-intervention." There was little he could do for the Turks and he found himself in a serious dilemma. While his fellow Muslims, feeling that the honor and integrity of Islam were at stake, advocated a *jehad*, a holy war, he realized the futility of asking the Turks to fight on and opposed such a move. When he said so in an interview in the *Times of India*, many Muslims were angry.

A peace conference was convened in London, broke up, and was reconvened to produce a treaty that imposed considerable territorial losses on the Turks. There was a *coup d'état* in Constantinople, followed by a second Balkan war. It was a confusing conflict. First the Bulgarians attacked Serbian and Greek positions; then Rumania joined Turkey against Bulgaria, which was quickly defeated. Albania was invaded by the Serbs, and the Turks recovered some of their territory. The Austrians intervened, a German general was appointed Turkish commander-in-chief, and in the end Turkey's alliance with Britain's enemies was almost complete.

By this time the Aga Khan was in the Middle East, another explosive conglomerate of races, religions, and alliances. On a rare visit to Syria he found some of his leading followers at loggerheads. The Joundi family sprouted two wings, one religious and one political, which were fiercely competing for one Ismaili seat in parliament. The religious Joundis won, the community was split, and the Aga Khan's attempt to mediate failed because Arab feuds are not easily abandoned. The two factions were never reconciled and fifty years later the ancient quarrel affected Prince Aly Khan even after his death.

CHAPTER V

At this time the Aga Khan's apartment at the Ritz was a beehive of activity. Visitors came and went in an unending stream, swallowed by the social scene in London's premier hotel. The British diplomats among them were content to remain anonymous because their mission was to solicit the Aga Khan's help for some of the more delicate and secret services important personages like him could render a country in time of international tension. He was more than willing. Envoys of several countries followed emissaries from his "spiritual children" in many parts of the world who wanted to hear his views and his wishes in case of an emergency.

As the situation was visibly deteriorating and Europe was drifting toward war, he had two main concerns. It was probably too late to prevent the impending conflagration, but it was important to strengthen the British Empire, with which much of his property and many of his personal interests—indeed, his whole life—were bound up. He was even more concerned with the well-being of the millions of followers who depended on his guidance. What was said of the British Empire in those days also applied to the Aga Khan's religious realm: The sun never set on it. In Asia, in the Middle East, in Africa, war would confront them with a deadly peril. He was anxious to visit those at the most distant end of the long lines of communication which would become precarious as soon as the first shot was fired.

Time was short, and he was in a hurry. His first destination was Burma, still under India Office rule, where mounting nationalism threatened to isolate his community. In Rangoon he gathered Ismaili leaders around him and laid down a new policy for his followers to take account of the changing conditions. He ordered them to adapt themselves to local customs, give up their strange-sounding Indo-Saracenic names, wear Burmese clothes, speak the Burmese language, and become Burmese in all but their religious beliefs. It was a historic decision. His directives to Burmese Ismailis in the early months of 1914 created the pattern for relations between Ismailis and indigenous populations and worked for their mutual benefit. Ismailis everywhere adopted the nationality and became loyal subjects of the countries in which they lived.

The Imam's next destination was East Africa, but while he was on the high seas, Austria's Archduke Franz Ferdinand was assassinated by a Serb in the little Balkan town of Sarajevo. Repercussions were bound to be grave; they were not long delayed. The news that Austria was marching against Serbia to punish her for the political outrage and that Russia was coming to Serbia's aid reached the Aga Khan in Zanzibar.

The fire spread quickly. The Germans intervened, declaring war on Russia and moving into neutral Belgium. On August 4 England declared war on Germany. Peace all but vanished from the earth. The Aga Khan went to see the British Resident in Zanzibar and offered his services to the British government. He was preparing to take the next boat out of Mombasa, but was warned that a German sea raider was operating in the Indian Ocean and advised to travel to England via South Africa. To leave no doubt about his sentiments, he returned the insignia of his German decorations to the Kaiser.

Never had a voyage seemed so slow. Arriving in London at

long last, the Aga Khan told the press that he would not mind
joining an Indian regiment as a private soldier, but his old friend
Lord Kitchener, now Secretary of State for War, had more
useful employment in mind for the Aga Khan's special talents.
Allied to Germany, Turkey was at war with England, France,
Serbia, and Russia and was trying to rally Muslims in a Pan-
Islamic movement against the Empire and the Western Allies.
Once more there was talk of a holy war and Indian troops,
including many Muslims who were fighting with the British,
found themselves confronted with *mullahs* sent out by Turkey to
persuade them to desert.

The Mediterranean, the Suez Canal, the Red Sea, the Indian
Ocean—the Empire's lifelines—would be under grave threat if
Turkey's campaign succeeded. Only a leading Muslim of the
Aga Khan's caliber, Lord Kitchener said, could help to foil this
plot and counteract the dangerous propaganda. After a confer-
ence with Lord Kitchener, the Aga Khan saw Prime Minister
Asquith and was received by the King, who was well informed
on this intricate subject.

Although he was not entirely uncritical of British policy toward
Turkey, the Aga Khan got his influential Muslim friends together
to support an appeal to Muslims everywhere not to follow the
Turkish call for a *jehad*. He described the Ottoman government
as a tool of Germany's aggressive, imperialist strategy. "Our only
duty as Muslims," the manifesto concluded, "is to remain loyal,
faithful and obedient to our temporal and secular allegiance."

British confidence in the Aga Khan proved justified. The idea
of a *jehad* collapsed; India's Muslims remained loyal to the
Aga Khan—and the British Empire. An even more delicate task
awaited him, this time in Egypt, nominally part of the Ottoman
Empire but, since 1882, under "temporary" British occupation.
The Aga Khan's own account of his mission suffers from excessive
tact toward the former Khedive, Abbas Hilmi, who had largely
created the situation that required his attention but who became his friend some years later.

Suspected of pro-German machinations, Abbas Hilmi was called to London but got no nearer than Paris and finally turned up in Constantinople. His moves created confusion in Cairo about the Muslim attitude to the war, and the Aga Khan's mission was to stabilize opinion and explain the Allied cause. In Cairo the palace was hostile. Prince Fuad, the future King, and some of the princes and ministers had strong German affiliations. The best policy would be to try to win over the powerful Muslim teachers of al-Azhar University, and who could better accomplish that than the descendant of the founders of the university? While Lawrence of Arabia worked among the sheikhs, the Aga Khan fought Britain's diplomatic battle in Cairo. That Egypt remained calm and stable while the war came close was in part due to his skill.

On a brief visit to Bombay he found his mother busily helping the Allied war effort, looking after Indian troops and working for the Red Cross, yet keeping a watchful eye on Ismaili affairs. The Imam attended to his religious and administrative duties before returning to England to be greeted with a most welcome piece of news. As a reward for his services, the King conferred on him the right to an eleven-gun salute and the rank and precedence of a First Class Ruling Prince of the Bombay Presidency. In imperial Britain no Indian could ask for more.

Presently it was suggested to him that he might make his headquarters in neutral Switzerland, an ideal base for a man with his international connections. He took a house in Zurich but had no sooner settled down when he found himself under attack on two fronts. Fellow Muslims criticized him for supporting Britain and helping to recruit Indian troops to fight against Turkish Muslims, and German agents, who were thick in Switzerland, naturally assumed that he was operating against German interests. The German press launched a vicious campaign against him while more sinister German plans were maturing. He had an inkling of what might happen when his cousin Aga Farrokh Shah was assassinated at the instigation of German agents while visiting Ismaili settlements in Kirman on his behalf. Now they seemed ready to kill him too.

The German attempt to rid themselves of a dangerous opponent came at a critical moment. The Aga Khan's health was giving him considerable trouble. "I myself was laid low with a difficult, painful and protracted illness," he wrote in his autobiography. His sight deteriorated further and his eyes suffered damage that proved to be permanent. His pulse was irregular, and though he was eating normally, he was losing weight rapidly. A French physician diagnosed Graves' disease and advised him to consult a famous Swiss specialist.

The Germans did not believe that their quarry was really ill and moved in for the kill. "With typical German thoroughness," as he put it, they had a bomb thrown at him, and to make doubly sure, arranged to have his coffee poisoned. The bomb did not go off and the Aga Khan did not drink the coffee. Under the glare of publicity, the Swiss police investigated the two attempts.

For the Aga Khan it was a difficult time. Although he was physically at a low ebb, he spent much of his enforced seclusion drafting an account of political developments in India which, in a way, was a reply to those who called him a British imperialist and suggested that his activities were not in the best interests of Muslims. But it was also a blueprint for the future in which he visualized India as an integral part of a South Asian Federation reaching from Malaya to Egypt.

While he was quietly working away in his study, the noise about his alleged activities and the German attempts on his life grew louder until it reached a new crescendo with the arrest of three suspects. The British authorities were embarrassed. "All the British government saw fit to do," the Aga Khan remarked with some bitterness, "was to request me to leave Switzerland." He gave up the house in Zurich, but instead of returning to London, decided to see the war out in his Paris residence.

His condition was still causing considerable anxiety. Eighteen months under the shadow of death—from bombs, poison, and

natural causes—had left a deep mark. A hundred medical reme-
dies must have been tried when a new investigation revealed
that the original diagnosis had been wrong. A fresh line of
treatment began to show results and put him on the slow road to
recovery. But as long as he lived, plagued by new infirmities,
constantly under the care of doctors, he would never again
meekly accept the verdict of even the most eminent authority
without demanding the most detailed explanation. Every doctor
who henceforth treated him was subjected to a barrage of questions about the diagnosis and suggested treatment. His troubled
health became the source of his fabulous familiarity with every
therapy under the sun, which turned him into one of the world's
medically most knowledgeable patients.

Between 1916 and 1918, while war restricted his movements
and illness confined him to his rooms, Ginetta saw more of him
than at any other time. They were together in Paris or in
Maisons-Lafitte, and little Aly, though his august father remained
a remote figure, began to feel not quite so overawed in his presence. Whenever the boy was taken from Cimiez to Deauville, he
visited "Papa," who always questioned him thoroughly about his
progress.

Aly was not too sure of himself. A succession of young tutors,
Swiss or French, taught him as much as he would absorb, but he
was no keener on his books than most boys of his age and easily
tired of a subject. French and Italian came naturally to him and
he was making good progress in English. An Ismaili scholar
acquainted him with the rudiments of Islamic history and the
basic tenets of his father's sect. As the heir apparent, important
religious duties would eventually fall to him, but the Aga Khan
remembered the ordeal of his own boyhood too well to allow his
son to be subjected at once to a high-pressure education.

The boy was moody—sometimes high-spirited, sometimes lost
in a world of fantasies. But he had an easy charm and a way of
endearing himself to people. His father encouraged him to take
exercise, swim, and ride. Aly's favorite tutor was M. Ed-

ʾin, a personable, talented young man who was father,
ᵇʳother, and friend to him. When Grin left the household to
start a teaching career, Aly took a tearful farewell of his beloved
"Professor." When they met again in the mid-fifties, Grin was
Rector of the University of Lausanne.

The book on which the Aga Khan had been working was published in 1918 under the title *India in Transition.* Emerging from
his sick room after a long absence from active politics, he joined
the peacemakers who were mixing cures for a war-sick world at
their conferences in and around Paris. The Versailles Treaty
between the Western Allies and Germany was about to be
signed. It inspired the Aga Khan with little confidence. India was
in a difficult situation, and it was unlikely that his suggestion of
a commonwealth of Asian states in association with Britain
would be adopted. Instead of swift progress toward responsible
government in India, prolonged deliberations only produced recommendations for harsh measures against political agitation and
sedition, which provoked a hostile reaction. India was restive and
on the brink of the same troubles that afflicted Ireland.

Although demonstrations were banned, there were many "unlawful gatherings" in Indian cities—in the course of one, in the
Jallianwala Bagh in Amritsar on April 19, 1919, police fired into
the crowd and 379 people were killed. It was a grave setback,
but the Aga Khan tried hard to calm tempers and encourage
negotiations. He joined the members of the Indian delegation at
the Paris Peace Conference, lobbied among British politicians,
and was in constant touch with Edwin Montagu, Secretary
of State for India.

As if to make up for the accident of history that had ranged
him against Muslim Turkey in the war, he took up the cudgels
on her behalf but found British policy as hostile to Turkey as
ever. The country's dismemberment was to be sealed by the Treaty
of Sèvres, but Kemal Ataturk, the new Turkish leader, refused to
submit. At this critical moment the Greek army invaded Asia

Minor to liberate Greeks under Turkish rule, captured Smyrna, and marched deep into Turkish territory. Britain and France sent expeditions to secure footholds in this troubled part of the world and a big row developed over British claims to an insignificant little city called Chanak.

It testified to the Aga Khan's skill and instinct that in the face of strong anti-Turkish sentiments he managed to secure the help of a most powerful political campaigner—Lord Beaverbrook, the Canadian multimillionaire who had turned the London *Daily Express* into a vital and highly successful newspaper. The Aga Khan could not have wished for a more sympathetic ally. "In the Graeco-Turkish conflict," Lord Beaverbrook wrote in *Politicians and the Press*, "with Britain backing the Greeks, nothing could be foreseen but disaster."

In August, 1922, Lord Beaverbrook visited Deauville. "At the Royal Hotel there," he recounted, "his Highness Prince Aga Khan discussed with me the disastrous character of the relations of the British government with the de facto Turkish government." Lord Beaverbrook did not conduct his campaigns from the ivory tower of his private office but decided to go to Angora (Ankara) and discover what the real intentions and terms of the new Turkish government were. With the Aga Khan acting as intermediary, he made arrangements for a meeting with Kemal and suggested that it would be a good thing if Churchill and Lord Birkenhead met the Turkish leader.

To tell the British government how strongly they felt about the Turkish question, India's Muslims sent a mission to London that included the Aga Khan. They were received by David Lloyd George, the Prime Minister, to whom they put the case for the return of Thrace and Smyrna to Turkey. After they had had their say, Lloyd George—according to an account by Sheikh Mushir Hosain Kidwai, a member of the mission—asked bluntly, "Now that the Greeks are in military possession who will turn them out from there?" Unable to restrain himself, the Aga Khan jumped up, wagged a finger at Lloyd George, and said, "Well, Mr.

Prime Minister, old though I am, I will go sword in hand and turn them out. We will charter ships, we will do everything. Leave them to us!" The Prime Minister was thunderstruck. "No, no, we cannot do that," he murmured.

But strong anti-Turkish forces in Britain rallied to resist this pressure. Lord Curzon frowned on the joint activities of the British press lord and the Imam of the Ismailis, and the conservative press published alarming accounts of their movements. The Turks themselves relieved their partisans from further exertions on their behalf. Taking matters into their own hands, they put an end to the presence of some three million Greeks in Asia Minor. Smyrna was burned and the Greeks who were not massacred got away with little more than their lives.

How the Aga Khan, who was constantly in the political limelight in these years, managed to squeeze his ample religious and private activities into a bursting timetable remained forever a mystery to his friends. Even in Europe he was constantly commuting between London and his houses in Deauville, Paris, and on the Côte d'Azur. Conferences in Lausanne and Geneva demanded his presence, and as if this were not enough, he was also fond of snatching a few days rest and privacy at Aix-les-Bains, not only to take the waters but also to enjoy the air and the scenery. Among his many friends in Aix were the Carron sisters, Marcelle and Jane-Andrée, daughters of a local hotel manager. Andrée, who was eighteen when he first knew her, often used to accompany him on long walks or drives in the foothills of Haute-Savoie. Later Marcelle moved to Paris and worked at a fashion house, Guérin, where the Aga Khan's wife bought many of her clothes. Andrée was also working in Paris, and he helped them to open their own establishment, Maison Carron-Soeurs. It enabled him to see much more of Andrée. As he said when their friendship became public, he had known her on and off for nearly a dozen years.

Four years of war without racing had whetted the Aga Khan's

appetite and he rarely missed a meeting. Horses to him were precious creatures. "Nothing," he said, "is more poetic than a man riding a beautiful horse, riding it to perfection, the man and the horse, like a centaur, carved out as one." To talk about horses was one of his favorite pastimes.

Gradually the idea of racing in England and France, which actually he had nursed since his very first visit to Europe, began to materialize. The decision came in the spring of 1921 and was the start of an important chapter in racing history. "I was dining at a friend's house in London," he recalled, "and my neighbor was Mrs. Asquith, one of Lord Oxford's daughters-in-law, who was the sister of Mrs. George Lambton." They talked about horses all through dinner, and Mrs. Asquith suggested that he should start racing in England and get in touch with George Lambton, who could help with training and management. "It was like a trigger being drawn on a cannon," said the Aga Khan.

Lambton came to see him at the Ritz and agreed to start buying mares for an Aga Khan stud. Through Lambton, the new recruit to English racing met Richard Dawson, trainer of the Derby and Grand National winners of 1903, and engaged him. In a parallel operation in Paris, he secured the services of the American trainer William Duke, who helped him buy French horses at Deauville. "The result of one chance dinner party affinity," the Aga Khan mused, "led to my becoming engaged up to my neck with horse breeding, bloodstocks, and with it naturally cattle breeding and farming in Ireland and France."

Although cautious with money, the Aga Khan was prepared to spend up to £100,000 in three years to build up a top-class racing stable. Richard Dawson looked after his horses at Whatcombe in Berkshire. Soon all eyes were on them. Among Lambton's first purchases was Cos, who cost five thousand guineas and promptly won the Queen Mary Stakes at Ascot, garnering nearly twice the amount of his purchase in stake money.

The Aga Khan and George Lambton were at the Doncaster

sales early in 1922 when a gray Sledmere filly came up for sale. She was a daughter of the Tetrarch, and the Aga Khan would not allow himself to be outbid. When the filly went to him for 9,100 guineas, cheap at the price, he christened her Mumtaz Mahal, after Emperor Shah Jehan's favorite wife, who lies buried in the grandiose Taj Mahal. On his visits to Whatcombe he admired her dappled gray coat, fine shoulders, strong legs, and powerful quarters.

Not satisfied with the Tetrarch's daughter, he also bought his son, Salmon Trout, paying 3,500 guineas. His faith in both horses was splendidly rewarded. The fastest filly the turf had ever known, Mumtaz Mahal (the "flying filly," the "spotted wonder") won every race but one that season and carried the Aga Khan's colors in the Queen Mary Stakes past the winning post ten lengths ahead of her nearest rival. Her amazing turn of speed was the talk of the town, and though she ran only one more season, she brought her owner £14,000 in stake money before she was retired to stud.

There was no holding the Aga Khan after that. He gave instructions to find a suitable home for his stud in Ireland and settled on a place in the Curragh, in County Kildare, which he named Sheshoon. He also bought another French farm at Marly-la-Ville, and this was only the beginning. Although he could command expert advice, he owed much of his success as breeder and owner to his uncanny instinct. George Criticos— "George of the Ritz"—the hall porter to whom the Aga Khan took great liking and who acted as his cashier, private secretary, and factotum in London, mentioned how His Highness on one occasion asked him to cable George Lambton to buy a horse called Papyrus. Neither Lambton nor Dawson shared the Aga Khan's high opinion of the horse, but it won the 1923 Derby.

When on the continent the Aga Khan often sent instructions to his stables through George Criticos, and George, in turn, telephoned him details of races in which his horses were involved. So fond was the Aga Khan of the Ritz concierge that he named a horse after him, Criticos (which did not come up to scratch and was soon sold), and even asked him to spend his holidays at the Deauville house. George proudly preserved a cutting from a London newspaper that reported in its gossip column, "Mr. George Criticos, head porter of the Ritz Hotel in London, is staying as the guest of the Aga Khan in Deauville. He is a cross between major-domo and grand vizier to the Persian potentate."

In his biography of the Aga Khan Stanley Jackson recounts the story of a punter who told the Aga Khan, "If you will give me a tip, Your Highness, I would willingly risk my shirt," to which the Aga Khan replied that the happiest man is often the one who has no shirt on his back. George Criticos says that he placed many bets on behalf of his famous patron, whose usual stake was £500, but double that amount when he thought he was on to a good thing.

For young Aly, his father's racing interests opened up a new dimension and brought him new friends. Soon he was as fond of Dickie Dawson as he had been of Monsieur Grin. At Whatcombe he tested his skill on a horse and proved that he was a worthy heir to the family tradition. Already he handled horses with great confidence and courage—perhaps too much courage. He was still very close to his mother (there were, incidentally, rumors that she and the Aga Khan had gone through a second, secret, marriage ceremony). She was not in good health, and it came as a shock to her when the Aga Khan decided that their son needed a spell of England to balance the Latin element in his mental makeup and the French influences of his environment at Cimiez and Deauville.

However painful the prospect of a long separation from Aly for the Begum, the Aga Khan's mind was made up. He was less certain about the kind of English education that would be best for the boy. As much as he admired English institutions, a fashionable school was not necessarily the most useful preparation for the life ahead of Aly. Private tuition to prepare him for entrance to a university seemed much more suitable.

The next move was to ask friends at the India Office to suggest
a man to take charge of Aly's education. They came up with a
very good choice—Charles Waddington, ex-officer of the Indian
Army and former principal of Mayo College at Ajmer, where
generations of Indian princes received their training as future
rulers of their states. Waddington, who shared the Aga Khan's
love of India and England and was living in retirement, agreed
to take Aly under his wing at his fine Sussex country house. He
saw that the boy, then in his teens, was taught style, self-
discipline, and savoir faire, though his head was never crammed
with academic knowledge.

The routine at the Waddington house was much the same as
the curriculum to which English boarding schools then subjected
their boys. Aly was instructed by tutors and spent his free time
riding, swimming, and playing tennis. Summer vacations he spent
with his mother in the south of France or in Deauville. During
other holidays Waddington's own children, two boys and one girl,
home from their schools, often kept him company.

For a little "English gentleman" in the mold in which the Aga
Khan hoped to shape his son, it was not unusual to suffer the
pangs of separation from his loved ones which clouded Aly's
life during his first few months at Sussex. But the warmth of his
new surroundings, though well controlled in the English style,
was no less comforting than the atmosphere in his mother's
homes. Waddington grew genuinely fond of Aly, whose charm
became even more evident as he grew older. He wanted to be
liked and was pleasant and well mannered, but a restless streak
and excess nervous energy found a happier outlet in physical activities than in desk work. He was good at games, prerequisite of
successful adolescence in England, and fortunate in that his agile
mind made up for what he lacked in application.

A great adventure was in store for him. Toward the end of
1923 the Aga Khan decided to take his wife and son on their
first visit to India. For Ginetta it was a tremendous event because she had never been at her husband's side when he faced his

followers as Imam. For Aly it was a romantic expedition into the mysterious interior of his father's religious empire, but his first reaction was unexpected. Standing on deck as the ship approached the landing stage in Bombay, Aly looked out on the Khoja dignitaries assembled by the quayside to receive the Imam. The boy was not easily perplexed, but their *jubas* (impressive crimson gold-embroidered gowns) and their *paqris* (golden turbans) puzzled him and he turned to his father. "Why have so many magicians come here?" he asked. The grandiose palace at Malabar Hill, his venerable grandmother, and her exotic court were pure fairyland for him.

Dressed in the style of a young Indian prince, Aly looked perfectly at home in the setting of his Eastern forebears. And when it came to visiting the *jamatkhana* with the Imam, he was well versed in the prayers and the ritual for which his Muslim teachers had prepared him and as familiar with Ismaili history as any Christian boy of his age with the Bible.

The extravagance with which the ordinary Ismaili venerated his father made a deep impression. An oriental writer, Ibn Zul Quarnain, caught the spirit of one of the ceremonies in honor of the Aga Khan when he wrote:

As far as the eye can see thousands are streaming across the countryside. At dawn the great pilgrimage began. Now it is late afternoon, yet still they come. Old men, young men, poor men and rich men, the lame, the halt and the blind. Some barefooted and in filthy rags, others on mules and those who are very sick in rough litters. They have come at the bidding of their High Priest.

Presently a huge limousine slides silently between the waiting thousands and from it steps an imposing figure in flowing Kashmir shawl robes and a Persian lamb headdress. A sigh, as soft as an evening breeze, runs through the immense throng who fall on their

knees, their lips moving in silent prayer. Rose petals
thrown by devoted worshipping hands fall like gentle
rain, and slowly the broad figure lifts one arm above his
head to bless them. Silently he blesses them. Then, as
suddenly as he came, he is gone and behind him he
leaves the multitude rejoicing; for have they not ful-
filled the life dream of every true Ismaili? Have they
not been privileged to set their humble eyes on the
mighty Aga Khan, direct descendant of Allah's greatest
Prophet?

Among his followers the Aga Khan, an impressive figure at
all times, seemed to grow in stature, making decisions and giving guidance with immense authority. The inspiration he derived from his office as Imam distinguished him from other men
and was impossible to explain except in terms of Sufi mysticism,
part of the Ismaili creed. "I am convinced," he said, "that
many Muslims . . . and that I myself have had moments of
enlightenment and of knowledge of a kind which we cannot
communicate because it is something given and not something
acquired."

In this spirit he tackled the problems of his followers with
the knowledge and insight that is the Imam's gift. He was in
constant correspondence with the heads (mostly hereditary) of
his widely scattered communities (in Hunza, for example, where
the Mir is an Ismaili and the religious leader). Local organizations were always strengthened as a result of his visits. On this
occasion, too, he streamlined the religious and administrative
institutions of Ismailis in India, adapted rules and regulations
where necessary, and gave his interpretation of the Holy Law.

Zakat still served the old Reform Party as a pretext for agitation. "When the Aga Khan visited Karachi in 1920," they told
all who would listen, "he carried away fifteen lakhs of rupees
after a stay of only twenty-six days." They claimed that on
another occasion he collected 1,540,000 rupees after a stay of

only two hours. As with his pet project, Aligarh University, he always collected money for a good purpose, and every Ismaili would have been mortally offended had the Imam refused his contribution.

Actually, had the Aga Khan granted his opponents a glimpse of his accounts, their case would not have stood up very well. He and Lady Ali Shah not only invested their followers' contributions shrewdly, but also the growing number of health, education, and sports centers testified to the community's social and economic advance under his regime. The value of land and property at the disposal of his followers was constantly going up, yet, with religious fervor, many of them insisted on giving more.

Though far short of the extravagant notions abroad (some suggested there was more gold in his coffers than in any European treasury) the Aga Khan's personal fortune had grown immensely as a result of clever management. One of the first to appreciate the potential of Middle Eastern oil, he acquired stock in American oil companies with concessions in the area. The value of these shares multiplied. His lucky touch was beginning to attract the attention of financial experts and his portfolio was an object lesson on how to grow richer every day.

Other people's money was of absorbing interest to him, and he was intrigued by the affairs of ex-Khedive Abbas Hilmi with whom he was now on friendly terms. He had always thought of Hilmi as a brilliant financier who had made a large fortune for himself after losing most of his capital in Egypt. To his great astonishment, the Aga Khan found out that dubious associates had relieved Hilmi of all he owned and that he died a poor man.

There was no risk of such a disaster befalling the Aga Khan, the least gullible of men. Even his hobbies were richly rewarding. Returning to Europe in the spring of 1924, he found his racing interests prospering and his fame as an owner spreading. As a politician, he received many honors—the Council of State in India recommended him for the Nobel Prize for Peace—but as a popular figure, he was also a target for good-humored music-hall jokes. Comedians were singing ditties about him. Whether referring to his beautiful women companions or to his sporting activities, they usually ended with a punning refrain about what the Aga can or Khant do.

CHAPTER VI

"It is a matter of concern to India, and more particularly to Bombay, that His Highness the Aga Khan should find happiness in his private life."

—*The Times of India,* December 8, 1929

THE AGA KHAN was in Aix-les-Bains—he was actually in his bath at the time—when news came that his horse Diophon had won the Two-Thousand-Guineas Stakes at 11 to 2, his first classic winner in England. Salmon Trout made it a pair by winning the St. Leger at 6 to 1. The green and chocolate colors were flying high.

These successes confirmed many of his idiosyncratic views on racing, about which he argued fiercely with friends. There was the question of mating: What was more important, the dam or the sire? On this he was in harmony with his old friend Lord Wavertree, partisan of the pro-dam school. Mollycoddling? He seemed to side with William Duke, who did not spare the horses. If a horse broke down during the preparation for a big race, it would probably have broken down in the big race.

William Duke or, for that matter, Frank Butters, who took over the training of his horses some time later, attached little importance to a horse's appearance. Both believed one yearling was as good as another as long as it had good health, nervous energy, and the capacity to rest and sleep. Duke hardly ever looked at a horse before he bought it.

Racing in the footsteps of Salmon Trout and Diophon, Teresina and Paola assured the Aga Khan second place among England's winning owners of 1923. In the following year Friar's Daughter and Voluse were the stars of a splendid batch that went to Sheshoon, where Sir Edward Greer looked after the Aga Khan's expanding Irish interests. The next stud farm he bought, Gilltown (Kilcullen, County Kildare), became the best known of all. There was no holding him now. He headed the list of winning owners for the first time in 1924 and repeated the performance in later years more frequently than any other owner.

His technique as a punter did not lag behind. When he entered the previous year's Irish Derby winner, Zionist, for the Lincolnshire Handicap, he warned young Charlie Smirke, the jockey, not to talk about the horse's chances. Smirke gathered that his owner had placed a bet of £500 at 100 to 1 on Zionist and agreed to allow the bookmakers time to "hedge" the bet. George of the Ritz thought the bet was £1,000 at 50 to 1, but then there were always at least two versions about everything the Aga Khan did.

A 9-to-2 favorite, Zionist faltered in the last strides and was beaten by a rank outsider. "He was a desperately difficult horse to ride," Smirke told a *Daily Express* racing expert years later. "I don't think it was my fault we were beaten, but the weight Zionist carried and had to give away was too much for us."

Of course, the Aga Khan had his eye on the Derby, but it was his ambition to win the great classic with a horse bred on his own stud. To him, breeding horses seemed infinitely more satisfying than buying them; it stimulated his imagination and became his main interest. He pondered a hundred theories about the making of a good horse, studied the conformation of thousands of sires and dams, and followed the history of their offspring through generations. This involved science had no more advanced scholar.

Big horses, small horses, horses with staying power, horses

Aga Khan III at the age of eight
at his installation as Hazar Imam (*Keystone Press Agency Ltd.*)

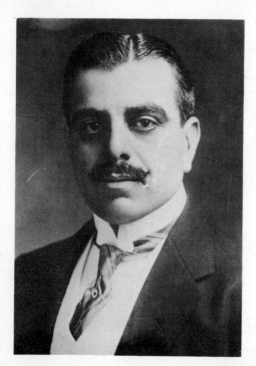

The young Aga Khan III
(*Keystone Press Agency Ltd.*)

Prince Aly Khan
with his mother,
Teresa Magliano
(*Keystone Press Agency Ltd.*)

Teresa Magliano (*Radio Times Hulton Picture Library*)

Aga Khan III with his third wife, Begum Andrée, at their wedding, 1929 (*Keystone Press Agency Ltd.*)

Aga Khan III and Begum Andrée
at Epsom, 1938 (*Radio Times
Hulton Picture Library*)

Aga Khan III and his fourth
wife, Yvette Labrousse, on
the terrace of the Palace
Hotel, St. Moritz, 1945
(*Keystone Press Agency Ltd.*)

Aly Khan and his bride, the Hon. Joan Yarde-Buller, at their wedding, 1936. From left to right: Aga Khan III; the bridegroom; Prince Sadruddin; the mother of the bride, the former Lady Churston; the bride; and the Begum Aga Khan. (*Keystone Press Agency Ltd.*)

Aly Khan and Rita Hayworth, his second wife (*Fox Photos Ltd.*)

Aly Khan and Bettina
(*Paul Popper Ltd.*)

Aga Khan III with Gandhi,
London, 1931
(*Paul Popper Ltd.*)

Aly Khan and his son
Karim at Harvard
(*Camera Press Ltd.*)

Yasmin,
daughter of Aly Khan
and Rita Hayworth
(*Keystone Press Agency Ltd.*)

Aga Khan III with Bahram, Derby winner, 1935 (*Fox Photos Ltd.*)

Aly Khan leads in Petite Etoile, Epsom, 1959 (*Fox Photos Ltd.*)

Aga Khan III in 1924
(*Radio Times Hulton Picture Library*)

Sir Eboo Pirbhai with Aly Khan and
Sadruddin Khan, East Africa, 1946

Sadruddin Khan and Nina Dyer at their marriage, 1957
(*Paul Popper Ltd.*)

Aga Khan III is weighed in diamonds in Bombay, 1946
(*Keystone Press Agency Ltd.*)

Drawing of Princess Joan Aly Khan by Drian

Prince Amyn, the Aga Khan IV, and their mother at Woking Mosque
(*Keystone Press Agency Ltd.*)

Princess Andrée, Bettina, and Begum Yvette
at the funeral of Aly Khan, 1960 (*Paul Popper Ltd.*)

Karim Aga Khan at his installation as Aga Khan IV
at Dar-es-Salaam, 1957 (*Paul Popper Ltd.*)

Begum Yvette at Yakimour (*Camera Press Ltd.*)

Chateau de l'Horizon, Cannes (*Camera Press Ltd.*)

The author (standing) with Amirali Fancy (right)
and Pakistan Ismailis (*Camera Press Ltd.*)

Karim Aga Khan at Charamillon in 1962 (*Paul Popper Ltd.*)

The Aga Khan and his bride at their marriage, Paris, 1969
(*Keystone Press Agency Ltd.*)

with speed, alert horses, lazy horses, energetic horses, horses with equitable temperaments . . . it was an exciting game, like choosing a couple of cards from a big pack and drawing a winning hand. So well versed a racing man was bound to encounter an echo in a like-minded expert. The Aga Khan met him in the person of Colonel J. J. Vuillier, the famous French breeder who operated an idiosyncratic points system. The Colonel accepted the Aga Khan's invitation to join him, but this did not mean that his calculations were always accepted without question. This particular owner was quite capable of adjusting the Colonel's findings in the light of his own views. Colonel Vuillier was installed at Marly-la-Ville, the Aga Khan's first French stud farm. He bought another, La Coquenne, in 1927, and a third, St. Créspin, two years after that.

In the winter of 1925 Kenya's Ismailis were excitedly looking forward to one of the Imam's rare visits, few with greater anticipation than Eboo Pirbhai, a young Indian-born Ismaili who cherished a childhood memory of seeing the Aga Khan in Bombay ("This is your Holy Imam," his parents told the boy at the Mosque where they went to pay homage to their leader). The family settled in East Africa before the First World War, then moved to Nairobi. After graduating from the Aga Khan Religious School, Eboo and his brothers, like most Ismailis, set up as small shopkeepers. Soon Eboo went his own way, bought a filling station, learned to drive, and established a transport firm.

Every free minute he devoted to the community, helping in the mosque, serving with the uniformed Aga Khan Volunteer Corps, working for the new Health Board. When jobs were allocated to followers for the Aga Khan's visit, Eboo was chosen "to drive His Highness." He was there, proudly at the wheel of his own car, when the Imam arrived to be received by the leaders of East Africa's Ismailis.

As was his habit, the Aga Khan soon engaged his driver in conversation. "He seemed to like me," was Eboo Pirbhai's im-

pression. The Imam asked him many questions, then said, "I
give you my blessing for your business—you will be a great man
in years to come." Eboo's pride knew no bounds when the Aga
Khan added that he hoped to see him again on future visits and
that he ought to be a member of the Ismaili Council. It was
like an accolade. Eboo's appointment to the Council was not
long delayed. ·

In this way the Imam encouraged the young men of his community, often linking exhortation with practical advice, bringing
a whiff of his European experiences to Africa, giving his followers new ideas and also good old-fashioned faith, which helped
so many of them to get to the top. The encouragement generated ambition; the prophecy became self-fufilling. The Aga
Khan's eye for ability and talent rarely failed him. He was
certainly right in this instance, because Eboo—now Sir Eboo
Pirbhai—has become the leader of East Africa's Ismailis and
owner of Kenya's biggest fleet of safari vehicles and taxis.

Recalling the fateful days of 1925 that launched him on his
spectacular career—Kenya Legislative Council, knighthood from
King George VI, great wealth and standing in the new Kenya—
Sir Eboo showed me over his fine bungalow, Dar-ul Amam
(House of Peace), in Nairobi's exclusive Muthaiga district, con-
taining foreign embassies and big private residences. His three
sons, Cambridge graduates, hold prominent positions in the
Ismaili community; his three daughters were educated at Chel-
tenham Ladies College, and his three grandsons at Harrow,
Winston Churchill's old school. The whole family feels strongly
that they owe their good fortune to the Imam, and Sir Eboo at
once made his statement of faith. "The Aga Khan is our leader,"
he said. "He is more than a Pope. What he says is for our benefit, and his guidance and advice is often years ahead of the
times. They are accepted, although he applies neither force nor
pressure."

In the mid-twenties, while the Aga Khan traveled, Aly continued his education and his sport. By the time he was fifteen,

he was familiar with most of his father's famous horses and frequently went to the Berkshire stables or, with Thomas and Nesbit Waddington, on excursions across the Irish Sea to visit Gilltown and Sheshoon. He was already beginning to live up to his father's notion of the ideal horseman. Though separation from his parents sometimes bothered him, he had thus far enjoyed a largely untroubled and uncomplicated boyhood.

His mother had been ailing for over a year, but he was utterly unprepared for the news that reached him at the end of 1926. It seems that her health had been failing, but the doctors had been unable to diagnose the source of her illness. In December in a Neuilly clinic they operated to remove her appendix but discovered that there was nothing wrong with it. She seemed on the way to recovery (she was, after all, only thirty-seven years old). "But one afternoon"—to let the Aga Khan take up the sad story—"I was driving in the Bois, and when I went back to the hospital I was told that she had died during my absence." The cause of death was an embolism.

The Waddingtons told Aly as gently as possible, but it came as a great shock. He traveled to Paris to join his father and attend the funeral rites in the new Paris mosque. Ginetta's body was taken to Monte Carlo, where she was buried by the side of her baby son, Mahdi Mohammed. Most of her considerable fortune went to Aly, who became the owner of the villa at Cimiez, the house in Deauville, the Paris residence in the rue de Prony, and the country place at Maisons-Lafitte. All this meant little to the boy and, of course, could not compensate for the loss of a dearly loved mother. He never mentioned her again, evidence—as every psychologist knows—that his pain was so great he could not bear to recall it.

Back in England with the Waddingtons, Aly plunged into ever more frenetic activities. He spent more and more time with his father's horses. From Michael Beary, the stable's leading jockey, he learned enough tricks of the trade to qualify as a first-class amateur rider. By the time he was old enough to ride to hounds, the Waddingtons eased him into the exclusive strong-holds of English fox-hunting. In Sussex and Warwickshire, where the best hunts pursued the finest foxes, houses were rented for the personable youngster with the swarthy skin and the slim, athletic figure. Aly entertained generously, was greatly admired for his horsemanship, and before he was out of his teens, the county girls began to cast covetous eyes in his direction.

When he was eighteen he was installed in a house in London, where the season's debutantes welcomed the exotic newcomer to the social scene. Prince Aly attended royal garden parties and missed few of the nonstop coming-out balls. There were whispers about this girl or that (each with an impeccable name) who was said to have put up no resistance at all to his charms, and some of them have since almost proudly confirmed the old rumors. So that life should not be all play—the idea of sending him to Cambridge having been abandoned—the plan was for him to study law with Charles Romer, a young London barrister with chambers in Lincoln's Inn.

Content to watch Aly's progress from afar, his father left the Waddingtons in full charge. Much of the Aga Khan's own time was now spent in the company of the attractive Mlle. Carron, whom he called Jane, although her friends knew her as Andrée. A whole year elapsed before he proposed to her. He was over fifty, she twenty years younger, and before she had time to give her answer, the press began to speculate about the new ro-mance. Reports said he had fallen in love with a girl who was selling candy in a sweetshop in Chambéry. "The girl in the candy shop had never met me," the Aga Khan growled. "She did not know me from Adam; my Mademoiselle Carron was someone quite different."

A thousand problems battled for his attention. He had been keeping aloof from India's sharpening struggle for independence. Mahatma Gandhi, whose nonviolent marches sometimes pro-voked much violence, was in and out of prison, Mohammed

Ali Jinnah was taking an increasing share in the Muslim leadership. In the long run, it was impossible for a Muslim of the
Aga Khan's stature not to be drawn into the conflict. In the
deteriorating situation a new initiative came from Viceroy Lord
Irwin (later Lord Halifax), who assured Indians that the British
government was seriously contemplating the attainment of Dominion status for India. A Royal Commission was sent to India
to prepare for a major conference. Its leader was Sir John Simon,
lawyer and statesman, and a future Labour Prime Minister,
Clement Attlee, was among the members.

For India's Muslims it was essential to get together and decide on a common policy. An all-Muslim conference was convened in Delhi and the Aga Khan asked to preside over it. He
was back in the mainstream of Indian affairs, working his charms
on delegates behind the scenes as well as carrying out his functions as chairman. After a great deal of maneuvering, the conference under the Aga Khan's guidance arrived at a common
policy and decided that a federal system was the best form of
government for India. Whatever the form of India's future administration, they would insist on the right to elect their own
representatives and press for a share in provincial and central
government. The Aga Khan could proudly claim to be the parent
of these important decisions.

Even the tremendous issues of India's future, however, could
not compete with the momentous developments in his private
life. After two years of courtship, Jane-Andrée agreed to become
his wife. In Europe, for the international statesman and popular
racing man, the portly but elegant *homme du monde,* to take
a wife was an interesting social event. For the Imam of the
Ismailis, marriage to a new Begum would be a great Muslim
occasion. In India, in Africa, and in the Middle East his followers
would hail the new Princess, celebrate with extravagant ceremonies, and shower gifts on their beloved leader and his spouse.

"I shall arrange for you to take the Muslim faith," he told the
"bewitching maid of the Savoy mountains." Jane shook her head.

She was a Catholic, her family was Catholic, and she had no intention of changing her faith. The Aga Khan was disappointed. It would have to be a civil wedding and there would be no Muslim ceremonies in Bombay and Karachi. By this time—September, 1929—he could be in no doubt that his prospective marriage was exciting tremendous interest all over the world and that it would be difficult to escape the attention of the press. But a great many problems remained to be settled before a formal announcement could be made. The heads of the community would have to be informed, his lawyers and bankers would have to make arrangements—he eventually settled £200,000 on his bride. He also had the difficult task of breaking the news to Aly. All these matters required thought, and the Aga Khan was the last person to allow himself to be stampeded. Yet he was too much in love to show real anger when, as most women would, Jane-Andrée let the cat out of the bag before he was ready. "I am going to marry Prince Aga Khan at Aix-les-Bains on November twentieth," she told French reporters. Her father would not be gainsaid either.

M. Carron told the Paris newspaper *Midi* that contrary to the tales about himself and his daughter, he had been managing hotels in Chambéry, Nice, and Paris. "My future son-in-law, the Aga Khan," he said, "desires complete secrecy." He, M. Carron, had two daughters and also two sons, one of them living in Belgium, the other in Scotland. His wife had died in childbirth. His elder daughter managed a dress shop in Paris and Jane-Andrée had been working in a perfumery at the time she met the Aga Khan at the house of one of her sister's clients. The Prince would marry her at the end of November or the beginning of December and the honeymoon would be spent in India.

The Aga Khan, however, left the matter shrouded in mystery in the best Ismaili tradition. The indefatigable reporters saw him emerging from Villa Victoria in Aix-les-Bains every morning with Jane-Andrée and driving to the local course for his daily round of golf. To escape the press, he left "for an unknown destination" which was, in fact, Nice.

When he returned to Aix-les-Bains a week later, the mystery cleared up. He called the reporters together and told them with a big smile, "I have refused to discuss my intentions until now because I had not made a definite decision. But the marriage is now decided upon. It will take place on December 4, and my friend Henri Clerc, Mayor of Aix, will tie the bond."

"No romance of recent times has created such world-wide interest," the *Daily Mail* wrote. Sheepishly, newspapers put the record straight and reported that Mlle. Carron had not worked in a chocolate shop in Chambéry but in a dressmaking establishment on the Boulevard Haussmann in Paris. The *Daily Express* summed up popular reaction: The announcement of the Aga Khan's approaching marriage was of great interest to the British people. The Empire had no firmer friend, and the British turf could boast of no more splendid and sporting patron.

Excitement in Aix-les-Bains was mounting as the day of the wedding approached. It was finally fixed for Saturday, December 7, 1929, and on the previous day Mlle. Carron talked to reporters. She was wearing a red and beige ensemble with a big diamond spray and looked most attractive. It would be a small wedding, she said. They had abandoned the idea of having the families. Hers was too big, his could not easily come from so far. Then she went to put flowers on her mother's grave at the local cemetery.

The Aga Khan was nowhere to be seen. It turned out that he had gone alone on a motor trip to Lausanne. When he returned that evening, stacks of telegrams and good wishes awaited him. He emerged, only to plead for a little privacy. He would not tell anyone where they were going on their honeymoon except that it would be somewhere in Italy. "After all"—he turned on the questioners—"you would like to be left in peace on your honeymoon, wouldn't you?"

On the great day the mountains surrounding Aix-les-Bains were covered with snow. An icy drizzle hung in the air, but the crowds armed themselves with umbrellas and made for the town hall, a medieval palace. By ten in the morning the photographers were in position and the streets outside chockablock with people. Mayor Henri Clerc, with his well-known love of the dramatic, could not have wished for a more romantic occasion. First to arrive were the bride's two witnesses, Maître Durand, a lawyer, and M. Borel, a French Deputy and Prefect of the Department of Haute-Savoie. They were quickly followed by two imams of the Paris mosque, Ali Yvahia Diu and Mohammed Ben Lahsei, resplendent in their white burnouses and turbans.

The bridegroom, by contrast, wore a light overcoat over his lounge suit, and the bride was dressed in the Aga Khan's English racing colors—an emerald-green mink-trimmed dress with chocolate-colored hat, gloves, shoes, and handbag. The Tricolor and the Union Jack flew side by side in the Mayor's parlor, and the table was strewn with roses and carnations. M. Clerc made the Aga Khan an honorary citizen of Aix-les-Bains before proceeding to pronounce the couple man and wife according to French law. The formalities completed, the Mayor's place was taken by the two *mukhis* and an interpreter. Ben Lahsei read in Arabic the *khotba* and the wedding address especially composed for the occasion and prayed with hands outstretched, palms upward, that Allah, the one true God, would pour the essence of his mercy on the Aga Khan, his representative on earth. Then he took the small gathering as witnesses of the marriage.

Leaving the town hall, the couple were mobbed as they made their way to the Pavillon Rivollier for the wedding breakfast. After the meal the Aga Khan gave a short newsreel interview before quietly slipping away with the new Begum. Their car was followed by another one carrying their luggage and servants and the cavalcade drove off toward Italy. The wedding guests were told that Aix-les-Bains' new honorary citizen had donated £2,000 for the city's poor.

The couple had not gone far before the Aga Khan told the chauffeur to forget about Italy and take the familiar route to Cannes, no more than 150 miles away. At Cap d'Antibes a thrilling surprise awaited the Begum. The car swung through high, ornate gates into a grandiose garden whose radiance even winter did not dim. Tall trees, manicured lawns, and decorative bushes surrounded the attractive house. "La Villa Jane-Andrée," the Aga Khan said.

He and his bride went along the wide, marble-paved loggia into the salon with the Persian silk carpets, seventeenth-century Flemish Gobelins, and precious objets d'art. The wood-paneled library with a Turkish motif, the dining room with the wrought-iron doors, heavy carved table, and silver candelabras, completed an ensemble as opulent as it was tasteful. The house, sumptuous and simple at the same time, resembled the man who provided it; combining an oriental taste with French elegance, it was full of museum pieces but eminently livable.

After the honeymoon the Aga Khan took the new Begum to London. One of their first excursions was to Fawley Manor, Richard Dawson's stables at Whatcombe, where Colonel Vuillier, George Lambton, and Michael Beary were awaiting them. This congregation of the mighty racing brain-trust could have one meaning only—the Aga Khan was going all out to win the Derby. The proud owner showed the Begum one of his horses, Blenheim, a son of Blandford, who had cost 4,100 guineas. Blenheim would be a runner, but the horse he confidently expected to win the greatest classic for him was Rustom Pasha. Michael Beary was certain the colt would be first past the post.

The Ritz Hotel at the time was like a branch of the India Office, and the Aga Khan's apartment there the scene of heated political and diplomatic discussions. He was desperately anxious to bring about a consensus of Indian opinion, but the signs were not encouraging. Indians wanted to be independent and free, but no two parties agreed on the kind of India they wanted, far less on how to realize their objectives. With London or against? Dominion status? A federal state, as the Aga Khan proposed? An orderly transfer of power or a violent separation? How soon, how quickly?

While politicians argued, the situation went from bad to worse. Gandhi's followers were out in the streets, bloody clashes were the order of the day, mass arrests filled the prisons. The Viceroy was in London for talks with the government, but only a stroke of genius could break the vicious circle of revolt and repression. The Aga Khan tried to rise above the conflict and talked to government officials, the Viceroy, the Muslims, the Indian princes, and Hindu leaders. The outcome was a British decision to hold a Round Table Conference about the future of India. For the moment, the tension eased. Lord Irwin's intention was to release Gandhi's supporters from jail, but negotiations broke down and Gandhi went on his famous march through the villages of Gujerat. His new campaign of civil disobedience and tax boycott was gaining momentum when he was arrested, prosecuted, convicted, and sent to prison. The prospects for the Round Table Conference did not look good.

For a brief diversion the Aga Khan turned to his horses. The fruits of a decade of endeavor were ripening. So far—up to the beginning of the 1930 season—he had won over £220,000 in prize money, but lavish purchases and stables and studs had devoured more money than that, and still the supreme triumph of a Derby win had eluded him. He did not begrudge the big outlay. Rustom Pasha was coming on splendidly and would not disappoint him. With luck, Blenheim might also finish in the money, and this ride was given to Harry Wragg, a strong and clever jockey known as Head Waiter because of his knack of waiting for the right moment and coming from behind to win.

At Epsom on Derby Day all eyes were on the Aga Khan and his Begum. Aly Khan was with them, very grown up at nineteen, an accomplished young horseman in his own right. The Aga's hopes—if not his money—were on Rustom Pasha, but the race was

only a few seconds old when they were doomed. In spite of
Michael Beary's efforts, Rustom Pasha faded early and was soon
out of the running. A horse called Diolite seemed to be heading
for victory when the Aga Khan was jerked from despondency by
seeing Blenheim, Harry Wragg astride, coming up fast to challenge. In an exciting finish the two horses ran together stride for
stride until, in the nick of time, Blenheim went ahead to pass the
boat with a length to spare.

"The Aga Khan! The Aga Khan wins!" From one end of the
downs to the other, punters joined in the happy chorus of the
bookmakers as the beaming owner led in his 18-to-1 Derby winner. Aly rushed to commiserate with the despondent Michael
Beary, but Dick Dawson was jubilant and ready to forget the
failure of his favored horse for the moment. The Aga Khan was
summoned to the Royal Box and congratulated by King George
V and Queen Mary. "How much did you have on it?" the King
asked with a knowing wink. "Not a shilling, Your Majesty," the
Aga Khan confessed.

Even without a winning bet, his rewards were not negligible.
In that year the Aga Khan won over £46,000 in prize money
alone. Rustom Pasha went on to win the Eclipse Stakes, and his
stable companion Ut Majeur took the Caesarewitch at odds of
100 to 1. By this time the Aga Khan's studs in France and Ireland were estimated to be worth some £2 million.

Watching Aly in London at close quarters in these days, the Aga
Khan learned more about his son than he had known for years.
Their common interest in horses brought them closer together, but
Aly was still in awe of his father and rather reserved in his pres-
ence. He was quite uninhibited when he plunged into the hectic
life of London, which was the most swinging city of the early
thirties. Young people, and some not so young, lived it up as in
few other capitals. He was seen at the Embassy Club in Bond
Street, the "400" in Leicester Square, the Café de Paris, the
Cavendish Hotel, where Rosa Lewis presided. This was Noel

Coward's London, Edgar Wallace's London, Evelyn Waugh's London—and Aly Khan's London.

If there was a world economic crisis on the horizon, it did not darken the skies over Mayfair. With the aristocratic racing set as his base and Michael Beary as guide and companion, Aly melted naturally into the colorful environment. More English than the English, except for the hint of a foreign accent, the oriental prince graduated from debutantes to more mature female partners.

He could dance through the night, each night with a different girl, and be off at the crack of dawn in his Alfa Romeo at breakneck speed to watch the morning gallops of England's finest horses at Newmarket, where his father's string was moved to Frank Butters' stables before long. Come evening and he was back in the little house in Mayfair which he shared with his Ismaili valet. He bought his first horse, Grey Wonder, a gelding, which had been only just beaten by one of his father's horses.

Having secured the Ismaili colors of Green and Red which had eluded his father, he wore them riding his own Cyclone in the South Down Welles Plate, his first race on an English course. Not much later he won the Berwick Welles Handicap on Grey Wonder. He went on to ride in a hundred races altogether, a gallant if not consistently successful amateur jockey. Daring as he was on horseback, he could be positively reckless at the wheel of his car. Being unpunctual and always in a hurry only made matters worse. On his way to a race in Brighton he was stopped by the police and fined for exceeding the speed limit. Returning from Newmarket not much later, he was involved in a motoring accident and lost three teeth, but was back in the saddle a few days later. The number of his near accidents was too big to count.

Extramural activities left him little time to study law and "eat his dinners." (Those reading for the bar examination must attend a certain number of dinners at the Inn of Court to which they belong.) To perfect his horsemanship, he went on a stiff advanced course at an equestrian school in Cambridge and promptly employed his skill for the greater glory of the barristers by winning the Bar Point-to-Point, a performance he repeated in the next two years. He had, his friends said, the love of the Arab for his steed and the skill of the Persian on horseback. But he was already aiming higher—his next adventure was in the air. He started training as a pilot and it was not long before he earned his "wings."

The Aga Khan thought this was as good a moment as any for his son to take on some of the religious duties of the Imam's heir. Aly had, of course, met leaders of Ismaili communities on their visits to his father in Europe, but the rank and file of the faithful had not set eyes on him since his childhood visit. Now the Imam decided to send his son on a tour of Ismaili centers in Syria which no Imam had visited in centuries. "I am sending my beloved son to you," he wrote in a message to his followers. "You should consider him as equivalent to my own coming."

At Beirut Lady Ali Shah was awaiting her grandson to guide his first steps in this difficult territory and introduce him to some of Syria's Ismailis, rough men of the mountains, who had traveled for days from their remote homes on mule or horseback to greet the son of their divine leader. Heirs of the tradition of Hasan-i-Sabbah, they matched the religious fervor and fanatical devotion of the men of Alamut.

Had there been doubt about the reception these primitive warriors would give the sophisticated and Westernized youngster, it was quickly dispelled. The Aga Khan never entertained such a doubt because he had a higher opinion of his son than Aly himself suspected and sensed the spark in his temperament that would quickly fire his followers. No sooner had the reception committee spotted Aly—His Serene Royal Highness, Prince Aly Khan, as he was styled in these parts—than the Aga Khan was proved right. The men prostrated themselves before the eminent visitor, tried to touch his clothes, sought his glance. Flushed with excitement, Aly responded warmly and joyfully.

The enthusiasm in the villages was even greater. Wherever he went, he was greeted by cheering crowds lining the dusty roads. Exchanging his Savile Row suits for the flowing robes of the indigenous Arabs, he joined his hosts in daring displays of horsemanship and quickly earned their respect. The tour reached triumphal proportions at Salamiyz, the Ismaili stronghold where he remained a favorite throughout his life.

His appearances were an astonishing feat of personality. "Aly's appearances always sent the marriage rate soaring," wrote Leonard Slater, who saw sex in everything Aly did. "Young men would speed their courting; young women would overcome their shyness." Sex appeal may have had something to do with it, but much of Aly's success was spontaneous popular reaction to a warmhearted, handsome young man with a genuine affection for people. From Syria he went on to Bombay and Karachi, where he visited *jamatkhanas,* led the prayers, and performed religious ceremonies with a touch as sure as that of an experienced *mukhi.* The tour was a great success.

In London the future of the people among whom Aly moved with such ease was under discussion and his father was in the thick of the diplomatic wrangle over India. The Maharajah of Baroda said that the issues involved were the prosperity and contentment of 350 million souls and the greatness and safety of the British Empire, but it would have been more correct to describe the moment as the beginning of the breakup of the Empire. India was on the verge of revolution; some of her ablest men were in jail, and the mood was so ugly that, as the *Daily Telegraph* commented, even British financial resources were insufficient to hold rebellious India, and to hold it by force would be foreign to the whole genius of British rule.

The 1930 Round Table Conference on India opened under a cloud because Gandhi and the Congress Party refused to attend. British and Indian leaders hoped that the Aga Khan would be able to allay some of the bitterness. He was in his place when King George V spoke at the inauguration in the House of Lords before delegates moved to St. James's Palace for their working sessions. The British Prime Minister, Ramsay MacDonald, presided over the imposing assembly of Indian princes and Muslim, Hindu, and Parsee leaders, each delegation bristling with historic names. Maharajahs in diamond-studded turbans and glittering coats included Baroda, Kashmir, Bikaner, Patiala, and Bhopal, all accompanied by their ministers. Facing Ramsay MacDonald and the British delegates, Lord Reading and Sir Samuel Hoare among them, was the Aga Khan and next to him Mohammed Ali Jinnah and the other Muslims. But a conference on India without Gandhi was like a performance of Hamlet without the Prince.

Try as he might, the Aga Khan could only postpone the inevitable end. As hopes of agreement between Muslims and Hindus—and the British—vanished, he concentrated on creating agreement among the Muslims, which was no easy task. Everybody trusted him, and he was asked to arbitrate on some delicate questions, but these were side issues and the free-for-all ended with the collapse of the conference.

A second gathering in the following year looked no more hopeful. The world economic crisis complicated matters, as did a change of government in England. Not even the presence of Mahatma Gandhi on this occasion made much difference. Again, the Aga Khan acted as mediator, and some of the more important talks took place not in the conference hall but at the Ritz. In the prevailing atmosphere, however, few expected Gandhi to visit the Aga Khan at his hotel. They soon learned better.

The midnight meeting of the two great Indian leaders took place behind the closed doors of the Aga Khan's apartment. At the outset he assured the Mahatma that were he to show himself a real father to India's Muslims, they would respond by helping him to the utmost of their ability in his struggle for India's independence. "I cannot in truth say," was Gandhi's ice-cold reply, "that I have any feelings of paternal love for Muslims. . . . I cannot indulge in any form of sentiment." The effect of this cold shower pervaded the whole meeting. Though the conferees discussed every

aspect of *swaraj* (self-government), the talks led nowhere. But
Gandhi paid the Aga Khan a compliment in spite of the acid
Hindu-Muslim communal conflict. In these troubled days, Gandhi
said, the Aga Khan displayed infinite patience, understanding,
and wisdom.

CHAPTER VII

A̲ʟᴛʜᴏᴜɢʜ ɪɴᴛɪᴍᴀᴛᴇꜱ ᴛᴀʟᴋᴇᴅ about his flashes of temper, his impatience with fools, and his imperious manner which brooked no contradiction, the Aga Khan, at the age of fifty-five, wealthy, respected, popular, bestrode the contemporary scene as a benevolent father figure. Though it was difficult to imagine him in the role of a devoted son, to him it came quite naturally. Early in 1932 he announced that his mother, Lady Ali Shah, would be paying her first visit to London.

When the grand old lady of Malabar Hill arrived, their reunion was an emotional affair. She wanted to see London, scene of her son's triumphs; above all, she wanted to see her son—even after all these years, separation from him was still painful. She was eighty-four years of age and not blind to the course of nature. "Death is inevitable," was one of the first things she told him, "but if it comes to me in your absence, it will be unendurable." The Aga Khan begged her not to worry. "You will breathe your last with your head in my lap," he promised, as it turned out, prophetically. But at this time she was far from death's door.

Stories of her vitality and strength were not exaggerated. She moved with complete assurance in her new surroundings, but rather than stay with her son at the Ritz, she moved into Aly's Mayfair house. Allah only knows what she thought of London life. Unlike her Westernized son and grandson, she was, as someone said, "a strict warden of the past who sees little that is worthy or desirable in the fruits of the present." Her face adamantly hidden behind the veil her son had encouraged Ismaili women to drop, she wore the traditional Persian-style silken trousers and soft draperies, which she preferred to European clothes. She ate sparingly, drank water only, and observed the fasts.

King George V and Queen Mary received her, Ismailis paid homage to her. But nothing pleased her as much as to be with her son, on whom her eyes rested lovingly. "Fate has smiled generously upon him," she observed, "but in his good fortune he has always been good to others." Fate smiled on him again—after an interval of twenty-two years he was going to become a father once more. Begum Andrée was expecting a baby.

Being in constant demand at political, social, and sporting functions, the Aga Khan seemed to be continually on the move from one highly publicized event to another, and some of his friends wondered whether he ever found time for contemplation beyond the next Indian difficulty. As if to give them their answer, he spoke on the radio; his subject was, significantly: "If I Were a Dictator." After exercising his pet theories on religion and education, he encouraged listeners to think good and beautiful thoughts. If he were a dictator, he said, the overclothing and overfeeding on which money was foolishly wasted would be replaced by rational diet and dress and the money spent on golf courses, tennis courts, cricket, football, and hockey grounds. Every European child would be taught an Eastern language, every Asiatic child a European one. His strongest plea was for the removal of barriers between peoples, mutual understanding, and above all, peace.

The practical terms for securing peace occupied his mind and there was no shortage of trouble spots in need of honest efforts

by men of his caliber. But goodwill was not enough. He wanted
to represent India in international councils but came up against
some stiff resistance. Being highly thought of in London did not
endear him to Gandhi and the Congress Party; his dedication to
Crown and Empire was a liability. In Delhi, even in Whitehall, he
felt sidetracked, and though he knocked on many doors, he
received no offers.

A whispering campaign damned him with faint praise. What a
splendid racehorse owner he was, but politics? Surely, his interests were mainly artistic and literary. His past political achievements? They were of benefit to Muslims only, and as Imam of the
Ismailis, was he not bound to put the interests of his followers
above all else? The man whom the public regarded as a living
success story was thoroughly frustrated. His great ambition would
have remained unrealized had it not been for Sir Samuel Hoare.
With plans for a Disarmament Conference in Geneva maturing,
Sir Samuel immediately thought of the Indian leader who
pleaded the cause of peace so eloquently. "I was appointed a
member of the Indian delegation," the Aga Khan wrote, "nominally as second in command to Sir Samuel Hoare, but to take
charge as soon as he left. I was also appointed chief Indian
representative at the 1932 Assembly of the League." Prospects for
the success of the conference were not auspicious, although
Stalin's Russia, represented by Foreign Minister Maxim Litvinov,
was trying to initiate contact with the West. The Germans,
predictably, sent a soldier to deal with disarmament, General
Werner von Blomberg.

Uninhibited by restraints that might have dictated caution to
a lesser man, the Aga Khan (how well I remember him from
these days!) shed the nimbus of a racing idol, the halo of a
religious leader, the ivory-tower airs of a philosopher, and jumped
with both feet first into the political whirlpool. He gave a
series of dinner parties to bring delegates together informally,
the biggest for Maxim Litvinov, which melted much ice. He
talked to Blomberg, undeterred by the signs that Germany might

soon be pursuing her "just aspirations" by force of arms. Altogether, the Aga Khan did a great deal of good in Geneva. But time was against the partisans of peace.

A peace operation was also required in his own bailiwick, where the troublesome Khoja Reformers were taking advantage of the Imam's long absence to keep opposition to his religious establishment alive. To counter a new campaign, the Aga Khan asked Aly to go to Bombay and Karachi and work his charm on the Khoja community. When they heard that Aly was on his way, the Reformers changed their tactics and prepared a document to present to the son of the absentee Imam. In a crude attempt to play off the son against the father, it suggested that the spirit of Alamut was alive in India and that the dagger was still the Imam's principal weapon against his opponents, some of whom had been murdered. The tone of the document was menacing; a veiled threat seemed to hint at counteraction.

If this was designed to put fear into Aly's heart, the plan was misconceived. Throughout Aly's whole life he followed Nietzsche's philosophy of living dangerously. He accepted the document, sent it through "proper channels" to his father, and forgot about it. Going about his religious duties with evident pleasure, he impressed his father's followers with his *joie de vivre*, enlivened ceremonial occasions with his boyish enthusiasm, and conquered the community by his easy manner. In the family tradition, he was anxious to support an educational institution and eventually adopted Karachi University, donating and collecting funds for it.

An even more spectacular demonstration of Aly's enterprise and daring was in store for the community. Long-distance air travel was still in an experimental stage when Aly put the finishing touches to a plan for a pioneer flight, a test for a regular air-mail service from Bombay to Singapore, ten thousand miles across an uncharted, inhospitable route. The aircraft was a tiny, fragile Moth, and he was accompanied by two friends, each in their own Moth: the chief instructor of the Bombay Flying Club and his father's erstwhile political adviser, Naoroji Dumasia, assistant editor of the *Times of India*.

The venture fired the imagination of Ismailis and non-Ismailis alike. At Rangoon Aly was given a triumphal civic reception and made a fine speech which pleased the Burmese. His two friends turned back, but he went on, as he said, in order to make people air-minded. The flight was a great boon for civil aviation. Other Indian princes became as enthusiastic as he, and aerodromes sprang up in Hyderabad, Baroda, Indore, and other Indian states. In his biography of Aly the diligent Leonard Slater gives another reason for the flight—a woman who was waiting for Aly at Penang. According to this theory, he flew all those miles across the jungle simply to keep a date.

On English race courses that year it was the Aga Khan who made all the running. With Frank Butters training his English horses, he was bound for another record season. After winning the Oaks with Udaipur, he entered no fewer than four horses for the St. Leger—Udaipur, Firdaussi, and Dastur (known as The Three Musketeers), and Taj Kasra. He fancied Dastur, who had stamina and speed and only needed a little more luck than had been his in his three classic races, in which he had finished second. Michael Beary chose the horse as his mount in preference to Udaipur.

Doncaster race course was packed; the Aga Khan's name was on all lips, but punters and bookmakers, even racing experts, had difficulty in telling his entries apart. Dastur carried a great deal of money at 6 to 1. After a smooth start it was difficult to make out the order of the runners in the distance, but as they reached the straight, the four horses were close together. A few more paces in the thrilling race and Beary with his chocolate cap was in front and the bookmakers' hearts sank. Then the others moved forward only to be overtaken by Harry Wragg on Udaipur, but in the end another horse with the Aga's colors emerged to pass the post a neck ahead.

Nothing like it had ever happened. One owner had four horses in the first five. The hapless Dastur was second again, Udaipur came in fourth, and Taj Kasra fifth. The winner was Firdaussi at 20 to 1. The Aga Khan was jubilant. "Let me lead him in," he said to Frank Butters, taking the reins. "He may not have been the favorite to win the race, but he is my favorite."

That year, 1932, the Aga Khan again headed the list of winning owners, with over £57,000 in prize money, more than he had ever won before. Colonel Vuillier, whose controversial breeding and training methods deserved a big share of the credit, did not live long after to enjoy the stable's triumphs. Before the year was out, his death ended the brilliant association between owner and breeder that is still a topic of racing gossip on both sides of the English Channel.

Colonel Vuillier's death coincided with the birth of one of the greatest horses he ever bred, Bahram (by Blandford out of Friar's Daughter), whose name was engraved on the roll of English Derby winners three years later. Madame Vuillier carried on her husband's work and in the late sixties was still keeping an eye on Karim Aga Khan's studs. A young man of German antecedents, Robert Muller, with an intuitive understanding of horses, who had been with the Colonel for some time, emerged to take an increasing share in the running of the French racing establishment.

The relentless routine the Aga Khan followed was taking him on another visit to India. He toured the main centers in a special train and his followers flocked to the stations to receive his blessing. Like others before, the tour produced many anecdotes, which soon made the rounds in India and Europe. Some amused him, others he shrugged off as the price of fame. One that annoyed him told of his train stopping in the pouring rain, while he, because he was indisposed, stayed inside, a *mukhi* placing one of his shoes on the platform for the veneration of the assembled Khojas, after which the purses they had come to lay at the Aga Khan's feet were piled around the shoe and gathered up by the *mukhi* before the train went on its way. According to another story, the Imam handed out letters of recommendation to the

Archangel Gabriel. Both these stories were figments of some lively imagination.

True, the community paid the traditional *zakat,* but more often than not the Aga Khan paid them back with interest by helping followers with their business ventures. In the spirit of the Prophet he took an active interest in the economic as well as the religious life of Ismailis, brought them into contact with the West, and helped them find customers for their fine silks, furnishings, and other products. New ideas he imported from Europe and the United States enabled Ismaili growers to produce better cotton and grain crops than their neighbors.

He made big investments in the jute industry, which expanded under his regime and has grown into a vital element in East Pakistan's precarious economy (Karim Aga Khan is a big shareholder in jute mills that employ some twenty thousand men). The devotion of his followers who benefited from his enterprise did not blind him to the sorry state of India, locked as it was in communal strife. He was angry with those he thought responsible for the violence that swept the country and said so in letters to the London *Times,* which was his favorite platform for airing his political views.

He returned from India in time for the birth of the Begum's baby. At the American Hospital in Neuilly, on January 17, 1933, she was delivered of a healthy boy. The Aga Khan was as jubilant as any man of fifty-six who becomes a father. He had already decided on a name for the baby—the name of a great teacher who had converted the ancestors of so many of his followers. The boy was called Sadruddin ("Shield of Faith") and prayers were said for him in the mosque in Paris. News of the event was sent to all Ismaili communities.

Leaving the baby in the care of his nurses, the Aga Khan took the Begum with him on another trip to India. She was thrilled with the reception she received from Ismaili women, who felt that the presence of the Imam's sophisticated wife advanced the cause of their own emancipation. The couple went sightseeing in

Bombay, Calcutta, Delhi, and Madras and were welcomed with garlands, loyal addresses, and obeisance. They stayed with the Maharajah of Bikaner and the Governor of Bengal. After three crowded months they returned to Cannes in April, 1934, to be greeted, the Aga Khan recorded, "by a much grown, healthy, strong little boy."

Was it the new baby who turned his mind toward dynastic thoughts? Was it the course of Indian affairs that inspired his wish to cement his spiritual dominion with territorial authority? The truth was that the Aga Khan, however remote from his predecessors, had inherited a desire to rule—perhaps from the Fatimids, perhaps from his Persian grandfather—which now came to the surface.

Through a question raised in the Indian Legislative Assembly it became known that he had discreetly asked the British government to grant him some territory in India over which he could rule. The official explanation was that a confidential communication had been received from His Highness the Aga Khan, but that its nature could not be disclosed. The matter was taken up in the British House of Commons in July, 1934, when Major-General Sir Alfred Knox asked Sir Samuel Hoare, Secretary of State for India, for his comments, but Sir Samuel had nothing to add to the disclosure made in India. When Sir Alfred Knox persisted and asked whether any other prominent supporter of the government's Indian policy had asked for an estate in India, Sir Samuel said that if this was meant to cast an aspersion on the motives of the Aga Khan, he was sure the whole House would say it was entirely misplaced.

One of the Aga Khan's biographers, Harry J. Greenwall, suggested that the land on which the Aga Khan had his eye was in the province of Sind and that he would have been content with a relatively small estate. In retrospect, Greenwall's theory that the Aga Khan wanted the territory for his son, Prince Aly Khan, sounds unlikely. The MacDonald government refused the request, but if only as a solution to his complicated, multinational tax problems, the Aga Khan never completely abandoned the idea, and his successor has been toying with it ever since his accession.

When, after yet another conference, the British government produced the Government of India Act of 1935, the Aga Khan was extremely critical. To everyone's surprise, his main objection was that it gave Britain too much influence (later he blamed the act for taking India into the war). In his view, it ended all hope of uniting India. He was, of course, quite right. This outburst was the Aga Khan's swan song in Indian politics. Hard as he had tried to keep India united and in the Empire, he had failed. He was a disappointed man.

For Aly, life held few disappointments. It was fast—fast aircraft, fast cars, fast horses—and full of women. If the stories circulating about him could be believed, he was changing his women as frequently as his cars and his horses and hopping from one bed to another. He was, in truth, for many years associated with a married woman much older than he, and was very loyal to her except for the occasional adventure one might expect from a young man of twenty-three. The reason for the many stories was that London's society women had a habit of boasting about their conquests, and what more romantic lover to boast about, truthfully or otherwise, than the rich and handsome oriental prince?

If at the time they did not hint at a liaison with him, they made certain to recall it in their autobiographies, the most intriguing of which, *Double Exposure*, was written by American-born Lady Thelma Furness and her twin sister, Mrs. Gloria Vanderbilt. Six years older than Aly, Thelma was the toast of London in the mid-thirties, a frequent partner of the Prince of Wales at dinners and dances. Before Wallis Warfield Simpson appeared on the scene, there were even rumors that the heir to the throne might marry her, but she met Aly in New York and he, according to Lady Furness, turned his battery of charm on her, showered her with roses, pursued her across the Atlantic to England, and courted her throughout a hectic London season.

Before leaving for the United States, Lady Furness was said to have asked an American friend, Wallis Simpson, to look after the Prince of Wales during her absence, and by the time she returned to Europe with Aly in tow, the Prince had fallen for Wallis. "Edward VIII might still be on the throne of England today if not for Aly," Elsa Maxwell pronounced, a little extravagantly. Supplanted in the Prince of Wales's affection, Lady Thelma Furness found consolation in Aly's arms and went with him on a European jaunt that ended—with Aly, almost inevitably—at the Deauville horse sales. However important women were in his life, horses often took precedence.

Romantic as the affair sounds in Lady Furness's recollection, for Aly it was but a brief interlude. Mayfair gossips were still talking about it long after his roving eye had come to rest appreciatively and fondly on another woman. In this case it was almost love at first sight. Even thirty-five years later, Princess Joan Aly Khan, when I talked to her in her Eaton Square apartment (where Prince Karim before his marriage used a suite of rooms as his London pied-à-terre), was as attractive, elegant, and haughty as she appeared to her future husband in the hot summer of 1934 in Deauville, where he found himself sitting next to her at a dinner party.

For seven years the former Joan Yarde-Buller, one of Lord Churston's daughters and through him descended from Edward III, had been married to Loel Guinness, the wealthy Tory member of Parliament for Bath, and they had one son. Aly was only dimly aware of all this and was not even certain of the lady's first name when he turned to her jokingly and asked her with mock seriousness, "Darling, will you marry me?"

Perhaps the story conveys something of Aly's technique. Joan Guinness might as well have said "Yes" then and there. They liked each other at once, met again, and when they returned to England, saw a great deal of each other. Aly, who was famous for making every woman feel that she was the only one in the world, had never felt as strongly before.

Aly's life was full and busy—as far as horses were concerned, busier than ever. The family's colors were prominent on both sides of the Channel. At Longchamp, Begum Andrée led in a winner, and at the same meeting Aly won the Prix Henri Greffühle with Anonyme, but the Aga Khan, whose Felicitation, Gordon Richards up, challenged Baron Edouard de Rothschild's wonder horse Brantôme for the Arc de Triomphe, was unsuccessful on this occasion. Now it was to the English turf that he and his son looked for triumphs. The Aga Khan, recently elected an honorary member of the Jockey Club, was full of ideas for improving the standard of jockeyship and other aspects of racing.

While his father remained at Antibes, Aly Khan kept an eye on his racing interests, dividing his time between London's unending social round and Fitzroy House, Frank Butters' stables at Newmarket, which sheltered some seventy of the Aga Khan's horses, a few of Aly's, and some registered in the name of the Begum. One stood out among them—Bahram, named after Omar Khayyám's hunter. Having miraculously recovered from a bout of pneumonia in early life, Bahram became the year's undisputed top two-year-old, winner of all his races, and the great white hope of 1935. His big test came with the Two-Thousand Guineas, the first of the new season's classics.

Bahram was in fine fettle. To double the stable's prospects Frank Butters entered Theft, another Aga Khan horse, for the same race. From the south of France the owner kept in constant touch with Aly and Butters; he was told that most of the money was going on a horse called Bobsleigh and that Bahram and Theft were second and third favorites. A detailed description over the telephone (since television was not yet available) enabled the Aga Khan to recapture the thrill of the race as soon as it was run. Both horses emerged halfway down the final stretch and were going ahead, with Theft looking a certain winner, when gallant Bahram stormed up to go first past the post.

The Aga Khan's attention was already turning to another potential star, Mahmoud, who ran at Newmarket a fortnight after Bahram's great victory but did not live up to expectations—not yet—and came nowhere. In the excited anticipation of the Derby, less than three weeks away, there was no time to dwell on this failure. Theft was again booked to accompany Bahram, the firm favorite, but a good deal of the public's money went on rival horses—Sea Bequest, Robin Goodfellow, and Hairan. There was no question of the Aga Khan's missing this race. He and the Begum caught the Blue Train from Nice. They stopped over in Paris and he found time and the peace of mind for a leisurely round of golf at St.-Cloud before going on to London.

He was up early on Derby Day, June 5, 1935, which was wet and cheerless, but on his way to Epsom he saw the sun breaking through the clouds. At the track a big cheer went up for King George and Queen Mary, who were celebrating their Silver Jubilee on the throne of England. Surrounded by the familiar faces of friends and fellow owners, the Aga, the Begum, and Aly basked in the general expectation that the next hour or so would bring them a great triumph.

They went to the paddock to take a closer look at Bahram, who seemed fit and well but was a little nervous and sweating. There was nothing to worry about. By the time he reached the start he was composed and moved magnificently. He was well away but boxed in awkwardly by the time the large field approached Tattenham Corner. Freddy Fox, his jockey, must have been wondering how he could possibly squeeze through and the Aga Khan was anxious too. He could not know about the little drama that was being played out on the course. A shout from Fox and Harry Wragg on Theft cleared the way to enable Bahram to surge ahead and win by two lengths (from Field Trial and Robin Goodfellow). For the Aga Khan it was one of the great emotional moments of his life.

That evening he was the guest of honor at a celebration dinner for Jockey Club members at Buckingham Palace for which the tables were decorated in the winning owner's green and chocolate colors, Queen Mary's idea. Mahmoud and Bahram could look forward to other great victories, but for the Aga Khan religious duties called.

From all over the world Ismaili delegations converged on his house at Antibes to pay him homage, for on August 18 he celebrated his fiftieth anniversary as Imam. The community had big plans for the auspicious occasion. On behalf of the Aga's Indian followers, Gulamali G. Merchant (whose sons are prominent in the Karachi community) humbly requested His Highness to approve plans for an elaborate Golden Jubilee ceremony during his visit to India later in the year. East Africa was making similar preparations.

The Aga Khan demurred, but a member of the delegation, a highly respected *mukhi* whose ancestors had been loyal Ismailis for generations, asked permission to tell the story of the Kaithiawar model state of Gondal, "small in size but great in the happiness and contentment of its people," and of Gondal's ruler, His Highness Maharajah Shri Bhagvatsinhji, who won the love and devotion of his subjects to a degree without parallel.

To mark the Maharajah's Golden Jubilee, the *mukhi* explained, the people of Gondal decided to perform the ancient ceremonial of *tula-vidhi,* or weighing, which is of historic Aryan (Indo-Germanic) origin and supposed to insure peace, health, and prosperity to the person weighed. Quoting instances from the golden age of Hinduism, when gods and heroes stalked the earth and inspired mankind to noble deeds, of monarchs who were weighed against gold at their coronations, the *mukhi* said that in all these cases the gold came from the royal treasury, its bestowal was royal largesse, and the precious metal was given in charity to the needy and the poor.

But the gold against which the ruler of Gondal was to be weighed would come from the humble purses of his subjects, the poorest vying with the wealthiest in order to provide the precious

metal for the *tula-vidhi* of their beloved paternal Maharajah.
Appealing to the Imam's understanding, the *mukhi* said that
fifty years, half a century, was a long time to be at the head of a
vast and prosperous community which owed the Imam a great
deal. It demanded tangible recognition, a token of gratitude
from every single Ismaili alive. Surely, what the people of
Gondal could do for their ruler, Ismailis should be allowed to do
for their Imam. The Aga Khan could do nothing but acquiesce
to this plea. He gave permission for the preparations to go
ahead but had his own ideas on how to employ the proceeds of
his followers' generosity for their own benefit.

Not a man to dwell on the past, he quickly turned to current
problems. By early September he was in Geneva attending a
meeting of the League of Nations Assembly. Japan had just
snubbed the League and Hitler's Germany was arrogantly
defiant. As for India, the Government of India Act had just been
passed, the last major piece of British Indian legislation before
the dramatic statute that ended the rule of the British Raj in
India twelve years later. The time for glib words had passed, and
addressing the Assembly, the Aga Khan spoke of India's concern
about the League's preoccupation with Europe, about the failure
of the Disarmament Conference, and about rearmament, which
was in full swing. A fortnight later Mussolini attacked Abyssinia,
and the Aga Khan's warnings were dramatically justified.

He was deeply involved in the proceedings when he was
called to the telephone and told that Bahram had won the St.
Leger. "It is the horse of the century!" he exclaimed jubilantly.
He claimed a new record. "I am sure I must have been the only
member of the Assembly of the League ever to be called away to
hear that his horse had won the St. Leger." No other horse had
won the triple crown since Rock Sand thirty-two years earlier.

In the absence of his father, Aly Khan led in the winner, but
even on this auspicious occasion he did not look as happy and
carefree as of yore. His own joy at Bahram's fantastic achievement was overshadowed by a feeling of gloom that did not long

remain hidden from his friends. By this time most people were aware of Aly's problem. Puritans were calling it a scandal and the shock waves emanating from the heart of London soon reached the Aga Khan in Antibes.

Suspicions, voiced more or less openly, received confirmation in the last week of November, 1935, when a brief notice in the British press announced that "A Decree Nisi was granted in the Divorce Court yesterday to Mr. Thomas Loel Evelyn Bulkeley Guinness, the retiring Conservative M.P. for the city of Bath, owing to the misconduct of Mrs. Joan Barbara Guinness, formerly the Hon. Joan Barbara Yarde-Buller. The suit was not defended. The co-respondent was named as Prince Aly Khan against whom costs were awarded."

The London-Antibes telephone lines bristled with acid conversations between father and son, but the Aga Khan seemed mollified when Aly assured him that this was not just another intermezzo in his turbulent love life. "Joan and I are going to be married as soon as possible," he said. As soon as possible was in six months' time when the decree nisi would become absolute. To escape the European winter and the London and Paris gossip, the young couple decided to await the great day in the sunshine of the Bahamas.

As they were westward bound, the Aga Khan was on his way to the East, traveling toward an ovation unequaled even in his triumphal passage through life so far. It came on January 19, 1936, when vast crowds in a festive but solemn mood were making for Mazagaon and Hasanabad. Over the years the Ismaili "Vatican" in Bombay had been the scene of many colorful celebrations, but the Aga Khan's Golden Jubilee Durbar they came to witness on this day was certain to surpass all previous occasions in splendor. So many people converged on the scene that it was obvious that large numbers of non-Ismaili Muslims were joining the Khojas on their great day. Although the available space did not allow more than some thirty thousand to reach the immediate vicinity, one eyewitness recorded that it seemed the entire population of Bombay were on their feet to see the unique spectacle.

A burst of affection greeted the Aga Khan as he came into sight precisely at the appointed hour of 11 A.M. Surrounded by Ismaili nobles, he looked splendid in his green bejeweled turban and purple robes on which shone the glittering insignia of a dozen high orders. Frail but upright, the aged Lady Ali Shah was awaiting her son on the raised dais with little Sadruddin by her side, but before they could get a glimpse of the Imam, the excited crowd pushed forward, bowling over women and children, many of whom were trampled underfoot. Coming to the rescue, Bombay's chief of police was injured in the crush. Luckily there were no fatalities and the Imam's dignified presence helped to restore order.

Amid noisy shouts of acclamation, he inspected the Khoja Volunteer guard of honor with the Begum, whose precious stones sparkled on her light-green sari. Reaching the dais, the Aga Khan took his place on the *gadi* (throne) embroidered in gold and decorated with his coat of arms. Those standing nearby thought they could discern a faint smile on his face as he glanced at a big structure, the giant weighing machine. Presently the Imam rose and asked to be heard on an important matter. With the noise it was difficult to understand the fragments of sound reaching the crowd through inadequate loudspeakers. He was saying that His Majesty the King-Emperor was gravely, critically, ill, and that he had, therefore, decided to cancel all but the religious ceremonies. Unless there was an improvement in the King's condition, none of the secular functions would take place.

Whether they could hear him or not, the crowd was obviously not in the mood for bad news. Again and again it demanded to see the Imam, who rose from his seat to show himself and acknowledge the enthusiastic acclamation. Talking and shouting subsided only when Gulamali Merchant read out the text of a telegram from Buckingham Palace extending the King's good

wishes for the Imam's future, probably the last message of a
reign that was coming to an end. Then the ceremony proper
took its course. Bowing deeply, Gulamali Merchant requested
His Highness to step onto the weighing machine. "On behalf of
Your Highness' followers," the Ismaili functionary said, "I most
reverently and respectfully request that Your Highness will
allow yourself to be weighed in gold on this happy and auspicious occasion, and to accept the gold as a humble token of our
love, devotion, and gratitude for all the unbounded bounty and
benefits that Your Highness' followers have derived during your
Imamate in the last fifty years."

The Aga Khan eased himself into the chair of the weighing
machine while prominent Ismailis slowly loaded the counter-
pan with gold bullion until it balanced the Imam's weight of just
over 220 pounds. Loud cheers greeted the announcement that
the value of the gold was 335,000 rupees, or about $125,000.
Slowly the Aga Khan rose. "I accept with great pleasure," he said,
"the gold that my dear spiritual children have offered me, and
give them my loving and paternal spiritual blessings." He had,
he added, decided to use the gold for their benefit and had
appointed Gulamali Merchant and other leading Ismailis to de-
vise the best possible scheme to apply the proceeds to important
projects such as scholarships, transfers of followers from con-
gested districts to better accommodations, infant care, and the
community's general welfare.

Next delegate after delegate stepped forward to present the
Imam of the Imailis with *nazerana* (valuable presents). The
Maharajah of Kutch offered a gold-bordered robe and one thousand rupees in silver, and the Nawab of Lunawada a beautiful
silver tea set. Diplomats from many countries brought their governments' good wishes. From Hasanabad the Aga Khan was carried in procession through the streets of Bombay and acclaimed
by more people than had ever paid homage to an Imam.

The following day ten thousand men and women from Ismaili
communities all over the world assembled on the grounds of

Mahaluxmi race course, which had been brilliantly illuminated. A silver casket mounted on four carved tigers standing on rare sandalwood—a replica of the Assembly Hall with the clock tower from which the Imam blesses his people—was handed to the Aga Khan. The casket contained a commemoration address that emphasized the great Ismaili tradition of learning, linking Al-Azhar University of 971 with Aligarh of 1936. Visibly moved, the Aga Khan once more exhorted his followers to "educate, educate, and educate their children."

The celebrations came to an abrupt end. When news of King George V's death reached him, the Aga Khan ordered the Jubilee program to be forthwith abandoned and gave instructions that all Khoja shops in Bombay be closed and business be suspended for three days. He exchanged his colorful robes for black clothes and told his followers to wear their national mourning dress. The Aga Khan's sorrow was genuine and deep. It was also nostalgic. He could not help feeling that there would not be many more British monarchs whom he could call King-Emperor. With the death of George V he mourned the India of his dreams.

CHAPTER VIII

IN SPITE OF ALL the tremendous events of 1935, the Aga Khan confessed that for him it was "Bahram's year." The aging Persian prince may well have hoped that 1936 would turn out to be "Mahmoud's year."

It did, but on his return to Europe other weighty topics soon diverted his attention from his beloved horses. Indeed, even while Aly's romantic problems were as yet unresolved, the Aga Khan was preoccupied with rumblings of another, more portentous, romance. Soon after his accession to the throne King Edward VIII received the old family friend, who happily transferred his loyalty to the fourth British monarch in his lifetime. The King appeared to be well briefed about the Aga Khan's work in Geneva and asked a hundred serious and searching questions. King and Imam, individualists both, both endowed with an easy social manner and attuned to the same environment, got on well. They talked for an hour and a half while, the Aga Khan recalled smugly, Lords-in-Waiting and India Office officials cooled their heels in the anteroom.

Soon they met again, first at lunch in the house of Philip Kerr, Marquess of Lothian, then at other private parties where the

King was accompanied by Mrs. Simpson. Although this association was, of course, not openly discussed, the Aga Khan was
aware of the imperial drama that was slowly and inexorably
building up. A friend of Queen Mary's told him that the Queen
wept bitterly whenever she thought of "the hidden, unspoken
catastrophe which loomed ahead" for her son.

The Aga Khan's son and Joan Guinness were back in Europe
by May 11. Her decree nisi became absolute and preparations
for their marriage went ahead. Many of his friends refused to
believe that Aly was about to give up his freedom, even after
the arrangements for a simple wedding in Paris were completed.
For the ceremony the couple chose the unprepossessing town
hall of the sixteenth arrondissement, not far from Aly's flat. The
date was May 18. The Aga Khan, who came to like his future
daughter-in-law, promised to be present.

The skies smiled and the sun was strong on that pleasant May
morning in Paris when Prince Aly Khan, still one month away
from his twenty-fifth birthday, and looking even younger, set out
for his wedding in a sober lounge suit with a white gardenia in
his buttonhole. He was kept waiting only a few minutes before Joan, accompanied by her mother and sisters, arrived. She
was wearing a trim black silk coat and a broad-brimmed black
hat with a white bow and looked as cool and composed as ever
as she greeted the Aga Khan, the Begum, and her groom's half-
brother, little Prince Sadruddin, whose blue velvet Lord
Fauntleroy suit provided a lively touch of color, the fashion
press observed.

After the brief ceremony the Mayor thanked Aly who, like
his father at his own wedding, had made a generous donation
for the poor of the district. From the town hall a cavalcade of
cars took the wedding party to the Ismaili mosque at the other
end of Paris, where *mukhi* Ben Khalifa awaited the couple in the
Hall of Prayers. They took off their shoes before entering and
settled on the mats on the ground. This was Joan's first encounter with the rituals of her bridegroom's faith. The Muslim

wedding ceremony with prayers and recitations from the Koran took no more than twenty-five minutes.

During the wedding breakfast father and son discussed Mahmoud's Derby chances. By a coincidence, as they were talking, Woodstock, a horse belonging to Joan's ex-husband, was running to victory at London's Alexandra Park race course. Mahmoud, Mumtaz Mahal's gray grandson, in spite of three fine wins among six outings in 1935, had not done well in his first race of the new season. In the Greenham Plate at the beginning of April the colt had failed to make an impression, and in the Two-Thousand Guineas, a fortnight earlier, he came second to Lord Astor's Pay Up. The Aga Khan told Aly that his confidence in the horse that was bred under his own auspices remained unshaken. On this note he parted from the newlyweds, who were off, the press was told, "on a secret honeymoon." Their destination was the Villa Jane-Andrée, but the honeymoon was short. Aly was firmly resolved to be at Epsom nine days later for Mahmoud's greatest test.

He was by his father's side as the field lined up for the 153rd Renewal of the Derby Stakes, as it is officially called, then worth £9,934 (over $40,000) to the winner. Pay Up was the 5-to-1 favorite, and Mahmoud, who was not thought capable of staying the mile and a half, rated odds of only 100 to 8. Even his trainer, Frank Butters, preferred Taj Akbar, the Aga Khan's other entry.

Watching the proceedings from the stands, Aga and Aly picked up Mahmoud when he was lying about eighth or ninth but going well and moving up. The gray colt looked conspicuous and was easy to follow as Smirke maneuvered him into a favorable position at Tattenham Corner. A 33-to-1 outsider, Thankerton, was leading the field by four or five lengths, followed by Bala Hissar, who rated no better odds than Mahmoud, and Taj Akbar, who was going great guns.

With a quarter of a mile to go, Smirke, who had been anxious to conserve his mount's doubtful reserves for as long as possible,

called on him for a spurt. A tap of his whip sent Mahmoud
flying forward (shades of the flying Mumtaz Mahal). Now he
was catching up on the leaders so fast that it looked as if they
were standing still, and though some experts still expected him
to fade before the finish, he easily passed the winning post first.
Three lengths behind, Taj Akbar was second, and Thankerton
came in third, ahead of Pay Up, the hapless favorite.

It was a tremendous victory. Doffing his silk hat to acknowledge the cheers, the Aga Khan's lips were seen to be moving and
he could be heard murmuring, "First and second, first and second." With the shouts of his Asian followers still ringing in his
ears, he was once more basking in the favor of a big crowd. He
celebrated his victory with a party at the Embassy Club in
Bond Street, one of Aly's haunts, which was decorated with
the unusual combination of chocolate-tinted carnations and roses
in bowls of green ink. Among the hundred guests were many
names famous in racing circles and society.

But the crowd's favor, as the Aga Khan found out, was fickle.
Popular acclaim turned to public criticism when it became
known that soon after his third Derby win he had sold Mahmoud's glorious predecessor Blenheim to the United States. The
price Blenheim fetched was £45,000, over $200,000, a great
deal of money for a stallion in these days, but for a man of
the Aga Khan's wealth not an amount so big as to outweigh the
loss to his blood line. The transaction provoked much speculation but no plausible explanation until thirty years later when
Marcus Marsh, the trainer, wrote in his autobiography (*Racing
with the Gods*) what a few initiates whispered at the time. In
selling Blenheim, the Aga Khan, according to Marsh, was moti-
vated partly by fear. "He was a man who lived very close to the
political pulse and, from the mid-thirties onwards, he was convinced that the German armies would one day engulf Europe.
He was quite sure that Britain was doomed. And so he came to
look upon the United States as a future refuge."

Marsh thought the Aga Khan probably planned, if necessary,

to rebuild his racing fortunes in the United States. Since later he also sold Bahram and Mahmoud to Americans for sums so small that there had to be a motive other than financial gain—this seems a plausible interpretation. Blenheim, incidentally, was most successful in the United States, where he sired a colt that won the Kentucky Derby.

The controversy was still raging long after the Aga Khan had left for Geneva, where, later in the year, King Edward called him on the telephone from London. The conversation, though "necessarily guarded," conveyed something of "the profound sadness and complexity of the drama" in the King's life. The Aga Khan never revealed what they discussed, but at this time the King, already preparing for the worst, was casting around for an inconspicuous place to stay after his inevitable departure from England. Switzerland was a distinct possibility, and the Aga Khan a most eligible potential host, but in the end Edward went to the estate of the Austrian Rothschilds at Enzersdorf near Vienna.

Deeply disturbed by the stormy course of the King's struggle for love and throne, the Aga Khan had the consolation of seeing Aly's life moving into calmer waters. He saw a great deal of his son, who was in and out of Geneva, where Princess Joan was installed in a rented villa, Le Soleil, to which she had moved from Paris to await the birth of Aly's child. Doris Lyon, a well-trained state-registered nurse, was with her, and Jean and Lucy Delporte, a married couple, did the domestic chores. A room was reserved in a private clinic in Geneva for mid-December, when the baby was expected to be born.

The Aga Khan was at his villa in the south of France on December 10, 1936, when the news of King Edward's abdication reached him. The final, irrevocable decision struck the Aga Khan as utterly tragic. With tears in his eyes, he listened to the King's farewell speech on the radio. The moving confession that he could not go on "without the woman I love" appeared to the sentimental Eastern magnate as the grand

climax in one of the great love stories of all time. "Set it alongside the imperishable, tragic and beautiful stories of Persian or
Arabian legends, alongside the stories of Antony and Cleopatra
and of Romeo and Juliet! Does it not stand forth as perhaps the
most moving of them all?" he asked.

Three days later the happy event in his own family circle
dispelled the gloom of the abdication. On December 13, 1936,
Princess Joan Aly Khan was delivered of a baby boy who was
pronounced strong and healthy in spite of his slightly premature
birth. In these times of political tension and imperial dramas the
birth in Geneva did not command much attention outside the
family and Ismaili centers, which were duly informed, but the
Aga Khan hurried to Geneva to congratulate his son and daughter-
in-law and to bless the baby. Looking down on the infant, he was
glad it was a boy who might one day follow in his footsteps as
the Imam of the Ismailis.

"What shall we call him?" the Aga Khan asked the boy's mother.
Though her answer was prompt, the matter was not resolved
without long discussions. Joan, who had been thinking about a
name for some time, had made up her mind to call the boy
Karim. "I thought it sounded beautiful in any language, in
Persian, in Arabic, in English," she told me. Considering the
boy's European family—Patrick, her son by her first marriage,
and her sister's numerous offspring—she did not want a name
that would be difficult to pronounce. The Aga Khan, however,
did not think Karim a suitable name. Princess Joan remembers
him saying that it had "something to do with alms"—actually,
Karim means "generous" and is one of the ninety-nine Muslim
names for God. Joan was adamant and prevailed on Aly to
support her. The Aga Khan, content that the continuation of the
line was assured, accepted defeat.

Early in the new year, mother and baby—and Miss Lyon, who
became a fixture in the household—moved to the family house in
Maisons-Lafitte, commuting to the flat in Paris. As soon as Karim
could talk, he was spoken to in English and French and became

bilingual. His first summer holiday, like many in later years, was spent in the house in Deauville. That winter Aly also rented a chalet in Gstaad, the skiing village in the Swiss mountains not far from Geneva, where Karim later went to school and acquired a big chalet of his own.

Children of perambulating internationalists like the Aga Khan's family rarely enjoy the company of their parents for long, and Karim was no exception. He was barely one month old when the whole family—Aga, Begum, little Sadruddin, Aly, and Joan —went off to the Golden Jubilee celebrations in East Africa, where Ismailis did not want to lag behind their Indian brothers in tangible protestation of their loyalty to the Imam. For almost eighteen months they had been preparing for the Aga Khan, in the words of a contemporary, to become the only man in history to be weighed in gold twice.

As so often with expatriates, the Aga Khan's East African followers felt even more strongly about their leader than the Khojas of India. They had made their home in an alien continent and "with the Imam's guidance" (as they never tired of saying) had prospered and taken root without shedding their religious beliefs.

From the four corners of Africa they converged on Nairobi for a ceremony that differed little from the Aga Khan's Golden Jubilee Durbar in Bombay: Even the amount they contributed toward the gold was almost the same—£23,000. Among those waiting to receive the Imam on arrival was the President of the Ismailia Council, Count Manji Janmohamed, and Eboo Pirbhai, member of the Council, now a prosperous merchant. Greeting Eboo, the Aga Khan smiled and whispered, "Did I not tell you that you would get on in the world?"

As in Bombay, the weighing ceremony in Nairobi was a joyful event. Prayers were offered for the health and happiness of the Imam, who blessed his spiritual children. Their cheers were full-throated and heartfelt. To honor the man who had abolished *purdah*, Ismaili ladies gave him a tea party, proudly

showing their unmasked faces for a photograph with their
Imam. They were joined by Aly's aristocratic English wife, who
took the Ismaili name Tajudowleh and decided to learn Arabic
and Urdu and study Ismaili history but never adopted the Ismaili
faith.

As in India, the Aga Khan ordered the funds to be used to
his followers' best advantage, but his approach was becoming
more sophisticated. He instructed the Council to form a Gold
Grant Committee to distribute the money to young Ismailis for
scholarships to advance their education abroad.

Among the Ismaili schoolboys from all over Africa who
benefited was Abdulali G. Tejpar, a third-generation East-Af-
rican Indian, who recalled to me how he first heard about the
scheme when he was a seventeen-year-old pupil at the Aga Khan
School in Mombasa, originally founded by the Aga Khan to give
religious instruction to Ismaili children, but which soon added
mathematics, bookkeeping, accountancy, and languages to its
curriculum. Encouraged by his teachers, Abdulali applied for
a grant and was awarded ten thousand rupees to attend the
Technical Department for Radio and Engineering at St. Saviour
College in Bombay for two years.

On his return to Nairobi, where skilled labor was scarce,
young Tejpar quickly found a job, kept it for eight years, then
started his own business. Following the advice and guidance of
the new Imam (Karim Aga Khan) to his followers to associate
themselves as closely as possible with independent Kenya, Tejpar
took African partners and now works well with them. Married,
with three daughters and one son, all of whom were educated at
the Aga Khan School in Nairobi, he wrote to the young Imam in
1968 that he would like to repay the grant that put him on the
road to success and good fortune. The Aga Khan told him the
Ismaili cause would be better served if he donated the money to
the Aga Khan Hospital.

Tejpar's story is typical of the effects of the old Aga Khan's
1937 tour and could be mutiplied many thousand times. At the

same time the Aga Khan had initiated the Jubilee Insurance Company for Ismailis, making a substantial personal investment. For East Africa in the thirties it was an ambitious scheme, and Sir Eboo Pirbhai confessed that he and other leading Ismailis felt a little out of their depth in this project. They were imaginative businessmen in their own trades but knew nothing about insurance.

"How do we go about it?" they asked the Imam, who told them to seek expert advice. An Indian insurance technician was invited to Nairobi to set up the company and train Ismailis. A campaign was launched to explain to followers throughout the country the advantage of insuring their property and their lives. Young men were sent overseas to study modern insurance techniques. To avoid the social problems that Ismaili prosperity could create among poverty-stricken neighbors, the Aga Khan founded the East African Muslim Welfare Society to provide funds for mosques, schools, and social centers for non-Ismaili Muslims, but cooperation between the different sects did not always run smoothly.

While Ismailis were still clannish and kept their affairs to themselves, even the Aga Khan's best friends in Europe knew little about the nature of the work that took him to Africa periodically. But when he accompanied the Begum on her first safari, French and British magazines soon took notice. *L'Illustration* of Paris carried a photograph of the Begum in Marlene Dietrich–style trousers, her shotgun pointing at a lion at her feet, one of two she had bagged besides a panther, a zebra, a wild boar, several gazelles, and "animals of lesser importance." The Aga Khan went only for the ride and did no shooting.

When he returned from East Africa, Europe was already shaken by the shock waves heralding the century's biggest political earthquake. It was an inauspicious moment for him to receive an otherwise richly deserved honor—he was elected President of the League of Nations Assembly. In his presidential address he quoted the great poet Saadi: "The children of

Adam, created of the self-same clay, are members of one body.
When one member suffers, all members suffer likewise." The
erudite President was unfortunately unable to apply Saadi's
thoughts to Nazi practices.

He was one of two names which Hitler and Goebbels noted as
of tremendous potential propaganda value to the Nazi cause—
the other was the Duke of Windsor's. It was probably no
coincidence that the ex-King and the Imam, leaders without
countries, should find themselves in Germany at the same time as
guests of Hitler, who was just framing the first of his "last territorial demands." The Aga Khan saw the Führer at Berchtesgaden,
where they talked about horses. Here is some dialogue as reported at the time:

Hitler: "How much is one of your stallions worth?"

Aga Khan: "Thirty thousand pounds."

Hitler: "Would you take forty German Mercedes cars
instead?"

Aga Khan: "What would I do with forty Mercedes—set myself
up as a motor salesman in Piccadilly?"

Although the Aga Khan was most emphatic that they not touch
on politics, there is reason to believe that weightier subjects also
came up. He saw Propaganda Minister Dr. Joseph Goebbels in
Berlin, and it was not long before the meetings between the
civilized Easterner and the fanatical Nazi leaders produced repercussions. Broadcasting on B.B.C. radio, the Aga Khan suddenly
voiced support for Hitler's demand that Austria and Nazi Germany should be united. It obviously did not occur to him that
the German clamor for the so-called Anschluss was the opening gambit in a cunning campaign to subjugate the whole of
Europe by one means or another. The Aga Khan's first false
step inevitably led to others.

Encouraged by connivance in high places, Hitler marched
into Austria and promptly made his next territorial demand,
which was for the German-speaking Sudetenland, part of Czechoslovakia. By now, many counted the Aga Khan among the

"appeasers," an influential but shortsighted group of British politicians who tried to buy off Hitler with concession after concession. At the invitation of editor Geoffrey Dawson, he contributed an astonishing article to the London *Times,* which was going through a dark phase. Referring to Neville Chamberlain's visit to Munich to meet Hitler and Mussolini and seal the destruction of Czechoslovakia, the Aga Khan wrote about "the glorious victory for peace with honor won by the Prime Minister."

"We are told that in *Mein Kampf* Hitler wrote this and that," the Aga Khan went on. "But every statesman . . . has said things and suggested courses that he never contemplated carrying out when in power." Obviously, Hitler would not attack France— what for? Hitler could not possibly attack the Ukraine. Hitler's live-and-let-live policy with Poland earned his commendation. (A few months later the Nazis virtually razed the country to the ground.) "What Hitler has achieved required outstanding qualities. . . . Why not take him at his word?" the Aga Khan asked.

It can only be said that in making these painful misjudgments he was in a large company which included the Duke of Windsor and the Marquess of Lothian at the time. Man of goodwill as he was, he could not visualize the length to which the Hitler gang would go to satisfy a mad ambition and had not yet diagnosed, as he did a year or so later, the Wagnerian death-wish at the root of the German character.

Death, in harsh particularity, now threatened his beloved mother in her eighty-eighth year. The Aga Khan was at Antibes when news reached him that Lady Ali Shah was gravely ill. All her life she had taken a Turkish bath once a week, followed by a massage, manicure, and pedicure at her house in Malabar Hill, where a special water system and heated alcoves had been installed. Coming out of her bath one day in November, 1937, she suffered a stroke which seriously impaired her faculties.

Determined that she should not die in his absence, the Aga Khan flew to Bombay. She was very ill and able to recognize him only during brief spells of consciousness. He knew that his mother wished to be buried in the soil of a Muslim state, so even though it was extremely difficult to move the sick old lady, he arranged for her to travel to Baghdad, where she was taken to a relative's house. While she held her own, he returned to Europe to join little Karim on his first birthday on December 13 in Gstaad and to see Joan's second baby boy, Amyn, who had been born three months earlier. "Grandfather" stayed for Christmas, which was celebrated for the children's sake, particularly Sadruddin, who was then five. In his unusual role as family man, Aly showered everybody with generous gifts.

Unlike his father, he was not given to worrying about politics. A man of action, he was prepared to do what was necessary when the need arose and went his own way undistracted by the gloomy international outlook. Moving about as restlessly as ever, he went on a safari with Joan, followed by a tour of Ismaili centers in the Middle East and India. As always, he was received with rapturous enthusiasm and again struck a chord in the hearts of Syria's Ismailis, who claimed him as their very own.

The Aga Khan was also on the move. He was in Cairo early in February, 1938, when he was again summoned to his mother's sickbed. Taking the next plane, he reached Baghdad and was by his mother's side at 3 P.M. For an instant her eyes opened and a flicker of joy lit up her features. Two hours later, her head resting in her son's lap, she went (to quote the Aga Khan) "on the safe and quiet journey from the midst of the living to achieve the peace and happiness for which all Muslims yearn." Though thousands of Ismailis attended her funeral, the Aga Khan, following Ismaili tradition, did not accompany his mother to her last resting place at Nejef, near Kerbela, where she was reunited with her husband fifty-three years after his death.

Aly, in the meantime, was up to his neck in horse-trading in the literal sense of the word. He brought off some notable coups but was liable to make mistakes too. When the hopeful three-year-old Bois Roussel came on the market, he bought him —not for himself, but for his friend Peter Beattie. Three months later Bois Roussel won the Derby. He also sold Beattie one of his own horses, Foxglove, which won at Ascot the very next day. Aly gave no hint of his disappointment. As he said, "Thoroughbreds never cry."

The nearest he came to contact with the appeasers with whom his father kept company was his friendship with the family of Joseph P. Kennedy, United States Ambassador in London. Like some of the Aga Khan's friends, Kennedy thought that Britain would crumble under the Nazi onslaught and would be better advised to make common cause with Germany. Aly met Jack Kennedy, the future President of the United States, like him then a young man about London town.

It came as a profound shock to the Aga Khan when "Hitler ripped off the veil of respectability" and gobbled up the whole of Czechoslovakia. So all this talk of self-determination and justice for German minorities was so much eyewash! The last few uneasy months of peace confronted the Imam of the Ismailis with problems not unlike the Pope's. His spiritual dominion was spread over nations which might soon be at war with each other. It was tempting to keep aloof, but when Mussolini's invasion of Albania brought several thousand Muslims under Fascist rule, he asked the India Office whether there would be any objection to his writing on their behalf to Il Duce, whom he knew personally. "Most of them belong to the Bektashi Order," he explained, "and I would like to plead on purely religious grounds for these people." The Foreign Office noted cynically that the Aga Khan's communication might help Mussolini ingratiate himself with his new Muslim subjects. They would have preferred to see the Duce antagonize the Bektashi, but of course did not tell the Aga Khan so, merely replying that the moment for his intervention was not opportune.

Then the flood gates of history opened, and for the Aga Khan, as for millions of others, Hitler's attack on Poland on September 1, 1939, ended an era. He was angry about Hitler's deliberate act of aggression. "However, it was not only Hitler's war," he wrote. "The terrible fact is that it was the German people's war." In spite of all their great qualities the Germans seemed afflicted with a romantic self-immolatory streak in their character which was never satisfied with mere success.

It was a difficult time for the Aga Khan, who even after hearing Neville Chamberlain announce that Britain and Germany were now at war still hoped against hope that an accommodation might be possible. While in Florence he made another attempt to sell his horses. As far as he could gather, Italy's Foreign Minister, Count Ciano, Mussolini's son-in-law, was in favor of buying them, but the Duce seems to have vetoed the transaction in the end. In the twilight of the "phoney war," the Aga Khan's Italian excursion inspired all sorts of rumors. As the Wehrmacht overran half of Poland and the Soviets occupied the other half, Hitler's emissaries tried hard to dissuade the Allies from continuing hostilities. They were reported to have approached the Aga Khan and to have had "peace talks" with him in Italy. It was a false report.

Equally false were the stories casting doubt on his loyalty to Britain. The instructions he sent to his followers at the outbreak of war were strong and unequivocal. The first of them was sent to the headquarters of Africa's Ismailis in Zanzibar, where they reached his representatives, Mr. Jindani and Abdullah Shariff. "Heartfelt, loyal, unstinted service must be given to the cause of the Empire which is the protector of our faith and liberty," the Imam's message read. He expressed similar sentiments in his communication to Nairobi's Ismailia Council. "It is our duty," he wrote, "to cooperate with heart and soul for the success of His Majesty, the King-Emperor. Such sincere and complete cooperation will also be in the best interests of Islam. . . ."

While he and the Begum were in India, the Aga Khan's racing empire in Europe lost its popular and able proconsul. At the first sound of the bugles, Aly Khan made up his mind to go to war. A British subject residing in France, he had no doubt at all whose side he was on and volunteered for the Foreign Legion, the only French unit that accepted foreigners. A fine linguist with intimate knowledge of Africa and the Middle East, he was a most useful recruit. As Sub-Lieutenant Prince Aly Khan, No. 4,702, he was posted to Beirut and attached to the staff of the French General Maxime Weygand.

The Aga Khan returned to Europe in 1940 and went to his house in Antibes. It was not a good moment. The German offensive in the west was imminent, and before he had time to settle down, the Wehrmacht's blitzkrieg on France was under way. He closed Villa Jane-Andrée and made for neutral Switzerland, leaving France in the nick of time before the Germans closed in. In Deauville, incidentally, they found a hundred of the Aga Khan's horses, which went the way of all German loot —to Germany.

War also uprooted Princess Joan. Having spent the last summer of peace in Deauville with Karim and Amyn, she worked for a while with the Red Cross before going to join Aly. She took the children by sea from Marseilles to Cairo, where a friend put them up, and went on to Beirut alone to look for a house. She found "a beautiful villa with a big garden and orange trees," about which she still enthuses, collected the children, and resumed her Red Cross work in Beirut.

May, 1940, changed everything and the stay in Beirut was abruptly cut short. Joan and Aly were dining with General Weygand the night before he was recalled to Paris. The mood was somber, the situation heavy and ominous. France was conquered and the French divided among themselves. Like other French possessions overseas, Syria faced an indefinite future. The formation of a pro-Nazi French government in Vichy split the military in Beirut, some of whom favored collaboration, while others remained implacably hostile to the Germans.

Aly was firmly with those who refused to admit defeat. Besides, once the French in Beirut made common cause with Germany, as British subjects he and his family would be in a delicate position, probably in immediate danger of internment. In spite of their status and wealth the descendants of the Fatimids were not immune to the agonies of war. They left Beirut in a hurry. While Aly made his way to Palestine with several like-minded French officers, Joan and the children went to Jerusalem, where they stayed at the King David Hotel, hub of the British presence in Palestine.

From Palestine Aly went on to Cairo to look for a new military assignment and joined the Wiltshire Yeomanry Regiment, among whose officers were many old friends including his brother-in-law, the Earl of Cadogan, husband of Joan's sister Primrose. He was attached to an intelligence unit where his influence with the Ismailis in sensitive areas would be extremely valuable.

Decisions on the future of the children had to await the advice of the Aga Khan, who was consulted on all important family matters. Communications were difficult and slow and it was some time before his wishes were known. Rather than take Karim and Amyn to England, where the evacuation of children from cities was in full swing, it was decided to send them to East Africa, where they would be among the Aga Khan's loyal followers. Princess Joan went with them to Nairobi and installed them in the family house on the Caledonian Road. The building, "semi-detached" and without great charm, was known as the Aga Khan Bungalow. Their mother soon left the children in the care of their nurse and rejoined Aly in Cairo.

CHAPTER IX

THERE IS NO MORE suitable setting for melodrama than a luxury hotel in a neutral country when the world around is at war; and certainly none with a finer ambiance than the Palace Hotel in St. Moritz, one of the most elegant, comfortable, and best run in the world. A fussy architectural mixed-grill with turrets, alcoves, and balconies, the Palace was a perfect home away from home for very wealthy people who wanted to opt out of the conflict. It was also inevitably a haunt of international busybodies and dilettantes playing the spy game. An occasional professional secret-agent on a busman's holiday gave it verisimilitude.

During the Second World War (as during the first) the Palace was also a most desirable residence for eminent personages like the Aga Khan who could not easily be fitted into a definite category. He was certainly rich, but exchange controls temporarily cut him off from his sources of income. The war, he used to say, put him in a position not unlike that of King Midas when everything he touched turned to gold but he couldn't eat it. How to get sufficient funds to Switzerland was one of his major worries.

He was, in these hectic months of 1940, an ailing man beginning to look older than his sixty-two years, and though he had
his books and his thoughts and his prayers to occupy him, his
active, wide-ranging mind accustomed to civilized combat in
drawing rooms or across conference tables lacked scope in the
remote valley where he and the Begum found refuge. The
Khedive of Egypt turned up, a kindred spirit in some ways;
wealthy Germans too were in and out of the place, usually up to
no good and without revealing how they obtained permission to
leave the well-guarded confines of the Reich at war and how
they found enough scarce, tightly controlled foreign currency to
travel in style in times like these.

One of the Germans was Prince Max Hohenlohe, one of the
Hitler peace scouts angling for contacts who were not averse to
justifying their expense accounts by highly colored reports to
their paymasters in Berlin. A personable man who spoke fluent
English and French, he talked to the Aga Khan in the relaxed,
enervating atmosphere of the Palace lounge.

Had the Aga Khan lived to see the versions of these conversations that Max Hohenlohe passed on to Walter Hewel, the
German Foreign Office official at Hitler's headquarters, as they
emerged from official documents after the war, he would have
been deeply shocked. Hohenlohe's reports made the Aga Khan
appear either a fool or a knave. At the very time when Britain
faced a Nazi invasion, Hohenlohe quotes the Aga Khan as saying
that he remembered his stay in Germany with much pleasure
and would be grateful forever for the consideration accorded
to him.

"The Khedive of Egypt," Hohenlohe continued in his account
of the Aga Khan's table talk, "had agreed with him [the Aga
Khan] that on the day the Führer put up for the night in
Windsor they would drink a bottle of champagne together. . . . If
Germany or Italy were thinking of taking over India, he would
place himself at our disposal to help organize the country. He
was counting for that on his well-known following and on

several young maharajahs. . . . In his opinion the Führer would attack England directly. . . ." The struggle against England, the Aga Khan was supposed to have added, was not a struggle against the English people but against the Jews in whose pay Churchill had been for years. If he were to voice such ideas in England, Churchill would lock him up despite his high rank.

"Although the Aga Khan is not always reliable," Hohenlohe went on, "his judgment has not been bad by any means. It should be further noted that, although he does not have his funds in England, he has placed them in such a way that he is now in Switzerland hard up for money to such an extent that he asked me whether I could afford to help him out with some cash for a while." Such words put in the Aga Khan's mouth did not sound like the view of an Indian prince who had worshiped the British royal family ever since the first weekend he spent at Windsor as Queen Victoria's quest. Nor would a man of his experience ever have expressed himself so openly and crudely. He was not such a fool.

Even Joachim von Ribbentrop, Hitler's Foreign Minister, to whom Hohenlohe's reports were sent, regarded the Aga Khan as a partisan of the British and more likely to pass on information to them than vice versa. The German consul in Switzerland was instructed to tell the Aga Khan, if the opportunity arose, that "we intend to destroy England." Finally Hohenlohe was told that the Aga Khan's views were noteworthy but his financial interests were so bound up with Britain that he could not be used. When the Hohenlohe reports were published after the war, Aly Khan was angry. "Ridiculous," he said. "My father was passionately pro-British."

While the Aga Khan became the victim of Nazi agents—although he never once left Switzerland during the war, they spread a rumor that he visited occupied Paris as Hitler's guest—Prince Aly was in Cairo, an even more ambiguous theater of military operations. Among the nonbelligerent Egyptians, some

friendly, others hostile, all suspect, the British garrison lived in
a twilight between war and peace. Looking west toward Rommel's Afrika Korps in the desert, looking east toward the un-
stable and uncertain Middle East, Cairo was supply base, leave
center, Intelligence HQ, meeting place, and melting pot of Free
French, Free Poles, and Free British under a military discipline
so relaxed that the war seemed a thousand miles away.

The social life of the British, in and out of uniform, owed
much to the customs and habits of the colonial overlords, on
which the Aga Khan had remarked during World War I. In 1940
and 1941 Aly took to it as naturally as he had to the nightclubs
of Mayfair or the *boîtes* of Paris. Joan made their luxurious
house at Gezira a favorite meeting place for cocktails or dinner,
and the popular couple were always surrounded by a large but
select band of friends.

Every morning Aly reported to his commanding officer, Major
Aldred D. Wintle, an unorthodox warrior like himself, a fierce,
imaginative little fellow who would have preferred to fight the
war single-handed. Between them they hatched all sorts of
schemes, not many of them practical, to carry the war into the
enemy's camp. To organize secret lines of communication with
Syria, which had fallen into the hands of the pro-Axis French
Vichyites, Aly recruited reliable men from among his Ismaili
followers, often crossing the frontier regardless of danger.

If the British were to drive the Vichyites out of Syria, Muslim
goodwill was essential, and Aly Khan was just the man to win
them over. From Jerusalem he broadcast an appeal to them on
behalf of Britain. "As a Muslim," he told his listeners, "I feel that
British democracy—whatever the differences between Muslims
and Britain—has given us religious freedom such as does not
exist in totalitarian countries." Action suited Aly better than
making speeches, but on these occasions words did not fail
him. "Some people in Eastern countries under British rule," he
said on another occasion, "may think they have not been given
the full independence to which they feel entitled. But I often

think they do not appreciate that what independence they enjoy would be fictitious but for British protection. Without British backing they would become easy prey for the aggressive militarist powers which are trying to dominate mankind."

Aly's propaganda broadcasts were part of the softening-up process that preceded the Allied move against Syria. Early in June, 1941, British and Free French forces of General Sir Maitland Wilson's army attacked across the border of Palestine. As they advanced, Aly's Ismaili friends welcomed Wilson's men with open arms. But there was a good deal of fighting. Although a member of the General's staff, Aly frequently raced up to the front by car, mindless of enemy fire, more like a sportsman hunting for prey than a soldier. Such courage earned him admiration and official recognition. Entranced by their brief encounters with the Imam's dashing son, local Ismailis were only too anxious to serve the cause he espoused. At the end of the successful operation, Aly asked permission to switch to the Free French forces. It was readily given, and General Georges Catroux, Free French High Commissioner in Syria, appointed him his *chef de cabinet*. He returned to Beirut, where Joan was soon reunited with him.

News of their two little boys in Nairobi was comforting. Karim and Amyn were kept so busy they had little time to miss their parents. From the children's point of view the Aga Khan Bungalow was an ideal home with its jungle garden full of parakeets and budgerigars, tennis court, and big lawns. Karim, Princess Joan remembers, had all his lead soldiers with him—a present from his grandfather—and fought the war on his own. Both boys adored Doris Lyon, their governess, and loved Kaderali, the young Ismaili missionary who became their tutor. "He was an enchanting young man," their mother recalled, "but though they loved him, they gave him a terrible time. He had only to turn his head and they were out of the window and in the garden."

Kaderali taught them their prayers and Arabic nursery rhymes, which are as charming and simple as European rhymes. As

soon as they could understand, they learned all about the
Prophet and the history of Islam, but there was no question at
this stage of acquainting them with the intricacies of the Ismaili
sect into which they had been born. As a boy, Karim was not
aware of the split between Sunnis and Shias or between Ismailis
and other Shias. "You learn your prayers, which do not reflect the
different nuances," Karim Aga Khan told me on one occasion.
"What we were concerned with as boys was the practice of
Islam, not the historical differences."

From the age of four Karim received the rudiments of an
English education from Miss Lyon. Amyn followed not far behind. Mrs. Bishop, the English housekeeper, completed the staff
at Nairobi. Eboo Pirbhai kept an eye on the boys, and his sons
often played with them. There were very few European children in Nairobi; one who came to tea now and then was
Princess Elisabeth, daughter of Prince Paul of Yugoslavia, who
lived in exile just outside Nairobi.

The routine was interrupted only on the rare occasions when
their father came to Nairobi to spend his leave with them.
Even as a child, Karim could feel the magnetism of his father's
personality. He made a dashing officer. "It was in uniform that I
first remember seeing my father," the young Aga Khan told me.
"I am still conscious of how impressive he was—his dynamism,
his life-force. He seemed so alive and alert and always on the
move." They played games. "He would go out and play a man's
game—badminton, football, tennis. He was a man's man," Karim
said. "To me he was a friend, even at a very young age." The
early impression persisted, and as Karim grew older, his friendship with Aly grew stronger. When he talks about his late father,
there is a tenderness in his voice that betrays deep affection.

The war, the distance, and several years still separated the boy
from his first conscious encounter with his grandfather, whose
contacts with the Ismaili communities and with his family in
East Africa were then spasmodic. The Aga Khan was commuting
between St.-Moritz, Zurich, and Geneva, but security measures

and censorship on all sides delayed news from the outside world. What trickled through frequently tempted him to bring his experience to bear on momentous events. When Iran, the land of his fathers, threatened to be drawn into the conflict, the temptation became irresistible.

Although the Major dynasty had long since given way to a new head of state—Reza Shah Pahlevi, a cavalryman and former Minister of War—the Aga Khan's concern was intense. Once the Soviets joined in the war against Hitler, the Western Allies would need a land connection with their new ally, but Reza Shah took the view that the passage of Allied troops and war materials across his territory would infringe Iranian independence. The Aga Khan was convinced that Britain could not tolerate such a situation and would try to bring Iran into line. Through the British Consul in Geneva he sent a telegram to the Shah, urging him to cooperate with the British and not to jeopardize his throne. Was it not better to enter the war as an honored ally than to be forced into it as a satellite? By the time the telegram reached Teheran, British forces from India had already entered Iran. The recalcitrant Shah was sent into exile, but his son, the current Shah, was allowed to succeed to the throne.

Before other deserving causes could lure him into the diplomatic arena again, the Swiss government asked the Aga Khan to refrain from all political activity. Worried lest he exert his influence on behalf of the Western Allies, the Germans, who had failed to recruit him, were thought to have asked the Swiss to muzzle him. What little he heard from India would have afforded him ample scope for intervention. Congress protested against Britain's taking India into the war "against her will," but Gandhi did not foreswear his pacifism and did not "seek an independence out of Britain's ruin."

Hindu pressure, nevertheless, increased so much that Mohammed Ali Jinnah made it clear that India's Muslims did not want to exchange a British raj for a Hindu raj. The Aga Khan saw British policy veering toward the Hindus when Labour and

Liberal members of the war cabinet made their weight felt and America entered the war and pressed Britain to give up her imperialist stance. The possibility of partition was already being discussed and the idea of a separate Muslim state called Pakistan was taking root.

The Aga Khan had to sit by idly, watching the confused situation from afar. Civil disobedience and arrests alternated with attempts to reconcile the warring factions. Britain's austere and pro-Indian Labour Minister, Sir Stafford Cripps, led a mission to India to offer independence after the war, but it failed because, in Sir Stafford's words, "past distrust has proved too strong to allow of present agreement." Angrily Congress called on the Indian people not to comply with British military requirements and demanded an immediate end to British rule in India.

In August, 1942, faced with the threat of widespread violence, the British government ordered the arrest of Gandhi. It was at this stage that the Aga Khan, to spare the Mahatma another spell in prison, offered his palace in Poona, Yarovda Palace, as "alternative accommodation." Gandhi appreciated the gesture but insisted on datelining his letters from the palace "Detention Centre, Poona."

The old Aga's gesture to Gandhi was his last wartime contact with Indian affairs. He had other problems to occupy his mind. So low were his finances that it was at this time he decided to sell Bahram and Mahmoud to America. The British racing community, with their almost proprietary pride in the Aga Khan's two most famous horses, was bitter. The Aga Khan's excuse was that he needed the money, but when he was called to account for his surprising decision, he maintained that he virtually gave the horses away. "I had to decide whether I should sell two of the best products of my stud or break up the whole stud by selling my mares and thereby selling bloodlines I had built up between 1921 and 1940 at tremendous cost."

Referring to his illness, his lack of funds in Switzerland, and the war restrictions, he added, "My bankers found out that if I produced new dollars and invested the same in England, they would be able to advance me enough Swiss francs to allow me and my family to live in Switzerland. . . . During those four and a half years, my family and myself lived on the sale of these two horses."

Even with his star stallions gone, the only news to bring a glimmer to the ailing Aga Khan's tired eyes were reports about his stud farms from Nesbit Waddington, who had taken over their management from his father. Frank Butters was supervising the Aga's and Aly's interests in Newmarket, and though father and son raced independently, they owned some horses jointly and often swapped or leased each other's horses. For the time being, however, Britain's most successful owner had to take comfort from minor victories.

Life offered few compensations. The Aga Khan's physical condition deteriorated. Surgeons and other specialists became regular visitors. He could no longer play golf or take walks, but it was a long time before the source of his difficulties was found —not, in fact, until after the war when he was examined in France and was operated on for a tumor which was, happily, nonmalignant. Ill health, combined with his restricted existence and his financial worries, put a strain on his marriage. Although living in close proximity in a small country, he and the Begum grew apart. Altogether it was an unhappy time for the Aga Khan, probably the worst in his life.

Thrown back on his own intellectual resources, he meditated more deeply than ever on health and marriage, so important to him and so disappointing; on racial conflict, which might engulf his followers in East Africa; on finance—his own and the community's. Being sentimentally attached to Britain, it pleased him that the number of Ismailis living in England was large enough to warrant the appointment of an Ismaili Council for Great Britain. He nominated Alnoor Kassim, a young Tanganyikan, as President, and later Mr. Kassim became a member of the secretariat of UNESCO. (But it was not until after the

war that a London house was acquired as headquarters and
hostel for Ismailis in Britain).

Pondering ways and means of improving his followers' prospects and introducing modern methods into the slow and slug-
gish African continent, the Aga Khan's fertile mind evolved plans
for a bank to finance the community's more ambitious business
projects. "We received a message from His Highness," Sir Eboo
Pirbhai told me, "informing us that he intended to found a bank
for Ismailis in East Africa as soon as he was able to come and
see us after the war." As in the case of the insurance company a
few years earlier, local Ismailis confessed that they knew nothing
about banking, but once more the Aga Khan told them, "We can
hire experts to start with, then our own boys can begin to
learn."

While such occasional exchanges were the Aga's only contact
with his followers, Aly was able to keep in personal touch with
many of them. Whenever he could get away from his military
duties, he visited Ismailis as representative of the Imam. The
affection of the Syrians was undimmed. They seemed to love
and admire him even more than the remote Imam. Aly's
speeches were brief, peppery but serious; though casual and
informal in some ways, he never allowed his attention to stray
from the prescribed religious rites. From Damascus he flew to
Bombay but managed to get back to Nairobi for a big occasion
in the life of Karim.

By the time he was seven, the boy had progressed well with
his religious education, and Kaderali was confident that he was
quite capable of leading the community in prayer. Easter of
1943 happened to be the date chosen for his debut in the
jamatkhana, and on the morning of the appointed day, amid
great excitement, he dressed in a gray *sherwani,* white jodhpurs,
and black Astrakhan hat to face his grandfather's followers.
Princess Joan was a little anxious as she watched him taking
his place at the head of the community. She had no cause for
worry. Her son did not betray his nervousness, was word perfect,

and came through the difficult ceremony without faltering. "A great accomplishment for such a small boy," Princess Joan said, heaving a sigh of relief in memory of the day.

Before the end of 1943 the Aga Khan's family received a piece of personal news from him that did not come entirely as a surprise. He informed them that his marriage to Princess Jane-Andrée was over, dissolved by mutual consent in a civil court in Geneva, but that their affection, respect, and true friendship for each other were in no way impaired. Custody of ten-year-old Sadruddin went to the father. To forestall comments about yet another divorce, the Aga Khan had a few pointed things to say about Western laws which often compelled people unhappy in marriage to stay wed and were as difficult to understand for Muslims as "the practical and contractual basis of the Islamic idea of marriage" was for Christians.

The family had been aware for some time of the Aga Khan's friendship with the tall, stately, and very beautiful Mlle. Yvette Labrousse, a French railway worker's daughter, born at Sète, near Marseilles, who grew up in a flat in Cannes overlooking the hill of Le Cannet. Elected "Miss Lyons" at the age of twenty-four, Yvette had gone on to become "Miss France of 1930," and as society opened its doors to this beauty queen of such charm and grace, was frequently seen in smart places on the shores of the Mediterranean. She lived in Cairo in the late thirties and was dining one evening at Mena House, the romantic hotel by the Pyramids, when the Aga Khan first met her. He was surprised to hear that she had adopted the Muslim faith, probably, as the Aga Khan put it, because of the complete absence of snobbery and prejudice that is basic to Islam. They soon met again in Europe.

According to Gordon Young, the respected British author and journalist (writing in the *Daily Mail* of March 24, 1953), there was an Islamic wedding in Cairo shortly after the Mena House meeting. The same author, who often talked to Yvette, mentioned in a later issue (April 9, 1956) that she and the Aga

Khan bought a site at Le Cannet, an abandoned olive grove
with only one living tree. "That was in 1937," Gordon Young
quotes her as saying. "I looked around the Riviera for a house
and failed to find anything I really liked, so I decided to build
one for ourselves. . . ."

Official records show that the Aga Khan entered into the state
of matrimony for the fourth time in 1944, thirteen months after
his divorce from Begum Jane-Andrée. His health was improving,
the war was moving into its final phase, there was even a
heartening victory on the turf—Tehran, leased from Aly, won
England's last wartime Derby for him. Marriage was another step
on the road to recovery. At thirty-eight, Mlle. Labrousse was
thirty years younger than her groom when they presented themselves at the parlor of the Mayor of Vevey, a small town on Lac
Léman. As on the previous occasion, the civil ceremony was followed by a Muslim wedding. The new Begum took the name Om
Habibah, after one of the Prophet's wives, and the Aga Khan
felt he had at last been granted "the real and wonderful haven
of a true union of mind and soul."

While a new wife shared his father's life in Switzerland, the
gossips of Cairo were busily spreading rumors about Aly's
amorous adventures. Like those circulating in London and Paris
before the war, they were often grossly exaggerated. He had
only to be seen talking to a woman over a cocktail or dancing at
a dinner party and it was assumed as a matter of course that he
was having an affair with her. Egyptian girls, Polish girls, French
girls—the historians of Aly's love life covered a wide area of
speculation. What fed the rumors was his habit of paying every
woman the most intense attention, as if she were the only woman
in the world.

One who fell into this category was a dark-haired girl
known as Christina Granville who was serving in the First
Aid Nursing Yeomanry, a cover organization for British secret
agents. The daughter of a Polish aristocrat and wife of a
Polish secret-service agent who had been killed by the Nazis,

Christina (whose real name was Krystyna Gizycka) made her way to England to fight against her husband's murderers and later parachuted into Nazi-occupied Rumania to organize the escape of several important people. After her return from this mission, she met Aly in Cairo and was immediately attracted to him.

Gossip about their association pursued him even to the small Tripolitanian town to which he was posted as military governor after the British Eighth Army had driven out Rommel's Afrika Korps. Although a lieutenant-colonel, he was, to quote A. J. Butcher, British journalist and former staff sergeant in North Africa, "unassuming and completely different from the descriptions in the more imaginative sections of the world's press." Mr. Butcher remembered Aly playing "Smoke Gets in Your Eyes" on a rather battered piano in the bombed-out local cinema. He was just as much at ease with senior NCOs, though they sometimes pulled his leg about his affairs of the heart, as with his fellow officers, who were a little inhibited in the company of such a famous figure.

On one of his flying visits to Nairobi, followed by a tour of Ismaili centers in East Africa, he stopped over at Mwanza by Lake Victoria in the British-mandated territory of Tanganyika (now Tanzania), where he stayed with the Fancy family, the city's leading Ismailis, who had come from India in 1937, started a grocery store, expanded into exports and imports, prospered, and come to own a cotton factory. Aly made friends with the son of the house, Amirali Fancy, who was devoting all his spare time to the community.

At Aly's suggestion, Amirali Fancy was appointed to the local Ismaili Council, the beginning of his rise in the community. He returned to the subcontinent when Pakistan emerged as independent and settled in Karachi to become one of the country's leading industrialists and head of the Ismailia Federal Council of Pakistan. "What struck me about Prince Aly," Mr. Fancy told me, recalling their first meeting, "was not only his tremendous

energy but his infinite goodwill and sympathy and eagerness to
help the community."

After his long spell in the desert, Lieutenant-Colonel Prince
Aly Khan was eager to get back to Europe, but it was a year
before an opportunity offered itself. It came when, soon after the
Allied invasion of Hitler's "Fortress Europe" across the English
Channel, Anglo-American forces were massing for an invasion of
southern France to take the German enemy in the rear. When
Aly found out that United States troops would be in the vanguard
of the new military venture, he asked to be transferred to the
U.S. Army. He was granted a commission and attached to a unit
about to cross the Mediterranean. He made the trip aboard a
landing craft, and drawn toward the Riviera like a homing bird,
he disembarked at St.-Tropez among the first Allied troops to set
foot on the soil of southern France. The date was August 15, 1944.

Christina Granville, too, had a part in the invasion. Before the
Allied landing she had parachuted into France, made contact with
the French underground, and helped to liberate three British
officers from a Vichy French prison (one of them was the writer
Xan Fielding). When Aly met Christina again, she told him her
fantastic story—how she had twice fallen into the hands of the
Gestapo, escaped twice, and succeeded in her dangerous work.
Christina's luck ran out after the war. She never found her way
back to a routine life, disappeared, and was not heard of again
until she was stabbed to death in a little hotel in Kensington,
London, in 1952.

Aly did not linger in St.-Tropez. He commandeered a jeep and
made off in the direction of Cannes. The familiar Carlton Hotel,
meeting place of Riviera habitués in happier days, was shuttered,
but when he presented himself at a side door he was greeted as a
liberator. His next destination was Cap d'Antibes and the Villa
Jane-Andrée, which had escaped seizure by the Germans because
a friend of the former Begum had spread protective wings over
it and kept the rapacious Wehrmacht at bay.

At the same time Aly learned that the Nazis had not allowed

the house in Maisons-Lafitte to slip through their fingers. Requisitioned soon after the conquest of France, it had become Field Marshal Erwin Rommel's private residence when Hitler transferred him from Africa to France. It would not be long before this house, too, would be restored to its rightful owners, but in the meantime Aly received a new assignment. It was to act as British liaison officer with an intelligence unit belonging to the U.S. Sixth Army Group with which he had come across from Libya.

His immediate superior was Lieutenant-Colonel Henry Cabot Lodge, former U.S. Senator from Massachusetts and member of a leading Boston family, himself destined to play a major role in American affairs. The two comrades-in-arms, although of vastly different backgrounds, hit it off splendidly. Colonel Lodge knew Aly's reputation as a playboy and was all the more pleasantly surprised by his dedication and stamina. Like everybody else, he was captivated by Aly's pleasant manner and he-man qualities. Gordon Grand, a major serving with the same unit, described Aly's three outstanding qualities as physical vitality, humility, and love of people. He told Leonard Slater that Aly was completely unpretentious and that money meant nothing to him.

As the unit moved on toward Germany, Aly's gift for languages brought him into closer contact with local people than most other officers had. Hard-working, untiring, dedicated, he smoothed out problems as he went. His status as the son of a religious leader never intruded on his army life except when he flew once more to India to meet leaders of his father's councils.

By the time the Germans laid down their arms, his unit had reached the Vosges mountains. By this time Aly proudly wore the U.S. Army Bronze Star. The citation, signed by General J. L. Devers, Commander of the U.S. Sixth Army Group, praised him for his "tireless energy, marked endeavor, and constant willingness to undertake any task regardless either of its

hazards or its irksomeness." The French gave him the Légion
d'Honneur and the Croix de Guerre with palm. The French
citation, signed by Generals Juin and de Gaulle, which reached
him after the war, spelled out his accomplishments: "Aly Khan,
Lieutenant-Colonel of the British Army, has shown in his functions as liaison officer for General Devers with the First French
Army military qualities as brilliant as those which he displayed
in 1939–40 as Second-Lieutenant in the Foreign Legion in Syria
and later as Intelligence Officer with the French staff. During the
period from August 15, 1944, until March, 1945, frequently sent
on missions to the front, he won the admiration of all by his
bravery under fire and complete disregard of danger, by his
intelligence, tact and character, and he was thus able to render
the highest possible service to the Allied army."

Alerted by Aly, friends in several armies moving in on Germany
were on the lookout for his and his father's horses, which the
Nazis had taken from their French stables as loot. He was delighted to receive a message from U.S. General George Patton,
whose storming finish had carried his troops farther east than
any others. The horses had been traced to the German National Stud at Altefelt from which Patton's troops were still some
distance away. Because Soviet armies were fast approaching, no
time could be lost. With a jeep and a horse-trailer and a single
G.I. to help him, Aly dashed across Germany but found the Germans still in control at Altefelt. It was a situation after his own
heart. At the point of a gun he demanded the return of his
horses. With Robert Muller, who had gone into German captivity
with the horses, he organized their removal, carting them two by
two across the French border in an expedition that took five
days and five nights.

Aly's jeep rides backward and forward across the bumpy,
bomb-scarred roads of Germany with the madly swaying horse-
box behind him were symbolic of his family's crisscrossing of
three continents as soon as the war was over, almost like a
Keystone Cops film with its crazy speed-up of movement. Aly

slipped into Switzerland for his first reunion with his father in five years to discuss the future. In a mellow, fatherly mood, the old Aga agreed to make his son a full partner in the control of the multimillion-dollar racing enterprise.

Even before the armistice was signed, but with France already safely in the hands of the Western Allies, Duff Cooper, the British Ambassador in Paris, enabled the Aga Khan to escape from his self-imposed exile and smoothed his path from Geneva to Marseilles. He and his new Begum accepted the hospitality of the U.S. Army, who put them up in one of the many requisitioned elegant and comfortable houses on the coast. From Marseilles, the couple soon took off for the better climate of Cairo.

Before their arrival Joan Aly Khan, who had been working with military welfare organizations in Cairo, went posthaste to Nairobi to pick up her sons Karim and Amyn. Accompanied by the loyal Miss Lyon, they stopped over in Greece before flying to Paris, where they opened Aly's house in the rue de Prony. After waiting several days for their luggage, which was too voluminous to come with them by air, it was decided to send the children and Miss Lyon to Switzerland rather than England, where conditions were still difficult and rations poor. They were installed in a rented chalet in Gstaad, the beautiful and invigorating mountain resort conveniently near the old Aga Khan's Lausanne residence.

Although he briefly contemplated making the army his career, Aly was soon on the move again. There was so much to do, so many matters needing his attention. Even before his demobilization he flew to England, went to the races, and traveled on to Ireland to inspect Gilltown, of which he was now part owner. He was full of plans for the studs and the stables and anxious to recapture the old glory of the famous colors. Then, a little heavy-hearted, he went to meet Joan. His extravaganzas had not remained hidden from her and deepened the estrangement that was the result of their long separation.

But more important than their problem was the future of the

boys. Joan would have preferred for them to be brought up in
England, where her son, Patrick Guinness, was being educated
and where her three sisters (Countess of Cadogan, Duchess of
Bedford, Lady Ebury) and their children provided a ready-made
family circle, but she realized that the destiny of an Ismaili
prince demanded a cosmopolitan background. After consultations with the old Aga it was decided to send Karim and
Amyn to Le Rosay—the "school of princes" at their doorstep in
Gstaad—where the Duke of Kent, several other boys of royal
antecedents, and the sons of many Eastern rulers had received
their education.

By this time the Aga Khan was back in East Africa, where he
and the Begum were met by an upsurge of affection and emotion. The Imam of the Ismailis was there in his religious role, but
his first concern was to prepare the community for the problems
of the postwar era and the severe competition in trade and industry in which only the fittest would be able to survive. What he
had mapped out in years of contemplation in Switzerland
could now be put into operation. The Imam called an economic
conference in Nairobi to launch a series of cooperative societies in
the East African territories—sixteen such societies sprang up as a
result. Next he introduced plans to disperse Ismailis into small
trading areas, reversing a trend toward congregation in the big
towns. He told his followers to get together and establish wholesale businesses. The head of East Africa's Ismailis, Bahadurali
K. S. Verjee, a Kampala lawyer, said, "Our Most Reverend
Spiritual Father has given us the fundamentals. . . ." He stressed
that Ismaili children should become thoroughly acquainted with
the role of the present Imam. "Real and true understanding," he
said, "will bring spontaneous loyalty to our Imam-e-Zaman, the
Lord of the Age."

The adoration was building up toward a great celebration to
mark the sixtieth anniversary of the Aga Khan's Imamate, his
Diamond Jubilee, when "our August and Spiritual Father" was to

be weighed against diamonds as he had been weighed against gold ten years earlier. The actual date of the Jubilee was August 18, 1945, but the Imam asked his followers to be patient. The immediate postwar period, he felt, was not an auspicious time for such a ceremony. He suggested—and the Imam's suggestion was an order—that the Diamond Jubilee should be celebrated in the following year, in March, 1946, in Bombay, and four months later in Dar-es-Salaam. For the Aga Khan it was a welcome opportunity to give his people a new outlook, a new mentality, a new direction in modern times.

What mattered most was that after the dark years of the war the Imam and his followers were reunited.

CHAPTER X

AT THE AGE OF nine Karim was a handsome, quiet boy with a fine physique and a serious bent, more studious than his brother Amyn; later, their mother told me, the trends were reversed. A mop of dark hair, soulful eyes, and a wide, pleasant smile communicated only the slightest hint of Karim's Eastern antecedents. Both Karim and his brother spoke English and French fluently, and both had a smattering of Arabic. M. Carmal, the headmaster of Le Rosay, whom Princess Joan went to see about the boys, was happy to accept them for his school. He already had a number of Muslim pupils, he told her, who were receiving religious instruction by private arrangements, but since Karim and Amyn were the grandsons of the Imam of the Ismailis, and since the office would eventually come down to Karim, it was thought important that he should continue to have individual religious tuition. Aligarh University, consulted by the Aga Khan, recommended a young student of Islam, Mustafa Kamul, who was summoned to Europe and engaged as Karim's religious teacher. (He now edits *Africa Ismaili,* a weekly published in Nairobi.)

Karim and Amyn quickly made friends with the other boys,

who called them "K" and "A," which is how the brothers soon referred to each other. From them the family adopted the practice—Karim's friends, his mother, his young wife, the new Begum Aga Khan, informally call him "K."

When the old Aga returned from Africa to stay in Lausanne, the boys were taken to see him. "An extraordinary relationship developed between my father-in-law and my elder son," Princess Joan recalls. " 'K' always talked to his grandfather as if they were contemporaries. There was a powerful bond between them." It was probably due to Grandfather's influence that Karim was mature beyond his age without foregoing the pleasures of a typical teen-ager's life. "K"—but not "A"—liked rowing, became very good with his sculls, and also played football well. Both he and Amyn liked skiing and tennis. Although very close, the brothers were different in character, and as their mother put it, "didn't collect the same things."

Young Karim spent the first postwar summer in the Villa Gorizia in Deauville but preferred Gilltown, which he also visited. Aly, who joined him on the stud farm, was dismayed because his elder son was not particularly interested in horses. Neither did his Eastern and religious associations play a great part in his early years; his closest friends were his numerous cousins on his mother's side and he often went to Scotland to stay with his aunt.

He saw little of his father, who was constantly on the move from country to country, from continent to continent, looking upon the south of France as his base. Aly paid £30,000 for the Château de l'Horizon, a fine, Mediterranean-style house on the sea between Antibes and Cannes which was originally built for the late American actress Maxine Elliot. Surrounded by a big white wall and separated from the main coastal road by the railway, which runs a little too close for comfort, the château with the terrace overlooking the sea and an outsize swimming pool was modern, informal, and comfortable rather than stately

and oriental. Aly, with his taste for objets d'art inherited from
his mother, furnished it and acquired some first-rate paintings,
including a Degas and some Utrillos and Raoul Dufys, which
were his favorites.

The large living room with the wide, long couch and a colorful
protrait of the Aga Khan on the wall was usually teeming with
visitors and there were rarely fewer than a dozen people for
lunch. Mario Magliano, a brother of Aly's mother, managed the
household, but some guests felt that he was not as hospitable as
his generous nephew would wish him to be. Two other fixtures
were Aly's Ismaili servant, whom he called Tutti, although his
name was believed to be Hussein, and Emrys Williams, who
acted as chauffeur and bodyguard. The energetic host swam,
played tennis, toured the Riviera high spots (preferring ice
cream to alcoholic drinks), and met his innumerable friends, some
of whom joined the roll of the château's guests at a moment's
notice and often stayed on long after Aly had gone off to Paris
or London or farther afield. Most of his trips were made
in hired aircraft until de Havilland built him a twin-engined
monoplane, which he later christened "Avenger" after one of his
horses. As pilot he engaged John Lancaster, a wartime friend
and frequent companion.

The Aga Khan also returned to the Riviera, where he stayed
at Yakimour, the villa he had built for the Begum and named
after her (from "Yaki," his pet name for her, based on her ini-
tials, plus "*amour*"). She preferred saris to European clothes and
owned three hundred of them, and as many pairs of shoes. The
jewels her husband gave her soon added up to a unique collection. She, in turn, looked after him with devotion and patience.
They made a happy couple.

Relations between the Aga and his son, on the other hand,
were far from harmonious. He did not approve of Aly's mode of
life and was apprehensive about his flights in the Avenger in all
kinds of weather, his reckless courage on fast horses, and his
driving at breakneck speed. If he was short-tempered with his

son, it was a reflex action due to his hidden fear of losing him. Aly was rarely at ease in his father's company.

There was no outward sign of tension early in March, 1946, when the whole family embarked for India and one of the great occasions in the Aga Khan's life. It was bound to be ample compensation for the deprivation and isolation of the war years. The Khoja community was in a state of mounting religious fervor as the committee of Ismaili nobles in charge of the preparations for the Imam's Diamond Jubilee reached the climax of many months' work. In the thirteen-hundred-year history of the sect only two of Hazar Imam's predecessors—one of them the Aga Khan's grandfather—had occupied the august office as long, and under no previous leader had the community made such spectacular progress. Much of it was due to the unique integration of religious and secular interests that the Aga Khan preached and practiced. "Ismailis are not like Hindus. There is no withdrawal from the world; they are not Yogis," I was recently told by A. M. Sadaruddin, an erudite Ismaili in East Africa.

The generosity with which the community approached the Jubilee was a measure of the regard in which they held their leader. Even before he and his family set out for Bombay, a British warship, H.M.S. *Devonshire,* was heading toward the Indian Ocean with diamonds worth £640,000, the amount the community had collected to hand over to the Imam as an outright gift. Kept in strong metal boxes and under constant guard, the diamonds were on loan from the London Diamond Syndicate. When the battleship's progress seemed too slow, boxes and guards were transferred to a flying boat for the final lap. They arrived at the same time as the Aga Khan.

For weeks ahead his followers had been converging on Bombay from every part of the subcontinent and even farther afield. At the appointed time—the afternoon of Sunday, March 10, 1946— over 100,000 of them were at the Brabourne Stadium, happily, expectantly, peering toward the raised platform in the center and the elaborate weighing machine with the big clock face more than ten feet above, one huge scale balanced against a base with a comfortable easy chair. Fourteen ruling princes, including the Maharajahs of Kashmir and Baroda and the Ruler of Nawanagar, were among the guests of honor. The family were in their places, but Prince Aly and his half-brother, Prince Sadruddin, a handsome, round-faced youngster of twelve, came to take a closer look at the precious boxes with the diamonds as they were wheeled up.

A tremendous cheer greeted the Imam as he appeared dressed in a long white silk robe spangled with silver and a turban threaded with gold. By his side, even more spectacular, the Begum was in a white sari studded with 1,200 diamonds worth some £45,000. Messages of goodwill from King Farouk of Egypt, the Shah of Iran, the King of Afghanistan, and Mahatma Gandhi were among those read out before the Mayor of Bombay started the weighing ceremony.

Only intimates were aware of the little drama that had preceded the occasion. Because those who made the biggest contribution would be the first to place boxes with the equivalent of their donations in diamonds on the scales—to be followed by those with smaller offerings—the amount of each donation was noted in advance and the notes placed in sealed envelopes. When they were opened, a modestly endowed printer appeared to have outdone Pakistan's richest Ismaili in generosity and earned the privilege of placing the first box of diamonds on the scales. Angrily, the rich man protested and wanted to increase his donation so as to head the list and be the first to pay homage to the Imam. The Aga Khan would have none of it. "I will not tolerate that," he said and refused to permit the change. The printer remained at the head of the queue of the diamond-bearing Ismaili nobles.

Seated in the easy chair on the scales, the Aga Khan looked on as the metal boxes, one after the other, were placed in position with slow deliberation and great formality to balance his weight, which turned out to be 243½ pounds, nearly 14 pounds heavier than at the Golden Jubilee celebrations of 1936. When the last box was on the scales, a wealthy Khoja lady broke ranks, mounted the platform, and produced a fistful of diamonds to add a personal gift to the communal offering.

Thanking his "spiritual children," the Aga Khan blessed the crowd before driving through Bombay's beflagged and illuminated streets to his floodlit palace. Pride and gratitude seemed to struggle for expression while his lips mumbled prayers. The diamonds were flown back to London and the equivalent of their value was handed over to the Imam, who announced that he was creating a trust fund for the community's economic and educational welfare. Not a penny went into his own pocket.

Preparations for a similar ceremony in East Africa in July were well on the way and enthusiasm among Ismailis there was as great. News of the mounting excitement reached the Aga Khan in Switzerland, but his doctors were concerned about the effects of constant travel and heavy ceremonial duties on his health. They prescribed a course of injections and advised him, if he insisted on carrying out his heavy program, to make arrangements for the treatment to be continued wherever he was. He was still in need of constant medical attention when he reached East Africa.

A big crowd of Ismailis greeted him on his arrival in Nairobi. One by one, the venerable leaders of the community, each a personality in his own right, came forward to pay their humble respects—Bahadurali Verjee, the Kampala lawyer with big interests in tea and coffee, one of the few of the old guard whose native wisdom was cemented by a formal education; Count Abdullah, an imposing man with a forceful character to match and fiery eyes that flashed violent disapproval (preceding an angry outburst) whenever he thought the best interests of the Imam were threatened; Count Fatehali Dhala, the Mombasa merchant who became the guardian of the community's pursestrings and made every Ismaili's personal needs his own concern;

and, perhaps the brightest of them all, the agile, quick-thinking little Eboo Pirbhai, owner of a growing fleet of safari vehicles and taxis, who was so well in tune with the Imam's progressive ideas on modernizing the community.

Taking up residence at the bungalow on the Caledonian Road where his two grandsons had spent the war years, the first thing the Aga Khan did was to look for a capable doctor to continue the treatment prescribed in Switzerland; he was advised to consult Dr. Guy Johnson, an English doctor who first came to Nairobi in 1935 for a year but liked the country so much that he stayed on and is still there. "I was asked to present myself at the bungalow," Dr. Johnson told me recently in his pleasant house on Sykes Road in Nairobi, where he keeps many mementos of the Aga Khan's 1946 visit.

Before he could continue his Swiss colleague's treatment, the Aga Khan developed pneumonia and had to be given penicillin every three hours, day and night. Dr. Johnson, who was running two practices and working long hours at the time because his partner was in England, offered to give the patient the daytime injections and arrange for a nursing sister from the hospital to administer them at 3, 6, and 9 A.M. "Not on your life!" the Aga Khan told him, "I am not having a nursing sister. You do it!" His word was a command. Dr. Johnson did as he was told and the Aga Khan arranged for his transport, back and forth, but after the 9 P.M. injection he told the doctor, "You can't go home now. Stay the night, sleep here, and we will call you at 3 A.M."

That night the doctor found a bottle of Dimple Haig whisky by his bedside. "I could visualize the Aga Khan thinking what he could give me," he mused. "He was the kind of big man with a very human touch, always thinking of little personal things to give pleasure to others." He was also usually meticulous about his treatment, but one evening when Dr. Johnson arrived at 9 P.M. sharp, the Aga Khan was in his dressing gown playing backgammon with the Begum. "Would you mind waiting?" he asked the doctor. "This is very important. I can't stop now—she is winning and I am losing."

When he recovered, he asked Dr. Johnson to accompany him to Africa. Dar-es-Salaam was crowded with followers including thousands of Indians who had crossed the ocean to live through "the experience of a lifetime" for a second time. From the Middle East, from Abyssinia, from the Congo, and from South Africa they had come to the big sports ground of the Aga Khan Club, which was packed with seventy thousand people, the British Colonial Secretary and the governors of Kenya, Tanganyika, and Uganda among them.

The final preparations for the weighing were completed and Dr. Johnson was giving his patient a last checkup when an attendant told the Aga Khan that a number of people wanted to see him to tell him how best to use the collected funds. "The Aga Khan was livid," Dr. Johson recalled. "He stamped his foot and refused to go on with the ceremony until he received a written assurance that this was a free and unconditional gift." As a small concession, he sent a message to say that these people could indicate how they thought the money ought to be used, but added pointedly that this did not mean he would necessarily obey their wishes. "I may agree to spend the money one way," he said, "or I may change my mind and spend it another way!" This little matter settled, he took the Begum's hand and led her out to a rapturous welcome.

After an address celebrating him as "one of the great figures of the age," he mounted the scales and watched the heads of Africa's leading Ismaili families, one after another, place the boxes with the diamonds on the scales. He kept a watchful eye on ceremonial details. "Tell the Boy Scouts to move into position now!" he told one aide. "Now is the time for the procession to start moving!" he told another. He was alert but obviously tired. His weight balanced the diamonds at 243 pounds—he had lost half a pound since Bombay four months earlier—and their value was £684,000 (then nearly $2,000,000). The Begum, Aly, and Sadruddin were also given gifts of diamonds.

Heaving himself up to address the crowd, the Aga stressed

that the gift to him was unconditional but added pointedly, "I do not wish to take this money for myself but want to use it as I think best for my spiritual children." As in Pakistan, he announced the creation of a trust, the Diamond Jubilee Investment Trust, to which he was giving the money as an absolute gift, the greater part of it to go toward a new financial structure for the community. Cooperative societies, banks, and building societies would be able to draw sums equal to their capital, mostly at 3 percent interest but at no more than 6 percent in any circumstances.

The celebrations went on for ten days. Dar-es-Salaam's towering coconut palms were lit up with gay fireworks at night, exhibitions showed the work of the community, Aga Khan Boy Scouts and Girl Guides gave displays, there were lectures on health, hygiene, child welfare, and domestic science. As Governor Philip Mitchell said, the Aga Khan was inaugurating a new era for Ismailis and beyond that for the people of Africa. The Governor of Tanganyika spoke in similar terms and the Governor of Uganda said that the British Empire as a whole had every reason to acclaim one who was both a great Imam and a great statesman.

"My grandfather," Prince Karim Aga Khan told me, "was determined that the funds presented to him should go toward creating great new community institutions and that what was given to him should be returned to the community." To get the trust going, the old Aga called the leaders of the community together and told them to stop petty trading. He pointed to Europe's business houses which came down from generation to generation. The community, he said, should concentrate on a housing program so that each Ismaili in East Africa would have a roof over his head and take root in the country of his residence. "We obtained the services of an adviser," Sir Eboo Pirbhai said, "and invited Mr. C. Grey of the Standard Bank to become General Manager of the Trust. His Highness told him that the trust's function was to administer the amount collected and its purpose to help the community." To bring it up to one million, the Aga Khan made a personal contribution of over £300,000.

After the ceremony he went on a tour of community centers, including a brief excursion to South Africa. In Mwanza Amirali Fancy acted as his aide-de-camp and honorary chauffeur. Throughout, as was his habit, the Imam kept up a barrage of questions about conditions, commerce, schools, hospitals. India was in the throes of a struggle for independence. What were the prospects in East Africa? "Not good for at least fifteen years," Amirali Fancy replied. "The people are not ready for independence." Hazar Imam congratulated Fancy on his work for the community and the cooperative societies he had organized in Lake Province; similar societies which came into being all over the country were the foundation of Ismaili prosperity. Impressed with his achievements, he appointed Fancy to the Supreme Ismailia Council for East Africa, to which he also appointed Eboo Pirbhai.

Hundreds of Ismailis cherish the memory of brief encounters with the Imam. A. M. Sadaruddin recalled meeting him on this occasion. "What is your job?" the Imam asked, and Sadaruddin replied that he was a writer and journalist. Shaking his head sorrowfully, the Aga Khan told him, "I am afraid you will never be rich." He patiently pondered the problems of his humblest follower; his advice was usually simple and direct, but he always backed it up. "Go and start a dress shop in Dar-es-Salaam," he told one Ismaili, "and send me a telegram when you have opened it!" When the telegram arrived, he asked the British Governor and other prominent friends to visit it and make small purchases. Others followed suit and the business prospered. Instructions, even when they affected the whole community, were not always written down but passed on by word of mouth.

The Begum thought the Aga Khan was doing too much and warned him that he was taking risks with his health. Once she berated him for going out in short trousers. She had reason to be worried. He was clearly overtaxing his strength. At Dar-es-

Salaam he fell ill and Dr. Johnson was called to his sick bed. He
strongly advised him to return home. A flying boat was chartered
to take him to Europe. "Have a good trip, your Highness!" Dr.
Johnson said and turned to go.

The Aga Khan flared up, shouting, "What are you saying? You
are coming along, at least as far as Cairo." At Shepherd's Hotel
in Cairo specialists were summoned to the Aga's bedside in the
middle of the night but they, too, thought he ought to return
to his own home. Accompanied by the Begum and Dr. Johnson,
he flew on to Marseilles and Nice, where Aly was waiting at the
airport. He was driven straight to Le Cannet.

Dr. Johnson kept telling the Aga that the prostate gland was
the cause of the trouble, but he pooh-poohed it. "One does not
argue with the Aga Khan," Dr. Johnson told me with a sigh. He
handed the patient over to his own doctor before the flying
boat took him back to East Africa. Some months later the Aga
Khan wrote that he had had a prostate operation. "You did guess
right!" he conceded. ("Guess?" Dr. Johnson commented.) In the
same operation surgeons removed a growth that had been the
source of much pain and discomfort.

After a brief convalescence at Yakimour the Aga Khan was
out on the Mougins golf links, trailed by his caddie, Maria
Giraldo, a quietly efficient girl who knew a lot about golf. He
liked her so much that he bought her a house and a small
motorcar in which she later drove to the course to play in her
own right.

The year 1947, as the Aga Khan noted, was India's year of
destiny. Though he had briefly seen the Mahatma and the Qaid-i-
Azam (Mohammed Ali Jinnah) at the time of the Jubilee, he had
had no part in the acrimonious final struggle for Indian independence. But when the British government recognized that
there were two different Indias and agreed to partition, an old
dream became a reality. Lord Mountbatten, one of Britain's outstanding war leaders, went to Delhi as Viceroy to bring British
rule to an end and hand over responsibility to two independent

states, India and Pakistan. The date set for the final transfer of
power was August 15, 1947.

The Aga Khan could justly claim that as the Battle of Waterloo
was won on the playing fields of Eton, the independent sovereign nation of Pakistan was born in the Muslim University of
Aligarh. But he was acutely aware of the immense problem
partition presented. To separate Muslims from Hindus, Sikhs
from both, and the princes from their states meant tearing apart
the very fabric of society. The authority of the police and the
army was undermined by the long-term power vacuum; in mixed
states (Bengal and the Punjab) which were cut in half by the
new frontier, there were communal riots, massacres, rapes, arson
incidents, destruction, and suffering on a frightening scale.

Refugees scrambled in all directions to find safety among
people of their own faith. Tens of thousands of Ismailis, taking
with them no more than they could carry on their shoulders,
made for the two separate parts of Pakistan to look for a roof over
their heads, even if only a tent or a piece of corrugated iron. To
give these hapless people a new start demanded a big effort
and not a few sacrifices from the Ismaili community. On the
other hand, this great new independent Muslim state also lured
many Ismailis who had gone out, as the Prophet commanded, to
other parts of the world to spread the gospel of Islam. Among
those who were now drawn back to the subcontinent and the new
Pakistan were members of the Fancy family. Amirali Fancy left
Mwanza and moved to Karachi, where he established himself in
business.

For the Aga Khan the Indian upheaval raised the question
not only of his personal properties but also of the assets of the
Ismaili community. His personal wealth was greater than ever,
testifying to his success in applying his oriental mind to the task
of administering his fortune in the Western way. Compared with
other Indian princes, he was neither ostentatious nor extravagant,
and although often regarded as a symbol of luxury living, led a
comparatively quiet and simple life.

Much as he liked to give the impression of owning less than

he did, even grumbling that he did not really have enough, he was, of course, very, very rich. Much of his property was held by companies and by trusts, such as those he established for the Begum, for his sons, and his grandsons. The situation was complicated because ever since the Haji Bibi Case the property of the community—hospitals, schools, sports grounds, *jamatkhanas* —had been registered in his name.

He had to consider the possibility of economic restrictions on Indian nationals or people resident in India. The application of Muslim law to his personal affairs demanded the attention of international lawyers with banking experience. At this turning point the Aga Khan decided to consult Lloyds Bank, whose branch managers in India, Paris, Nice, Le Touquet, and Geneva, all conveniently near the social centers in which he moved, had often previously advised him on matters of investment and connected legal problems.

The Lloyds official dealing with his account in London since the end of the war was the young French-born head of the Legal Department, André Ardoin, who had graduated from Paris University in Law and Economics before coming to England, where he continued his studies and joined the bank at the age of twenty-five. Maître Ardoin was the obvious choice when the distinguished client wanted to discuss certain financial matters and asked for a bank official to visit him at the Hôtel Royale at the French resort of Evian, where he was staying with the Begum.

For Ardoin it was a terrifying assignment. "The Aga Khan was a much revered public figure with a strong personality, the head of a religious community with followers all over the world," he recalled, confessing, "I was afraid." The young lawyer took the sensible precaution of preparing himself thoroughly for the meeting. He turned to a volume which still occupies a special place on the shelves of his elegant office on the Avenue de l'Opéra in Paris. Entitled *Mohammedan Law: The Personal Law of the Mohammedan,* it was compiled by Syed Ameer Ali, Member of the Judicial Committee of His Majesty's Privy Council, and was first published in India in 1929.

Ardoin flew to Geneva, where a car was waiting to take him to
Evian. "The meeting was informal," he said. The Aga Khan told
him, "I want to make a will," and proceeded to explain his
intricate position. Discussing a problem rooted in oriental history
and complicated by religious law, he was yet fully alive to Western financial concepts, full of ideas that in the context of his
Middle and Far Eastern preoccupations could only be
described as revolutionary. "He was vital, direct, and to the
point," Ardoin said. "He asked questions, listened to the answers, asked more questions. Once he had mastered the problem,
he devised new techniques—he was an innovator."

Some of the answers he sought were found in the chapter of
Mohammedan Law entitled "Succession and Status" which related a legatee's creed—in this instance, the Shia Muslim faith—
to his personal position in the community. Among Ismailis no
such question had arisen since the Aga Khan's own accession to
the *gadi* in 1885, when conditions were vastly different. That the
young man from Lloyds Bank had come so well prepared to
discuss these important matters impressed the Aga Khan. "He
was the kind of man who liked a face and trusted a man whom
he liked," Maître Ardoin said modestly. He was also a good judge
of ability and character, of course.

The difficulties of preparing the will of a man with such
worldwide and peculiar functions proved considerable. The Aga
Khan was extremely secretive. "It was an oriental atmosphere
and he had secret contacts here, there, everywhere," Ardoin said.
But as their meetings continued, he put his trust in his young
legal adviser and often it was a matter of "just between us." On
many occasions even the Begum was not allowed to know his
arrangements. Ardoin maintained liaison between the client and
the bank, whose management gave him a free hand, although
legal experts were often consulted. He drafted a provisional
document which became the basis for further discussions. It was
not long before the Aga Khan asked Maître Ardoin to give up his
job at the bank and take charge of his affairs. Ardoin agreed and
their association has lasted, in a manner of speaking, beyond the

Aga Khan's death. He not only prepared the will but was also concerned with the execution of its complicated provisions after the Aga Khan died.

For the old Aga Khan, who was putting his house in order, matters of property and wills immediately raised the question of domicile, and he wished sometimes that he had a territory to call his own. Not that he saw himself as a latter-day Fatimid or ruler over a big province like his grandfather, the first Aga Khan. What inspired the idea, which had fleetingly cropped up before the war, was his anxiety to safeguard the status of the Ismaili community and its property that was in his name. Might not the breakup of India yield a spot that could be allocated to him as an administrative center, a principality, a Vatican-like Ismaili state, small, neutral, and inoffensive? At the time he even considered purchasing such a territory, but confidential approaches to the British and other governments met with no response and the plan was abandoned—for the time being.

In Maître Ardoin's view, had the Aga Khan been younger he would have pursued the project more vigorously because it would have considerably simplified the matter of death duties. European countries made no provisions in their tax laws for the peculiarities of Muslim conditions and the question arose whether death duties should be paid on *jamatkhanas,* hospitals, schools. However valuable the land, who would buy a hospital in Nairobi, who would purchase a mosque? "The difficulty was that the problem had no precedent," Ardoin said. "With regard to all these public places for the use of the community, the Aga Khan was not a trustee, he was the owner."

A formula had to be found that would be in keeping with his functions, but the Aga Khan did not want change. The solution was to divide his property, some of which was personal, some of which was held by virtue of his position as Imam. A line had to be drawn between his personal and his vocational income. It was important that he should be able to dispose of his personal assets as he wished.

On Maître Ardoin's advice, the Aga Khan decided to take up legal residence in Switzerland and gave instructions to look for a suitable house for him in the neighborhood of Lake Geneva. "He wanted a small house," Ardoin said. "He always wanted small places, four or five rooms." Sometimes his advisers had to remind him that a man of his wealth and position had to keep up a certain appearance. Although he owned Yarovda Palace in Poona and Honeymoon Lodge in Karachi, whenever he visited India he stayed with the Governor or in hotels. By the same token, he could never understand why his son wanted so many residences. "Don't buy all these properties!" he used to tell Aly, who at one time maintained thirteen homes.

There is, incidentally, one territory which is an Ismaili state in all but name—Hunza, beautiful land of dark ravines, deep canyons, and snowy peaks (many twenty-three thousand feet or more above sea level) alongside the Pamirs, known as the Roof of the World. It is ruled by the Mir of Hunza, Mohammed Jamal Khan, hereditary chief and a loyal Ismaili who acknowledges the Aga Khan as his spiritual leader, as do most of the country's thirty thousand inhabitants.

Romantically remote and sometimes inaccessible when melting snow turns rivers into wild torrents, Hunza—model for James Hilton's Shangri-la—is popular with a few adventurous tourists, who receive a friendly welcome from the fair, tall people with curly hair who love music, chant war songs, strum mandolins, and beat kettle drums to produce effects not unlike some Western rock groups. They make first-class soldiers, and the Mir, following an old military tradition, is a major general in the Pakistan army while his nephew is commander-in-chief of Pakistan's paratroops. The Mir and his Rani, close friends of the Aga Khan, live in an imposing castle several stories high, built of sun-dried bricks and massive timber, which commands a magnificent view and has been a stronghold for centuries.

The financial complications that the division of the subconti-

nent created for the Aga Khan and his community did not
dampen his joy in the emergence of independent Pakistan. "Now
Islam rises once again!" he exclaimed and described the new
state as "a mighty infant, the greatest child of Islam." He was
full of praise for Mohammed Ali Jinnah, his erstwhile adversary, now Paksitan's first Governor-General. When he visited
independent Pakistan for the first time, he was generously
honored. The new ministers sought his views and he was
consulted by the rulers of Kalat and Hunza. For the social
occasion that followed, the Begum dressed in Hunza national
costume. As a token of his confidence in the future, the Aga
Khan decided to make major investments in Pakistan.

One shadow over the triumph of Pakistan's independence was
the death of Mohammed Ali Jinnah in 1948. The idea of building
the simple, dignified marble mausoleum where he lies buried
and which remains a landmark in Karachi came from the Aga
Khan, who also initiated the establishment of a new mosque
and an Islamic research institute as a fitting memorial for the
founder of the country.

CHAPTER XI

A LY WAS BACK in his element. Reluctant as he had been to leave the army, he found civilian life not lacking in adventure, even managing to invest his visits to the Syrian Ismaili community with excitement. In 1947, as his green and red aircraft swooped down on Salamiyya airport some distance from the city, crowds of loyal followers cheered themselves hoarse, hailing him more like a conquering hero than a religious leader. Switching from aircraft to automobile, he traveled along unmanageable roads into the interior until he and his party had to take to horses and mules to reach the remoter settlements. The farther he went, the more ecstatic his welcome, followers prostrating themselves to kiss the seam of his Arabic burnous. His mission completed, he stopped in Beirut and Cairo before returning to the south of France.

The racing season was at hand and most of his time was taken up with consultations with Frank Butters, Madame Vuillier, and Robert Muller. One reminder of these days is a painting of a horse carrying Aly's green and red colors past the winning post. It hangs in Muller's office at Lassy, the Aga Khan stud farm near Chantilly.

"It's Avenger," M. Muller said. Aly first heard of the horse in 1947 and asked Muller and Madame Vuillier to look him over. They inspected the horse and worked out the pedigree. "For a maiden which had never won, he was very expensive," Muller recalled. He did not seem in very good condition either. Aly ought to see for himself, they suggested. The result was a remarkable encounter. Avenger put his head on Aly's shoulder. "Look! He wants me! He's mine!" Aly exclaimed and told Madame Vuillier to buy the horse. Six weeks later, watching Avenger win the Grand Prix at Longchamp, Aly was so exuberant that he squashed Madame Vuillier's hat in his excitement.

To see their first English Derby since the war, Aly and Aga came together at Epsom. They had high hopes for their horse, Migoli—a descendant of Mumtaz Mahal—whom Frank Butters had nursed for the occasion, but when asked to tip the winner, the Aga Khan diplomatically named the favorite, Tudor Minstrel, his own Migoli, and the Maharajah of Baroda's Sayajirao in that order. A special cheer from the crowd showed that his popularity was undimmed. Watching the race, he saw the favorite going ahead soon after the start and still leading at Tattenham Corner. Then Pearl Diver, a little-fancied colt, went ahead. Migoli came up fast in the end but was only able to get into second place. Sayajirao was third.

Neither Aga nor Aly showed their disappointment. They were determined to do better at the next attempt. Aly flew to the United States in search of new blood, visited South America, talked to breeders, trainers, jockeys, stable lads. One of his scouting trips in England took him to Egerton House, near Newmarket, to see Marcus Marsh, who had recently taken over as trainer from his uncle, the great Fred Darling. He and Marsh got on well together.

Soon after seeing Migoli run, the Aga Khan suffered a relapse, and Aly was left in sole charge of their racing interests. Although constantly on the move between Newmarket and Deauville, the Curragh and Paris, London and the Riviera, that summer he readily accepted an invitation from Elsa Maxwell, America's legendary social impresario, who was gathering the big names of the Côte d'Azur for a party at the Palm Beach Casino in Cannes. Everybody seemed to be there, but the evening held no special attraction for Aly until his alert eye was riveted by a truly grand entrance. "Good heavens—what a beautiful woman!" he exclaimed. It was Rita Hayworth, who, it turned out, had come to the party only after much persuasion and after hurriedly buying an evening gown because she had just arrived.

Seeing and meeting her changed a great deal for Aly. They spent the evening together, danced and talked, and when the party drifted toward the baccarat tables, went off to the more congenial surroundings of Aly's favorite nightclub, where they stayed until the early hours.

In the south of France news of such an encounter spreads faster than forest fires. Before anything had happened, the gossips were already talking of the great new romance between Aly and Rita. They were right, but premature. Rita was not really in the mood for romance, but Aly, with the instinct of an *homme à femmes,* had caught her at the moment many women are most susceptible to a new man's charms.

Though he had seen her name in lights and some of her films, Aly did not know much about her background. That evening Rita told him the story of her life. Working backward, as it were, from the unenviable situation in which she found herself, she said her husband, America's spectacularly talented Orson Welles —writer, actor, director, intellectual, and universal genius—was due to arrive in Cannes within a day or so. Their marriage was in trouble, but she wanted to make one more attempt to mend it for the sake of their three-year-old daughter, Rebecca. They had been married for four years, during which time Orson had tried to interest her in the things that occupied his lofty mind. She had worked her way through volumes of history and philosophy, but as she later put it, "it is difficult to live with a genius." They were known in Hollywood as "the Beauty and the Brain."

She had tried hard to live up to his standards, but her show-business background was probably against her. She was not ashamed of it. Her grandfather, Antonio Consino, was a good old trouper, and her father, Eduardo, a superb practitioner of Spanish classical dancing; her mother had also been in the theater. Born in New York, christened Margarita, she had come up the hard way, first dancing with her father and then graduating to small films in Hollywood. Yes, she had been married once before, to Eddie Judson, a middle-aged, imaginative American auto salesman who literally remade her, shortening her first name to Rita and changing her surname to an adaptation of her mother's maiden name, which was Haworth.

Judson made her dye her black hair red, take lessons in voice production and deportment. She attracted the attention of Harry Cohn, president of Columbia Pictures, who could recognize a "hot property" when he saw one, and he carried on where Judson left off. A fashion expert was called in to advise her on clothes; a professional publicity man spread the gospel of her remarkable vital statistics: height 5 feet 6 inches, weight 120 pounds, bust 36, waist 26, hips 35, thighs 19, eyes brown, hair titian. These were the measures of predictable success for Hollywood's new Love Goddess. Unlike other actresses on the way up, Rita was pliable, willingly accepted advice, and soon reached the top. She became Fred Astaire's leading lady and earned over six thousand dollars a week. Her marriage to Eddie broke up, and Orson came into her life, but she did not find happiness with him either.

Rita's reunion with her husband was not a success. Twenty-four hours later Orson Welles was gone. She felt miserable and was not even cheered by Aly's flowers, which filled her apartment. At Cap d'Antibes that week, she was introduced to the Shah of Iran, who asked her to lunch at Eden Roc, the Hôtel du Cap's elegant promontory. She accepted, and an American magazine photographer who got wind of the assignation lay in wait with his camera to capture the thrilling rendezvous. The photographer—and the Shah—waited in vain. The table was laid, the champagne was on ice, but Rita did not keep the appointment. Instead, she went to the Château de l'Horizon and joined Aly Khan. They stayed together for most of their time in the south of France. Gordon Young, who has chronicled the Aly-Rita romance in great detail, quoted her as saying to a mutual friend, "Aly has asked me if I would marry him when he is free. We talked a great deal about his family, especially about his wife and sons."

Even in the throes of a big new romance, Aly could not banish the thought of his horses from his mind for long. As much as his father, who was recuperating at Yakimour, he was determined to make the 1948 Derby theirs, but they agreed that their entry, Noor, a progeny of Nearco, although a product of their own stud trained by Frank Butters, did not stand a very sound chance. They saw a glimmer of hope in a horse appropriately called My Love, which belonged to the French millionaire M. Léon Volterra, a showman with a considerable flair for racing. My Love had done nothing really outstanding but was a half-brother of Pearl Diver, winner of the previous year's English Derby.

Convinced that the horse could emulate his half-brother's feat, the Aga and Aly decided to make M. Volterra an offer for My Love, but the shrewd French owner would go no further than to sell them a half-share. Anxious to win his fourth Derby at almost any cost, the Aga Khan agreed and the deal was struck in the nick of time. The ailing Aga was confident that he was on the threshold of another triumph for his colors, and even the Begum could not prevent his making the arduous trip to England. He tipped My Love to the porters at Victoria Station when he and the Begum arrived in the Blue Train.

On Derby Day, Baroda's My Babu, winner of the Two-Thousand Guineas, was the favorite at 4 to 1, and Monsieur Volterra's Royal Drake was also much fancied, but My Love soon attracted support from women who liked its name and from punters who always put their money on the Aga Khan's horses. A crisp telegram—"My Love to all"—preceded the arrival of Raw Johnston, the Australian jockey who was engaged to ride him.

Johnston got his powerful mount well away at the start, and the Aga Khan, watching the race with Aly by his side, was thrilled to see Noor also moving very smoothly. My Love caught up fast to Royal Drake and passed him in the last furlong to win by a length and a half. Noor came in third, relegating My Babu to fourth place. The King congratulated the Aga Khan— neither had backed the winner. M. Volterra was disappointed about Royal Drake's failure and none too pleased with himself for having agreed to let My Love run under the Aga Khan's colors. His share of the prize money was £6,492. The Derby win brought the Aga Khan's wins in stake money for the season to over £46,000, but to quote Stanley Jackson, "The winning of his fourth Derby was the sweetest victory of all."

As soon as My Love was past the winning post, Aly was on his way back to the south of France and his love. He was wooing Rita more ardently than he had any woman before her—and not meeting much resistance. She fell in with his hectic mode of life. She enjoyed the sense of freedom that the use of a private air- craft engenders. One day the Avenger took them to Paris, the next they flew to Rome or Madrid. In Madrid their romance captured the imagination of the afficionados. At a bull fight the crowd chanted "Aly" and "Rita" instead of the names of their favorite matadors. The glamorous couple fled to Biarritz with the press in hot pursuit, then escaped to Cannes and the comparative privacy of the Château de l'Horizon.

Contract negotiations demanded Rita's presence in Hollywood, but Aly could not bear to be separated from her for long and followed her to the United States. Still, characteristically, on his way to California he stopped over at Saratoga for the yearling sales and bought horses worth $200,000. Then he moved into a rented bungalow in Beverly Hills opposite Rita's house. They spent hours discussing their problem, but the press would not give them time to make up their minds whether they were ready for marriage. Aly countered persistent questions with the conventional "Miss Hayworth and I are just good friends" but could not resist adding, "There exists a wonderful and healthy relationship between us." The pressure was beginning to tell, so they decided to make another run for it, went to Mexico, and ended up in Havana.

Soon after their arrival there Rita's lawyers signaled that her divorce from Orson Welles had come through. She also received frantic calls from her studio, which was anxious to exploit the publicity and start on a new Rita Hayworth film forthwith. When she did not respond, she was threatened with suspension, which put her $30,000-a-year income in jeopardy. For her, it was more important to be with Aly, who after a fortnight was impatient to return to Europe.

While Aly was constantly in the news, the Aga was trying to get away from it all. He went on a safari in East Africa with the Begum and Sadruddin, too young to be a problem. Their comfortable expedition to the Serengeti National Park started at Marseilles, where a chartered forty-five-ton flying boat (with some exquisite provisions in special refrigerators) waited to take them to Mombasa. Africa's finest hunters guided the party, which struck camp in the bush. The big marquee with electric lights, the Aga's own porcelain bath, easy chairs and tables, fine linens, glass, and silver became an oasis of Western civilization. Fresh supplies were flown in daily over a distance of two hundred miles, but the Aga's precarious health deteriorated, and by the end of the six-week safari he caught a chill, which forced him to cancel visits to his communities. He was flown back to Europe and arrived at Yakimour just when the publicity about Aly and Rita was at a new pitch.

The celebrated couple decided to speed their departure from America. Aly booked passages for himself and Rita on the liner *Britannic*, which was due to sail for Cobh, County Cork, Ireland. To avoid the press, Rita and little Rebecca were smuggled aboard via the crew's gangplank and made their way to their stateroom through the galley. The voyage was peaceful until the *Britannic* reached Cork harbor, where reporters were waiting to board her. They cornered Aly, who denied that he planned to marry. Rita said she was "spending Christmas with some friends over here."

They kept apart on the tender that took them ashore and drove off in separate cars. Once away from the harbor Rita quickly joined Aly in his car, leaving her car to block the road against their pursuers while they went on to Gilltown in the other. Though they were quickly traced to Aly's stud farm, they kept up the pretense that they were not together even when observers discovered them in a Dublin cinema watching one of Rita's earlier films. From Gilltown they flew to London, spent the night at the Ritz, and on the following day went to Paris to Aly's house in the Bois de Boulogne.

Dining at the Tour d'Argent restaurant overlooking the Seine, they found themselves two tables away from Orson Welles.

Thoughtlessly, Aly was about to give the social hyenas new cause for chatter. He was on his way to Switzerland to see Karim and Amyn, who were due to spend part of their winter holidays with him. Their mother collected them from school in Gstaad at the end of the term and booked rooms at the Palace Hotel to await Aly's arrival.

They had been in touch about divorce proceedings and matters concerning the boys, but Joan expected Aly to come alone. When he arrived with Rita, they were immediately caught in the glare of publicity. Joan withdrew hastily, muttering "What a sordid business" for all to hear. It was suggested that Aly had brought Rita deliberately to stage a confrontation with Joan. Puritanical women's organizations in the United States launched a violent campaign against Rita, threatening to boycott her films if she continued her illicit association with Aly. Aly countered that he and his wife had been living apart for three years and that divorce proceedings were pending. "As soon as they are finished," he added, giving the first direct indication of his plans, "Rita and I will stabilize our situation."

Six weeks later, in February, 1949, Joan's divorce action was filed in Paris. As grounds she gave "serious insults" and "incompatibility." When her petition was granted, Aly was given custody of the two boys—with a Muslim father and future Imam of the Ismailis involved, any other arrangement was unthinkable. Karim and Amyn admired their father, who was staying with them in Gstaad—no sons could wish for a more dashing, sporting, comradely, and indulgent parent. Though they were well-mannered and polite, they did not take kindly to their future stepmother. Rita lacked the intellectual equipment to get on good terms with two teen-agers who would naturally harbor resentment against the woman who had replaced their mother in their father's affections.

Otherwise, they spent an enjoyable holiday skiing, toboganning, and romping with their father in the snow. Karim, particularly, loved winter sports. At the age of twelve he was already a practiced skier who won prizes in school races and junior competitions. For Aly the holiday ended with a serious accident when he suffered a complicated fracture of his leg. But by the time they left Gstaad, the sky was clearing for him and Rita. They went to Cannes to see the Aga Khan, who later said that he had advised them to marry as quickly as possible. In the face of the newspapers' running commentaries about his son, he kept a stiff upper lip. Asked by a British reporter what he thought of the impending marriage of two divorcees, he answered curtly, "There are 150,000 divorces in Britain every year. Why criticize my son?"

Even before the divorce became final, Aly provisionally fixed the date of his wedding for May 27. The divorce papers came through at the end of April. Rita flew to Paris and he took her to the salon of Jacques Fath to choose a wedding dress. When news of their impending arrival got around, the staff was thrilled. Bettina, one of Jacques Fath's top models, later recalled how she and the other mannequins watched the famous couple through a chink in the door. During the parade Rita appeared indifferent and sat there with what Bettina described as "that

look of nonchalance so often seen on much-admired women."
Aly was talking and laughing. When it was Bettina's turn, her
eye caught Aly's—he seemed warm and sympathetic. She was
showing a bridal gown, and the late Robert Capa, a famous
American photographer who happened to be in the salon,
snapped her picture as she passed in front of the Prince. It was
a prophetic photograph, but for the time being Bettina did not
give Aly another thought.

She and two other Jacques Fath models were asked to go to
the rue de Prony the following Sunday to show Rita some more
dresses. Cutting into their rest day, it was an inconvenient assignment, but at least Rita chose one of the dresses Bettina
showed. "I found Aly most likable," Bettina said when I talked
to her about the occasion years later, "but I had no premonition, and would have been most astonished if anyone had suggested, that I would share Aly's life with him one day."

Aly would have been no less surprised at such a suggestion.
He was completely wrapped up in his wedding plans. To avoid
another burst of publicity, which was bound to displease his
father, he asked the Prefect of the Alpes-Maritimes Department
to permit the civil ceremony to take place in the privacy of his
château but was turned down because French law demands
that all weddings must be conducted publicly at a *mairie*. Re-
luctantly he settled for the town hall of Vallauris, a local village
in the hills where Picasso made his pottery.

Although a staunch Communist, the Mayor of Vallauris, M.
Paul Derignon, threw himself wholeheartedly into the preparations for the wedding of the millionaire Muslim prince and the
Hollywood Love Goddess. Rita's manager, Lee Ellroy, who flew
in from Hollywood with a handful of her friends, was no less
dedicated to the task. Mayor and manager gave half a dozen
interviews a day and issued as many denials, handing out press
passes to reporters and photographers, who were arriving in
growing numbers.

With his knack for handling big social occasions, Aly meticulously prepared the wedding reception and sent invitations to a hundred guests who reflected his many-sided interests—aristocrats (half a dozen princes and princesses among them), South American millionaires, famous figures of the turf, and other sportsmen, socialites, and hoteliers. The Riviera's best-known caterers and bartenders volunteered to minister to the guests. Legend has since distorted the details concerning the food and drink which were taken to the château in truckloads—one report which mentioned six hundred bottles of champagne, fifty pounds of caviar, a hundred pounds of cold meats, and as many pastries and cakes probably came nearest to the truth.

Early on May 27 a hundred photographers and as many reporters were lying in wait for Aly and Rita outside Vallauris Town Hall. As the morning wore on, they were joined by local people and tourists, who blocked the way to invited guests. The crowd was over a thousand strong when Aly arrived in a sports car driven by his brother Sadruddin. He was wearing a beautifully tailored morning coat, striped trousers, and gray topper and was acclaimed in several languages. A cheer went up when a white Cadillac disgorged the bride in her dainty ice-blue Jacques Fath dress and an enormous picture hat which framed her reddish-gold hair. The Aga Khan in his traditional all-white summer suit and the Begum in one of her famous bejeweled saris also received a friendly welcome.

By Aly's side upstairs was his best man, General Catroux, under whom he served in the war. Mayor Derignon conducted the ceremony with as much decorum as was possible in the crowded hall. All went well until Aly slipped a slim platinum band on Rita's finger and, disregarding protocol, impetuously kissed her hand. Carried away with emotion, guests and reporters shouted "Bravo," "Vive Aly," and "Vive Rita." After the ceremony the Aga kissed Rita on both cheeks and the Begum was the first to offer Aly her good wishes. Gaining the street, the couple was confronted by a phalanx of professional photographers battling for vantage points with camera-swinging tourists.

At the château a band by the swimming pool greeted them
with Aly's old favorite, "Smoke Gets in Your Eyes," to which
the violins on the roof replied with "La Vie en Rose." A flower
arrangement of white carnations in the shape of the letter M
(for Margarita) floated in the swimming pool, which had been
sweetened with the scent of gallons of eau de cologne. Yet the
worry about his father's obvious disapproval of the ballyhoo all
but spoiled the day for Aly. Rita, surrounded by her husband's
friends among whom she was a stranger, was not at her best
either. She went through the rest of the day in a daze and later
confessed that she had been nervous throughout, that it had
been worse than facing the film cameras.

That Aly gauged his father's reactions correctly emerged from
the Aga Khan's comment on the Vallauris wedding. "This was
a fantastic, semi-royal, semi-Hollywood affair," he growled in
his autobiography. "My wife and I played our part, much as she
disapproved of the atmosphere with which it was surrounded."
Compared with the tumultuous civil wedding, the Muslim ceremony conducted at the château two days later by two *mullahs*
from the Paris mosque and attended by Ismaili nobles from many
parts of the world was a solemn, dignified affair.

The tense days of Cannes were followed by a relaxing trip
to England for the racing season. In addition to a big diamond
ring and a sports car, Aly presented his wife with a racehorse,
Skylarking, which was doing extremely well. Aga and Begum
joined them in England and went with them to the Derby,
although their entries had little chance. The Aga had not been
back in Cannes for long when he received the news that Frank
Butters had been run over by a truck while riding a bicycle in
Newmarket and had suffered severe injuries. Leading specialists
whom he sent to his old trainer's bedside reported that Butters
would never recover sufficiently to resume his work.

It was, among other things, to discuss this tragedy with Aly
that the Aga Khan and the Begum decided to fly to Deauville.
With chauffeur and maid they were leaving Yakimour for the

airport when their car was pushed off the road by a black Citroën. Three men jumped out, threatened the Aga Khan with tommy guns, and brusquely asked the Begum to hand over her jewel case. They knew what they were doing—the jewels in the case included a twenty-five-carat diamond ring worth $125,000 and a bracelet worth $200,000. The total value of their haul was three quarters of a million dollars.

As the bandits turned to leave, the Aga reminded them that they had not taken his wallet, which contained $600, and handed it to them. One of them said, "*Soyez braves et laissez-nous partir!*" ("Be good sports and let us get away!") They did get away. There were rumors that the robbery was the work of American gunmen, but a French policeman said in a fit of injured national pride, "There were no foreigners on this job, no Americans, no Italians, no nothing. This was a job conceived, planned, and executed entirely by Frenchmen." The jewelry was insured by Lloyds of London.

The problem created by the Butters tragedy remained. The Aga and Aly were forced to look for a new trainer and approached Marcus Marsh for whose services two other leading owners, Lord Derby and Marcel Boussac, were already competing. Marsh was undecided. The Aga Khan's two-year-olds were well known, he reasoned, and were expected to do well. If they did, the owner would get the credit; if they did not, the new trainer might well be blamed. He sought advice from the senior steward of the Jockey Club who told him, "The Aga is, after all, the top owner in Europe—if not the world—and if you don't accept his offer, I am sure you will come to regret it." Marsh decided to talk to the Aga Khan and flew to Yakimour to see him. He was most courteously received.

How frail the Aga looked, he thought, but when they discussed terms and he asked for a five-year contract, the old gentleman shook his head. "No," he said, "three." Suddenly, Marsh observed, he did not look frail at all. His eyes were hidden behind dark glasses, but the stubborn cast of his lips and chin

was "reminiscent of a good old-fashioned Irish horse dealer."
March concluded that it was no use arguing and accepted the
contract. On his way back he went to see Aly at his house in
the Bois. Alone, except for Emrys Williams, Aly was in his usual
leisure wear of cavalry twill trousers and black polo-neck
sweater. He told Marsh about the race he had ridden in St.-
Cloud when he came in last but one. They discussed classic
hopes for 1950, particularly Palestine for the Two-Thousand
Guineas. The outcome of the trip was that Marsh bought a new
establishment, Fitzroy House, and took thirty-five of the Aga
Khan's horses.

Leaving Aly to complete the arrangements, the Aga Khan
escaped the European winter to Pakistan, where his community
was making great strides. One of the leading Ismailis who
looked after him was Captain Amirali Currim Ebrahaim, who
had held a commission in the British Army during the war
("Our Prince Aly Khan was an officer and desired our people
to join"), and following a family tradition, looked after the Aga
Khan's estates in Pakistan. He still acts as honorary estate agent
to Karim Aga Khan. His brother Zulfikarali Valiani, an eminent
lawyer, was in attendance when the Aga wanted to show the
Begum the crocodiles in the hot sulphur springs some twenty
miles from Karachi. He arranged the excursion and joined the
Aga Khan and the Begum on their drive. When their car stopped
at a crossing on the outskirts of the city, they were approached
by a beggar.

"Give him a hundred rupees," the Aga Khan told Valiani.
Having no cash on him, Valiani explained to the beggar that he
would come back with the money a little later, but the beggar
was doubtful and protested tearfully. "Promise him two hundred rupees," the Aga Khan commanded, and turning to the
beggar, spoke to him in Urdu. "Don't worry! This man will be
back in an hour and will give you three hundred rupees!"
Valiani arranged for the man to get the money quickly. "His
Highness," he said to me good-humoredly, "might easily have

raised the stakes to one thousand rupees." The Aga was extremely generous, and the community was generous to him. In the course of his visits rich followers presented him with big amounts well in excess of their payments in *zakat* and *khums*, but almost invariably the donations were devoted to community projects.

On his return trip he stopped over in Teheran to see the young Shah, who conferred the style of a royal Prince of Persia on the descendant of the previous dynasty. It entitled the Aga Khan to the address "Royal Highness," which also applied to Prince Aly and eventually to Prince Karim, who is "His Highness" in Europe but "His Royal Highness" east of Suez. The Aga Khan's Iranian nationality was confirmed, enabling him (and his descendants) to hold an Iranian as well as a British passport.

In Europe a new grandchild was awaiting him, a half-sister for Karim and Amyn. Giving the lie to the gossips who had predicted a much earlier birth, Rita's baby girl was born on December 28 at the Montchoisi Clinic in Lausanne. Aly told reporters that his wife had had a difficult time. The baby weighed five and a half pounds and would be called Yasmin, Arabic for jasmine.

Yasmin's first few months were spent in Gstaad, where Aly took a cottage and gathered the family around him. Karim and Amyn were once more enjoying winter sports with their father until he was laid low by another skiing accident. Although his leg was broken in three places, his spirits were as high as ever. Persuading Karim to help him out of bed, he commandeered his father's wheelchair, and before many days went by, insisted on being taken to the airport, where he propelled himself to the Avenger and was maneuvered aboard. Rita, Rebecca, Yasmin, and a nurse went with him to Cannes, but even though he could not walk, he was soon on the move again. Wheelchair or no, he flew to Newmarket to see Palestine run—and win the Two-Thousand Guineas.

Marcus Marsh had been placing bets for him. "Have you won anything for me?" he asked, and Marcus said, "Yes, over £2,000." According to Marsh, Aly lost that much in the next few days, but in racing finance these were not big amounts. Palestine won £12,982 in stake money, and when the colt defeated American-bred Prince Simon, American offers for him poured in, among them one for £158,000. The Aga Khan declined them all and sent Palestine to stud at Gilltown. His services as a stallion were syndicated at £120,000, divided into forty shares of £3,000 each. Almost in passing, Aly bought Wilfred Harvey's Sandwich stud of some sixty mares, stallions, and foals, concluding the deal within twenty-four hours and signing the documents as he was leaving the London Ritz for Paris.

Whether in London, Paris, or Gilltown, Rita felt as ill at ease among Aly's racing associates as among his socialite friends. Accustomed to top-star billing, she did not enjoy playing second fiddle to her famous husband, who preferred her to be known as Princess Aly Khan rather than as Rita Hayworth and who did not like the name Rita and called her Margarita. He would not deny her any wish—her dress allowance was £4,000 a year—but there was no disguising the fact that his style of life did not suit her.

Around that time he announced that he was giving his house in the rue de Prony to the community as a European center for Ismaili students (a house in the Kensington district of London was acquired for England's Ismailis). To replace the rue de Prony residence he took a town house in Paris on the Boulevard Maurice-Barrès which was always filled with his friends but was never home to Rita. He was still the talk of the town, any town, and the latest crop of rumors had it that he was short of cash and had been spending too much on his houses, his aircraft, his yacht, his gambling, on unsuccessful horse deals and diamond necklaces for dancing girls.

These were the kind of rumors that attach themselves to many sons of rich fathers who are still alive and control the purse strings. They were fed with new conjectures whenever Aly sold some of his paintings, but the gossips never took into account the value of his property and his share in the racing establishment, which was still expanding. He certainly had enough funds at his disposal to buy another big stud farm, Haras de Lassy, not far from Chantilly. Buying and selling properties, buying and selling horses, winning and losing while constantly on the move, Aly's approach was casual and he tended to be late settling some of his accounts. His creditors, reluctant to press such an important customer, sometimes grumbled but did not send reminders. If Aly was occasionally short of an odd £10,000, he was certainly not broke.

A tour of Africa was next on the agenda and Rita tagged along dutifully but without great enthusiasm. It went off to a poor start. At Cairo she thought Aly was spending too much time playing bridge while King Farouk paid court to her with embarrassing persistence. When the King's minions brought her a "royal command" to present herself at his palace, she and Aly left Cairo hurriedly for East Africa. Rita was not cut out for the role of an Ismaili princess and found the community etiquette unnerving. By contrast, Aly, who reveled in his duties, addressed his followers and attended conferences with the leaders, covering a lot of ground.

Whenever Europeans asked the couple to parties, Rita was anxious to accept, but Aly was far too busy with the community. "That's what we are here for," he would say. At a Portuguese Consulate function, on the other hand, Rita's angry eyes flashed extreme displeasure when he danced one dance after the other with the host's wife, who was of African blood. Regal as she was on the screen, Rita did not cut a good figure at gatherings of Ismaili ladies with whom she had so little in common. Conversely, when she wanted to go sea bathing at Mombasa, community leaders hinted that an Ismaili princess ought not to show her figure in public.

A short while earlier Aly had asked Columbia to stop issuing pinup pictures of Rita. Now stories emanating from Hollywood suggested that she was about to return and resume her career in films. They were variously confirmed by Aly—perhaps it was his secret wish—and denied by her. Husband and wife were now completely out of tune with each other, and the longer they traveled together, the further they drifted apart. She refused to join him on a safari, and while he was hunting, left East Africa rather abruptly for the south of France to join—or rather collect—Rebecca and Yasmin at the Château de l'Horizon.

Aly went on with his tour. The visit of the Imam's son being a carefully arranged official affair, he could hardly do otherwise. A little later he said that he had no idea his wife intended to leave him, but her sudden departure obviously marked the final break. At the end of his tour he returned to the south of France just in time to see her taking off with the children for Paris and Le Hâvre en route to the United States. Whether he was upset or relieved is difficult to say. The Aga Khan, who was on his way back from another Far Eastern trip and missed seeing his granddaughter, on whom he had not set eyes since her birth, was angry with Rita. "She could surely have delayed her departure," he complained, "and let me see the baby."

Tens of thousands of words have been written about the parting of Aly and Rita, but the Aga Khan's terse few words summed up the end of the affair quite adequately: "I thought Miss Hayworth charming and beautiful but it was not long before I saw, I am afraid, that they were not a well-assorted couple." Aly, warm-hearted and gregarious, was always surrounded by friends, while Rita looked upon marriage as a haven of peace and rest from her professional work. In the Aga's view, the collapse of the marriage was inevitable.

Having decided to end the marriage, Rita was apparently haunted by fear that the powerful Aga Khan and his son might deprive her of Yasmin, perhaps even kidnap the child. "Had Miss Hayworth made more enquiries," the Aga commented, "she could have found out what in fact are the Ismaili religious laws and the code which governs all my followers and my family in these matters." Under this code, young children are entrusted to their mothers whatever the circumstances of the divorce. "Unless we were criminals"—again, the Aga Khan—"we could not have comtemplated taking the baby Yasmin from her mother." Muslim boys at the age of seven pass into their father's custody, but girls remain with their mother until puberty, when they are free to choose. The Aga also rejected the insinuation that he had failed to make provision for his granddaughter's future, explaining that under Islamic law the child's father was obliged to leave her a share of his estate. Since it was unlikely that Aly would die penniless, the Aga said, there was no urgency about providing for Yasmin. Privately he was heard muttering, "If Aly could only choose his women as he chooses horses. . . !"

From the Château de l'Horizon Aly sent a long letter to Rita ("My darling one") telling her of his astonishment and sadness that she had left him so suddenly. He had no thought of any other women or of divorce, he wrote, but explained the conditions of a legal separation. "If you should ever change your mind," he ended, "this separation could not prevent your light returning to my life."

CHAPTER XII

Although four or five years beyond the biblical life-span of three score and ten and indifferent in health, the Aga Khan continued to travel between continents, turning up in Asia, Africa, and the Middle East as frequently as in the watering places and racing centers of Europe. Aly was moving about as restlessly—"restlessly and sometimes recklessly searching for happiness," to quote Gordon Young, "which for most of the time seems to have eluded him like a shadow." But the paths of father and son crossed frequently.

They were together in Cairo early in 1951 when they met Ismaili leaders from Pakistan, India, Burma, and East Africa who came to ask the Aga Khan's permission to weigh him in platinum in 1955, the seventieth anniversary of his accession, and promised to raise a record amount. Though he might well have wondered whether he would live to celebrate the day, the Imam approved their plans because the money would help to finance valuable welfare projects for the community.

An invitation to attend the wedding of the Shah of Iran to the beautiful Soraya Esfandiari took him to Teheran for the second time in two years. It was more than a festive occasion.

A visit to Iran meant a return to his ancestral roots and made him more conscious than ever of his Iranian background. The Teheran palace the Shah put at his disposal was sumptuous and comfortable. In Mahalat, seat of his ancestors, thousands of Ismailis from all over the country assembled to pay him homage. The women, he noticed with great satisfaction, had given up the *chaddur*, the Persian version of *purdah* (though in remoter areas through which he passed, they still hid their faces).

His next station was Karachi, the city of his birth. He addressed the World Muslim Conference, breaking a lance for the Arabic language. "Should not the powerful Muslim state of Pakistan make Arabic its national language?" he asked. "While Arabic will unite the Muslim world, Urdu will divide and isolate!" He defended Islam against all comers, and when the London *Times*, which he sometimes treated as if it were his house organ, spoke of Islam as "an intolerant religion which teaches the duty of shunning foreign influence," he denounced "this sweeping generalisation" as untrue and unfair. Did not Islam practice *hilm*, which means tolerance, forbearance, and forgiveness? As if to show that he meant what he said, he exhorted his fellow Muslims to learn from Europe "those secrets of power over nature, of scientific, economic, and industrial development which have made the West so powerful."

He backed up his sermon with hard cash for research and scholarships and sponsored a technological institute in Dacca, East Pakistan, modeled on one he had seen in Switzerland. He would modernize the cotton mills and start new industries with the help of European associates, he promised, and at once put up funds for 150 huts for homeless refugees to be built on the outskirts of Karachi. He gave permission for Honeymoon Lodge to be used as a convalescent home for ailing Ismailis—the only convalescent home in Pakistan—and started a fund for the maintenance of old mosques. He donated £20,000 toward a new mosque in London, which turned out to be a very long-term project; by 1970 the mosque had not yet been built.

Presiding over small lunch and dinner parties, the Aga Khan, as usual, quizzed his guests about every subject under the sun. In the course of this visit he approved final plans for the Ismaili Pak Insurance Cooperative Bank, which opened the following year with a capital of twenty-five *lakhs* (2,500,000) of rupees and admitted only members who were "loyal and practicing Imami Ismaili followers of His Royal Highness The Prince Aga Khan and His Successors." It has since sprouted branches in many Ismaili centers. In a family transaction he transferred the ownership of the Karachi Gymkhana, a big sports and assembly ground, to his son Aly.

The strain of work and travel across the vast subcontinent was beginning to tell. On his way to Calcutta the Aga suffered a heart attack that brought the tour to a premature end. He was flown back to the south of France in care of the Begum and two nurses. To step into the breech, Aly was rushed back from South America, where he had been looking for horses. Continuing the program on behalf of his father, he stamped the tour with his peculiar brand of *bonhomie*. Instead of grasping the outstretched hand of an Ismaili leader who addressed him humbly as "Prince," he embraced the man and told him, "Don't call me Prince, call me Brother!"

Aly insisted on visiting the smallest villages, consumed an incredible amount of ice cream as he drove from place to place, was completely tireless and content with two hours sleep a night. In Karachi he inaugurated a housing colony for Ismailis with a capital of forty *lakhs* (four million rupees) at 15,000 rupees per flat. Although he returned to inspect the work when it was in its early stages, he did not live to see the completed "Prince Aly Khan Colony," which houses some two thousand people in flats with modern bathrooms and kitchens of a much higher standard then their non-Ismaili neighbors enjoy.

Convalescing at Yakimour, the Aga Khan devoted himself to his family, keeping a wary eye on the younger generation. After a spell at Lausanne University, Sadruddin was sent to Harvard to study for a Bachelor of Arts degree (one of his contemporaries was Edward Kennedy). The plan was for him to go on to the Centre of Middle Eastern Studies. Soon the old gentleman was well enough to discuss the forthcoming racing season with Aly, who, incidentally, was being seen with the French *chanteuse* Lise Bourdin, who was helping him to forget Rita Hayworth. One of the decisions the father-and-son racing partnership made was to buy the Italian three-year-old Nuccio, for whom they paid £50,000. The paramount aim that inspired all their scheming and planning was to win the Derby for the fifth time. The horse carrying their hopes for the 1952 stakes was Tulyar.

Ismaili leaders frequently traveled to the south of France to pay their respects to the Aga Khan. One of them, Zulfikarali Valiani, on his way to the Villa Yakimour was given a lift by Aly Khan. "How did you get here?" the Aga Khan asked him when he arrived. When Valiani replied, "Prince Aly gave me a lift in his car," the Aga frowned and asked sternly, "Do you want to end up in hospital?" He would not allow him to return with Aly. Valiani recalls Aly driving from Karachi to Hyderabad at eighty miles an hour and changing his coat without slowing down. No wonder Aly's friends shared his father's misgivings. "I will do anything in the world for Aly," Elsa Maxwell said, "except get into a car when he is at the wheel."

Like other Ismailis, Valiani occasionally visited Le Rosay to see how the Imam's grandson was getting on. The Aga Khan told him he wanted an independent view on how the boy was progressing with his religious and language studies. "When you see Prince Karim," he told Valiani, "try to talk to him in Urdu, so he gets some practice." Karim, who was playing football when Valiani arrived, stopped and ran up to his visitor. They had a talk—in Urdu—after which Karim continued his game. Inaugurating the Urdu University in Karachi several years later, Prince Karim recalled "the burdensome duty of instructing me in Urdu" which fell to his professor at Le Rosay. "After some time," he said, "I was in the fortunate position of being able to appreciate, if not fully understand, the beautiful language."

Though he did not know it, he was the subject of long dis-

cussions between his parents and his grandfather. His time at
Le Rosay would come to an end in 1953, and decisions about
his future had to take into account the possibility that he might
become Imam of the Ismailis sooner or later (in the light of
what happened it is likely that his grandfather was thinking in
terms of "sooner" rather than "later"). "I was in favor of 'K'
going to the Massachusetts Institute of Technology," Princess
Joan told me. "He had talent, was a very good draftsman, and
drew some excellent pictures," she said, pointing to the walls
of her drawing room, which bear witness to young Karim's efforts
as a painter and sculptor. He was equally interested in archi-
tecture and science. "Mathematics was my strong point," Karim
Aga Khan confirmed when we discussed these days. And so he
started classes in engineering in 1952.

His grandfather seemed to be thinking of a broader educational basis. The old Aga thought highly of the boy. Whenever
he was at Villa Barakat in Geneva, he sent for Karim and talked
to him at great length, subtly introducing him into the deeper
meaning of the Ismaili faith and instilling in him the sense of
mission which became apparent to all not many years later.
Prince Karim himself remembers his grandfather asking questions about his religious instruction, testing his knowledge. "He
could extract more from a human being in a short conversation
than anybody else in a lifetime," he mused. But there was also
something completely inscrutable about his grandfather when it
came to important matters. "Yet when he took a decision, one
did not have to ask him for his thinking process; one felt sure
it was taken with full knowledge of all aspects." Young Karim
found his grandfather jovial, but joviality never turned into
flippancy. He could be playful and gay and light-hearted, was
not at all formal, and was very rarely morose. "If he had serious
matters to discuss, he would make it quite clear from the start."

With the approach of the English Derby, the heart of the
grand old man of the turf beat a little faster. He was thinking

of Tulyar, whom he came to regard as the greatest horse he ever owned, although it was difficult to assess the limits of the colt, who never seemed to do more than just enough. Not everybody shared his optimism. Tulyar disappointed Marcus Marsh, who did not run him in the Two-Thousand Guineas. Later he was converted when the colt proved its worth as a stayer in another race. If only he were not such a lazy horse! While Aly was at Fitzroy helping to exercise the horses, he and Marsh talked a lot about policy; though the best of friends, on racing matters they no longer saw eye to eye.

There was a heat wave and the going was hard, which was thought not to suit Tulyar, but after one gallop over a bone-dry patch, jockey Charlie Smirke found no cause for complaint. "This one will do for me at Epsom," he told Marsh. Obviously, rain or shine, Tulyar was a very hot tip indeed. A rumor that the colt would be withdrawn because of the hard going was swiftly denied by Aly. "He will run and he will win." Marsh felt that he was working for the most powerful and demanding stable in Europe and that his reputation was at stake. The challenge from eight high-class French entries did not shake his confidence.

On Derby Day Tulyar was his sleepy self and looked small and fragile. He was drawn number sixteen and it was up to Charlie Smirke to keep him out of trouble if he could. After a good start Monarch was taken into the lead by Gordon Richards, the famous rider who was trying to win his first Derby in his twenty-eighth attempt. Monarch was followed by Bob Major with Tulyar third, according to March "a perfect position." Then the two front runners slowed down and were overtaken by Tulyar, who, contrary to stable plans, raced ahead. Smirke managed to keep him there. Defeating a powerful challenge from Lester Piggott on Gay Time with a brilliant maneuver, Smirke and his mount reached the post half a length in front.

For the Aga Khan's stable, the fifth Derby win was a complete triumph. The stake money of £20,587 was divided among trainer, jockey, and stable lads, but Aly, as Marsh put it, "clipped the bookmakers for £40,000." Not much later, when Marsh gathered from a casual conversation with Nesbit Waddington that Aly proposed to move most of his horses to another stable, he tackled the Aga Khan but was told that this was entirely up to Aly. He, the Aga Khan, did not want to lose Marsh's services and would give him £50,000 a year to buy yearlings. Marsh was critical of some aspects of the Aga Khan's approach to breeding and racing, but felt there were things "you just could not say to a demigod."

Aly traveled to the United States in a glare of publicity and made up with Rita, whose lawyer, Bartley Crum, announced condescendingly that the Prince had asked for six months' grace to rewoo his client. Laden with toys and packages, Aly arrived in Hollywood, where he and Rita were plunged into a potentially tragic situation when Yasmin swallowed some sleeping pills, thinking them to be sweets, and had to be rushed to a hospital. Fortunately, the little girl was soon out of danger.

When Aly returned to Europe, Rita followed him and moved into his house in the Boulevard Maurice-Barrès. The atmosphere was not conducive to a genuine reconciliation. Reporters and photographers kept a constant vigil so as not to miss a single move in the intricate game, but Aly continued to see his racing cronies and business associates, which suggested to Rita that he had no intention of "reforming." Leaving him for a second time, she moved to the Hotel Lancaster, off the Champs Elysées, and told reporters, "I am bored with Aly's friends." Then she headed for Hollywood—and divorce.

There followed an embarrassing period of legal wrangling about the terms of separation and what the press called "Aly-money." Rita's lawyer asked Aly to set up a trust fund of $3 million for Yasmin. Eventually she was awarded $40,000 a year for their daughter's upkeep. Protracted arguments also went on about Yasmin's upbringing—Christian or Muslim—and about the child's visits to her father in Europe. Still preoccupied with the absurd notion that the child might be kidnapped, Rita's lawyers demanded a bond of $100,000 every time Yasmin left the United States. An allegation that Rita was neglecting both her children, Rebecca and Yasmin, received wide publicity. She finally obtained her divorce on January 27, 1953, after a hearing in a Nevada court lasting seventeen minutes.

Public interest in Aly's matrimonial affairs was only rivaled by curiosity about Tulyar's future. "Will he be sold for stud?" the Begum was asked. "Who can tell?" she answered politely, and added, "We have so many mating problems in this family." Tulyar's sale, in fact, was imminent. Returning to England from South Africa early in 1953, Marcus Marsh was spending his last day aboard the liner when he heard on the radio that "the Irish National Stud today purchased last year's Derby winner, Tulyar, for a quarter of a million pounds, a record fee." He was bitterly disappointed to lose the colt and thought he was at least entitled to a percentage, but when he put this to the Aga Khan he received a curt reply. "I have never given a percentage on sales yet, and I don't intend to start now."

However aggravating the rebuff, Marsh's personal relations with Aly did not suffer as a result. Aly called him a few weeks later and said he would like to come and spend the weekend with him. "Good," Marsh replied, "we'd love to have you." It emerged that Aly was bringing a girl friend who wanted to remain strictly incognito. She turned out to be another Hollywood star, the delicately handsome Gene Tierney, who had made her name ten years earlier in Otto Preminger's excellent film *Laura*.

There was good reason for discretion. Freed from matrimonial bonds, Aly was once more fair game—it was not so much what he did but the role he played in the imagination of others that made him so attractive. Like cowboys impelled to test their strength against the West's deadliest gunslinger, women threw themselves at him and told the newspapers turgid tales about their alleged association. Publicity men tried to squeeze the last ounce of juicy innuendo from Aly's most casual and fleeting contacts—one story making the rounds was that the aging French music-hall singer Mistinguette, whose performance he went to see, could only with difficulty be restrained from falling on his neck.

Elsa Maxwell's contribution was to confess that she had had no sex in her life but that Aly was one of the two men who attracted her. Zsa Zsa Gabor talked about the affair she did not have with Aly, and another nonevent in his life received a great deal of publicity—his withdrawal from the Mille Miglia motor race in Italy when the Aga Khan asked him not to take part. Young Karim winced whenever the headlines brought the tittle-tattle about his father home to him. It was in these days that he first formed his aversion to publicity and resolved to give the press as little cause for comment about his personal affairs as humanly possible. That he would grow up to hate not his father, but his father's playboy image, was a foregone conclusion.

Around this time one of Aly's friends brought Bettina to the Boulevard Maurice-Barrès for drinks. As so often happens, the guests arrived before the host. Aly was always late but always apologized so handsomely that he was soon forgiven. He took Bettina out to dinner at the Pré Catelan, his favorite restaurant, and later met her once more, briefly, in the south of France. She was already strongly attracted to him but could not help noticing that he was constantly surrounded by a bevy of girls. Was it a coincidence that he took Gene Tierney to Givenchy, where Bettina now worked as a model? After the Grand Prix de Paris everybody went to Aly's party, and when he gave another one in Cannes a few weeks later, his father was among the guests, giving the lie to rumors that they had fallen out. The Aga saw Aly paying court to Gene.

Like Rita Hayworth, Gene had been married, but she was divorced from her husband, a leading American couturier. Unlike Rita, she found it easy to adapt to Aly's mode of life and fitted in as easily at Gilltown, where she joined him on his early morning rides, as in the casinos of the Côte d'Azur, where she watched him gambling for high stakes. Inevitably, Elsa Maxwell came into the act. According to one story, the Aga Khan used her as an intermediary to warn Aly that he was failing in his duties to the Ismaili people. (This is about as likely as the Pope asking Walter Winchell to call his cardinals to order for him.) The gossip and the alarums around Aly and Gene Tierney died down, and so did their romance. Gene suffered a mental breakdown, retired to a quiet life in the United States, and received psychiatric treatment before making a triumphant comeback to the screen in another Preminger film.

With the Aga Khan ailing and aging, the management of the racing establishment was almost entirely in Aly's hands. One problem he had to solve forthwith was the choice of a successor to Nesbit Waddington, who was due to retire as stud manager at the end of 1953. He had already investigated several possibilities and virtually made up his mind to invite Major Cyril Hall, manager of the National Stud in Ireland, to take on the job. They knew and liked each other. Major Hall was no stranger to the Aga Khan either and had met young Karim on some of his summer visits to Gilltown. Aly summoned him to the south of France and asked him point-blank whether he would be prepared to take over the management of the studs. His terms were generous; the opportunity was tempting. Major Hall's mind was quickly made up.

As soon as the directors of the National Stud released him, he took charge of the Aga Khan's seven Irish farms—Gilltown, Sheshoon, Ballymanny, Sallymount, Ongar, Williamstown, and Eyrefield. "At that time the Aga Khan and Prince Aly between them had 180 horses," he said. "They probably represented a value which, at a guess, would be three million pounds today."

While Aly looked after the horses, the Aga Khan spent most of his time studying reports from Ismaili centers. Their keynote was progress. Local leaders sought his approval for new projects and asked for his advice; humble followers turned to the Imam with their personal problems. Dictating his replies, suggesting solutions, stimulating new thinking, he continued to guide the lives of millions. While conditions in the Indian subcontinent had become more normal, he foresaw great political changes in East Africa.

As Britain's colonies moved toward independence, Ismailis were growing in stature. They would have to play their part in the transformation of their countries. He discussed the subject with many of them who came to see him in the south of France or in London, where he continued to frequent the Ritz Hotel. Among the happiest memories of a great many Ismailis are their encounters with the Imam-e-Zaman, who received them when they came to Europe. For instance, at that time Eboo Pirbhai, member of the Legislative Council of Kenya, visited Buckingham Palace with his family to receive a knighthood from the Queen, and the Aga Khan conferred on him the Ismaili title of Count.

Another arrival in London was Karim, who at the age of seventeen left Le Rosay, not sorry by any means that his schooldays were at an end but sad to leave Gstaad, his beloved Swiss mountains, and the winter sports at which he excelled. He was bound to come back again and again. "Skiing," he said to me years later, "is the one sport which leaves one no time to worry about one's obligations or about anything else. It is compulsive concentration."

Having been accepted for admission by the Massachusetts Institute of Technology without taking an entrance examination but solely on the strength of his school record, he was spending the holiday with his parents, staying with Princess Joan in London before going to join his father at the Château de l'Horizon. Although he and Amyn would be separated for the first time, he would not be without family support in a strange land because his uncle, Sadruddin, was at Harvard, studying Middle Eastern history, and was a popular figure on the campus and founder of the Harvard Islamic Association, and Patrick Guinness, his mother's son by her first marriage, was working in the United States.

"I was happy about the prospect of going to M.I.T.," Prince Karim said. "Everybody was happy!" Not everybody, really. When the subject cropped up in conversation with his grandfather at Yakimour, the Aga Khan only said absentmindedly, "Yes, yes, yes." But the following week Karim was called to Yakimour again. "You are going to Harvard," the Aga Khan told him in a friendly but firm tone that brooked no contradiction. "I was too young to ask his reasons," Prince Karim told me. "I did not dare to ask him then, and never did."

The young man did not know whether his grandfather was already thinking of him as the next Imam. At this stage, however, there was no question of the Aga Khan changing his plans, and Karim took his entrance examination for the Department of Engineering at Harvard, passed it, and was admitted for the autumn term of 1953. At a school dance in Gstaad at the end of term, he danced once or twice with the dark-haired handsome sister of Fernando Casablanca, one of his schoolmates at Le Rosay. Her name was Sylvia and her parents—father Mexican, mother Swiss—lived in Geneva, where she and Karim saw each other occasionally. They met again in the south of France, and young as they were, a romance developed which in those carefree days remained unnoticed and unrecorded.

That autumn Karim went to America, but for the next four or five years, whenever he returned to Europe, he saw Sylvia, whose family assumed that they might one day be married. It was a little early to make wedding plans for the Aga Khan's grandson, who, like most youngsters of his age, was meeting a great number of girls. At a party in London that was attended by Princess Margaret and attracted a certain amount of attention, he was seen with a pretty debutante, Countess Bunny von Esterhazy, stepdaughter of a Hungarian-born race-horse owner. For a time she was referred to as his girl friend.

None of these social engagements or romantic entanglements in Europe even remotely interfered with his studies. Karim liked the life at Harvard and completely immersed himself in his studies. Though his interest in mathematics, chemistry, and general science never subsided, it was not many months before he began to look to history for answers to questions he was constantly asking himself. Intellectually, he was attracted to Islam, which had played such an important part in his upbringing, and was impressed by Harvard's exceptionally excellent orientalists, Sir Hamilton Gibb, Professor Philip K. Hitti, and Professor R. N. Frye (who later occupied the Chair of Aga Khan Professor for Iranian Studies, endowed by Prince Sadruddin). They offered a large choice of courses on Islamic matters.

Slowly the idea of switching from engineering to Islamic studies matured in his mind. Was it his grandfather's wish that he should study Islam? Years later, when he had already been Imam for over a decade, Prince Karim was still sensitive on this point. "I never discussed the switch with my grandfather," he said. "It was a personal decision that had nothing to do with either my father or my grandfather."

It laid the foundation for Prince Karim's astonishing range of religious knowledge and, equally important, his sense of proportion about these delicate matters. "At the university," he said, "there were discussions which exposed me to all aspects of Islamic studies. The scope was very wide. I read extensively and acquired an overall view." Because it was tested by other influences and did not develop in a glasshouse atmosphere of isolated Ismaili doctrine, his faith grew all the stronger.

Obviously, he does not accept the views of every author whose religious works he studied. In the light of his Shia Ismaili persuasion, he became critical of many works that interpret the history of Islam in Sunni terms. He has the greatest respect for Professor Hitti, a Christian Arab, whose classes he attended. "His achievement lies in the compilation of a great many facts and figures which have never been collected before," he stated. This does not mean, however, that the young Imam's conclusions coincide with the Professor's on all points or that he accepts Hitti's interpretation in every detail.

"K. Khan of Harvard" was only just beginning to come to terms with the university's approach to the theory of Islam when, as Prince Karim-al-Huseini, he was called upon to undertake an official mission on behalf of his grandfather. Separated from Ismaili contacts by the Atlantic Ocean, he had to acquaint himself with the events leading up to the situation into which he was about to be plunged. It appeared that a campaign of abuse and vilification against the Aga Khan and Aly Khan was unsettling Ismailis in East Africa, where collections for the Platinum Jubilee were under way. At one point it reached such a pitch that Mr. Oliver Lyttleton, the British Colonial Secretary, was asked to investigate. Community leaders from Kenya, Tanganyika, and Uganda traveled to Evian, the French spa, to attend a council over which the Aga Khan presided. They decided that all Ismailis should be asked to sign a pledge of loyalty.

Important voices were raised in defense of the Aga Khan. "These fanatics and hotheads do not realize that the Aga Khan gives us far more than we give him," said Ibrahim Nathoo, a prominent Ismaili who was Kenya's Minister of Works. Sir Eboo Pirbhai assured reporters that the community in Africa was "completely loyal" and denounced the "purely mischievous" anonymous attempts to damage the Aga Khan's name. The community itself would take action against the slanderers. In Kenya, mass meetings of Ismailis passed resolutions condemning the "unknown individuals under fictitious names and bogus organizations" who carried on a subversive campaign against "the august person of the head of the Ismaili faith, His Highness the Aga Khan, our religion, and Ismaili leaders."

The family rallied to the Imam's cause. In scorching heat, the Begum went to Mecca, the first European-born woman to make the exhausting pilgrimage. Clad in the *ihram,* the long, white, rough cotton garment of the pilgrims which makes it impossible to distinguish rich from poor, she worshiped at the shrine of Islam. In Paris Prince Aly had discussions with leading Ismailis, and Karim and Amyn were dispatched to East Africa to tour Ismaili centers with a personal message from the Aga Khan. In Nairobi Prince Karim addressed a large gathering, bringing home to Ismailis and non-Ismailis how much his grandfather had done for the community. (At that moment 104 schools in East Africa were maintained by grants from the Aga Khan, who wanted as many students as possible to enter the teaching profession.)

Returning to Harvard, the Prince quickly settled down again among fellow students who remained happily impervious to these events. Having switched to Islamic studies in his sophomore year, he roomed at Leverett House dormitory with John Fell Stevenson, son of the ex-Governor of Illinois who had been the Democratic Presidential candidate of 1952. " 'K' Khan," Stevenson said, "was a charming fellow with a cracking wit." According to his roommate, he did not go in much for clothes and became known as "that guy who had only one pair of shoes." "During the time I knew him," said Stevenson, "he owned two suits, but I never saw either of them pressed. He had about two dozen neckties, but they were all the same color."

The teaching staff regarded him as "intelligent and serious but rather shy." Professor Frye said that he had immense capabilities and was a well-rounded student, "liked by all of us here." Senior Tutor Richard Gill thought him an awfully nice guy, one of the best fellows at Leverett. Everyone testified to his keen mind, but one instructor suggested that he did not work all the time as hard as he could have. He dropped chemistry after a two-semester struggle but collected an impressive number of top grades, and his name appeared regularly on the Dean's List, an index of high scholastic achievement. His room at Leverett House, with a wide view of the Charles River, reflected his cur-

rent preoccupations. Records—his favorite was music from Tchaikovsky's opera *Undine*—were stacked side by side with volumes of philosophy and history to which he turned, to quote Stevenson, "with casual concentration."
Fellow students were impressed by his talent with the bongo drums. "He'd practice drumming on anything available," Stevenson noted, "waste baskets, automobile fenders, desk tops. If there wasn't anything to hit, he'd snap his fingers." Unlike many of his contemporaries, Karim did not run a car and usually walked or hitched a ride, never failing to get one because he had so many friends. He belonged to several clubs, including the exclusive Delphic, the Signet, whose members must demonstrate intelligence (fellow members: T. S. Eliot and John Rockefeller IV), and the Hasty Pudding. In summer he rowed on the Charles, in winter he spent most weekends skiing at Stowe, Vermont. Occasionally he went to New York to see a play or have dinner with a girl friend (Jane O'Reilly, pretty daughter of an American millionaire, was one of them) or a relative. His mother came from England to visit him and Amyn soon followed him to Harvard. Uncle Sadruddin's reputation on the campus was that of a dashing, flamboyant young man. By contrast, Karim's life was one of comfortable obscurity.

For the Aga Khan, the position was reversed—prominence and discomfort were the order of the day. The Far Eastern Platinum Jubilee celebrations were scheduled for February, 1954. So as to be equal to the strain of another long trip and the elaborate weighing ceremony, he submitted himself to a course of C.T. (Cell Therapy) injections by Professor Paul Niehans, the famous "rejuvenator" whose clinic, La Prairie, was not far from Villa Barakat, near Geneva. The treatment was effective, and by the time he reached Karachi, the Aga Khan's condition had improved. He was received with royal honors as the Governor General's personal guest and paid homage by the large and prosperous Ismaili community.

On the day of the ceremony the specially built stadium was sardine-packed with sixty thousand people and all the roads leading to it were filled with crowds unable to gain admittance. Escorted by his *wazirs* and councillors in scarlet and gold robes and gold turbans (except for the Mir of Hunza, who wore black velvet and gold), the Aga Khan appeared in a ceremonial high-sided black cap, a white tunic, and a brown embroidered robe. Aly wore a black cap, white jodphurs, boots, and spurs. The atmosphere was almost lighthearted. Sitting between the Begum Aga Khan and his own wife, Prime Minister Mohammed Ali recorded the whole ceremony with his 3-D camera, frequently "shooting back" at the photographers.

After the recitations from the Koran the Aga Khan rose and raised his hands in prayer before resuming his seat. Listening to the messages from kings and heads of state and to the long address of welcome, he seemed to be tiring. The afternoon sun was blazing down and one of the Governor General's household held a sunshade over the Imam. But when the Aga Khan rose to deliver his *irshad* (advice) to his "spiritual children," the man remained in his seat and left him unprotected. At the Aga Khan's signal he got up but still held the shade so awkwardly that it provided no protection.

Watching the incident from below, the Begum's anxious expression reflected her husband's obvious discomfort. The smile disappeared from her lips. "What a fool," she said under her breath and motioned vigorously at the man. When he took no notice, she at last managed to attract the attention of an official, who tilted the shade at a proper angle.

The Aga Khan started by saying how proud and happy he was to have been born in Karachi, which was also the birthplace of the late Qaid-i-Azam, the Father of the Nation. Nostalgically, he mentioned that, shortly before his death, Jinnah had asked him to take charge of Pakistan's diplomatic representation in Europe and America, but his health had not allowed him to accept the offer. The speech culminated in an appeal to Ismailis to make their patriotism and loyalty active and practical. "If every Ismaili living in Pakistan remembers and interprets his citizenship, howsoever humble his contribution may be, with the spirit of courage and devotion, then indeed I am happy to think that after many years of surgical operations and illnesses, I am still alive to give you this fatherly advice."

The value of the platinum used symbolically in the weighing ceremony was three million rupees. "This must not be frittered away," said the Aga Khan. "It should be the beginning of something like the Investment Trust in Africa, to be built up so that by a target date, say 1960, you will be able to reach a position by which Ismailis both in East and West Pakistan can be sure of employment." His aim was a prosperous Pakistan in which Ismailis could fully share in the prosperity. This attitude of enlightened self-interest in which patriotism is a basic ingredient still guides Ismailis wherever they live.

Willpower alone enabled the Aga Khan to hold out until the end of the ceremony. Once in his suite in Government House, he was near collapse, ran a temperature, and the doctors insisted on his taking a complete rest. The Begum watched over him with great solicitude, but not even she could restrain him. He was haunted by the needs and the problems of the community. One evening after the Begum retired, he heaved himself to his desk and wrote a long personal letter to Amirali Fancy in which he set out his ideas and plans on how to advance the fortunes of his community and raise their standard of living. He was adamant that his followers should be assisted financially but should, at the same time, learn to stand on their own feet. He wanted them to feel proud of themselves. "I do not believe in giving them charity," he wrote. "Financial assistance should be given only for the purpose of making them independent."

"It was 2 A.M. when His Highness' Iranian aide-de-camp delivered the letter to me at my house," Amirali Fancy told me.

"His Highness wants a reply at once," the aide-de-camp said. "It will have to be done very quickly so that the Begum does not find out he has been working at nights." Fancy wrote a reply on the spot. "His Highness' letter remains one of my proudest possessions," he said.

Amirali Fancy, *kamadia* and member of the Ismailia Supreme Council for West Pakistan at the time, started the ball rolling with an investigation into economic opportunities for Ismailis. "I called a meeting of the Council," he said, "and we discussed the most favorable areas." Some leading Ismailis went into textiles, others into the export-import business, with less well-endowed Ismailis taking up shares in their enterprises. "I went into steel," Amirali Fancy said. Like all those who followed the Aga Khan's advice, he did extremely well. His rolling mills are among the biggest in Pakistan.

A project to which the Aga Khan had been heavily committed since the early fifties was the jute industry in East Pakistan. He had a growing stake in the Crescent Jute Mill in which Prince Sadruddin also took up shares. Its value has more than trebled in the intervening years. "If anyone wanted to buy it today," Amirali Fancy said, "he could not get it for less than £8 million." Then came the People's Jute Mill, set up by the Aga Khan and local Ismailis with the government taking a 33 percent share. The mill is estimated to be worth another £8 million and the Aga Khan and the community retain a controlling interest.

The project arising from the Jubilee that helped to spread benefits more widely among the community than any other was the Platinum Jubilee Finance and Investment Corporation. "It owed its existence entirely to the Aga Khan's generosity," Amirali Fancy told me. Having accepted the three million rupees as a gift from the community, His Highness promptly returned them to be used for the betterment of his followers." This is how the corporation came into being. Amirali Fancy became its first chairman. The beginnings were difficult, but by 1969 there were ninety-five Ismaili cooperative credit societies in Pakistan and, says Fancy, "no bad debts."

So as to leave his father basking in the community's undivided homage, Aly kept in the background, which started a rumor that the Imam was deliberately downgrading his son and discouraging any inclination to regard him automatically as the Imam's successor. At this stage the rumor did not seem to have reached the ears of Aly. Back on his European stamping grounds he was cheerful, in great form, his touch as sure as ever. Two days before the Grand Prix de Deauville he heard that a four-year-old filly, Rosa Bonheur—a good filly without a great pedigree—was on sale. On Friday evening, rather than join a party of friends for dinner, he drove into the country to inspect the horse and bought it for a modest price. On Sunday afternoon it won the Grand Prix—and ten million (old) francs. Not one to hide his feelings behind a mask of supersophistication, he was exuberant.

Another rumor pursued him, this time about his finances. Marcus Marsh claimed that Aly owed the casinos "something in the region of a quarter of a million pounds." As most things that were said about Aly, this was probably an exaggeration. Marsh also mentioned the magnitude of Aly's racing transactions: "During his spell with me," the trainer wrote, "he sold horses to the value of £600,000 and this, coupled with prize money, must have raised something close to the million mark." (The pound was then valued at $2.80.)

When Aly missed the annual conference at Yakimour, where the next season's stud and racing operations were discussed, there were rumors about disagreements between him and his father. The Aga presided over the two-day talks, which were attended by Mme. Vuillier, Robert Muller, and Major Hall. "We reported to His Highness," Major Hall said, "and gave him a detailed picture of the position." The Aga asked questions, and many ideas came up. Some eighty hard and fast decisions were made. "One of the problems was to arrange for a nomination for the Queen's stallion Aureole," said Major Hall. The Aga Khan decided to send Neocracy, who had bred Tulyar, and the result was St. Créspin, who eventually won the Imperial Produce and the Eclipse Stakes in England and the Arc de Triomphe in France but failed in the Derby.

CHAPTER XIII

Eᴀꜱᴛ Aꜰʀɪᴄᴀ'ꜱ Iꜱᴍᴀɪʟɪꜱ were preparing to match the Karachi Jubilee celebrations with spectacular weighing ceremonies in Kampala, Dar-es-Salaam, and Mombasa when, early in January, 1955, grave news reached them about their Imam. While staying at the ornate Cataract Hotel in the Egyptian resort of Aswan, where the climate is even kinder than on the Riviera, the Aga Khan became bedridden with bronchial pneumonia and a high temperature, a calamity for a man of seventy-seven. The Begum was with him, and Aly hurried to his father's bedside. Ismaili leaders expecting to accompany him on the last stage of his journey to East Africa anxiously watched his progress. Although his condition improved, doctors would not even hear of a compromise plan to restrict the celebrations to one single ceremony in Kampala. There could be no question of the patient traveling the fifteen hundred miles. It might well result in his death.

The dreaded word symbolized the gravity of the situation. It was no secret that the Aga Khan wanted to be buried at Aswan and had already chosen his tomb of rose-red granite. "The Aga Khan wants to sleep in the hot sand overlooking the waters of the Nile," the Begum told a friend, "and when I die, I want to

lie beside him." To banish the thought of death, which seemed
so near, a villa was bought for him at Aswan, a white house on
red basalt rock by the Nile with a view of the city. It was
named Noor-el-Salaam (Light of Peace), but there was no saying
whether he would ever be well enough to occupy it. At the
moment he just managed to sit through a token Jubilee ceremony in the lounge of the hotel, and the East African celebrations went ahead in his absence. Reports that his days were
numbered raised the question of his succession, a talking point
among his friends the world over. The community could not
help wondering, the newspapers were speculating, and Aly's
name was bandied about in a manner that caused him severe
embarrassment.

The matter came to a head when David Burk, of the London
Daily Express, ran into Aly in the lounge of the Cataract and
bluntly confronted him with the rumors about his future. The
Aga Khan was said to be still upset about his son's two divorces,
not to speak of the prospect of his marrying another Hollywood
film star, although this no longer seemed likely. Had there been
a quarrel? "There has never been the slightest disagreement
between me and my father on this subject," Aly told Burk. "I
know there are rumors, but someone must have dreamt them up."
When Burk mentioned that some people doubted whether he
would succeed his father as head of the Shia Ismailis, Aly re-
torted, "Why should there be any doubt?" He said he had
regularly visited Ismaili communities and loyally performed his
religious duties as his father's representative.

Published in the *Daily Express,* the interview was interpreted
as Aly's way of saying that he fully expected to succeed his
father; however, Aly could not possibly have overlooked the
significance of the Aga's persistent harping on his fast driving,
flying in all kinds of weather, and risking his life as an amateur
rider. The Aga had made no secret of his premonition that his
son's life would not be a long one.

The answer to the question about the succession was hidden
among fifteen thick volumes of documents and deeds which

listed the Aga Khan's properties and made up his last will and testament. In consultation with English and Swiss lawyers, Maître Ardoin, the faithful adviser, prepared a final version which was completed and signed in May, 1955, when the Aga Khan was back on his feet and visiting London for a few days. It was deposited in the vaults of Lloyds Bank, and until opened after the Aga's death, no one except Ardoin and the solicitors, Slaughter and May, knew whom the Imam had designated as his successor. Speculation was also rife about the financial provisions, although the Begum, Princess Andrée, Aly, Sadruddin, Karim, Amyn, and Yasmin were known to have been provided for by individual trusts.

"The will mentioned a few million pounds," I was told by Maître Ardoin, "but the bulk of the property, real estate, shares, and other assets were held by companies and trusts." Some of the Aga Khan's accounts were overdrawn because his advisers thought it financially useful. Conversely, literally hundreds of properties, many of them covering land of great value, came under the heading of the community but were designated for specific purposes, such as sports grounds, hospitals, schools, mosques. "Who would buy a hospital in Nairobi?" an Ismaili leader asked, "Or a mosque or a school?" Although the value of these properties was immense and they were all in the Aga Khan's name, they were not really negotiable.

Owing to his grave condition, plans to provide him with a permanent home on Swiss territory were speeded up. The choice (the Begum's) fell on La Rivière, a charming villa in Versoix, on Lake Geneva, which used to belong to a wealthy hotel owner. It was very near Evian, where the Aga Khan used to take the waters, and arrangements for a "carrier" to take a quantity of the precious water to Versoix every day were made. The house was renamed Villa Barakat (*barakat* means blessings) and was renovated and furnished. Aly Khan acquired a piece of land to build his own house on Swiss soil, and Sadruddin bought the Château de Collonges-Bellerive.

When the Aga Khan's condition improved and he returned to

Europe, talk about his health, fortune, and succession subsided. With the agonizing moment of decision fading into the distance, the weight of uncertainty also lifted from Aly's shoulders. The winter of discontent was over and his mood was once more in harmony with Paris in the spring. Impetuously, he telephoned Bettina, who had lingered in his mind since their brief encounters, but she was too busy to see him. When he persisted and tracked her down in the middle of a photographic session at the studios of the Paris magazine *Elle,* they arranged to meet at his house.

Rushed as usual, doing too much, seeing too many people, and trying to be in several places at the same time, Aly was late and Bettina left angrily before he arrived, but he sent his car to bring her back and took her to dinner and to see a Western in a movie theater on the Champs Elysées, where, to her immense astonishment, he promptly fell asleep. Afterwards they went dancing, and when Bettina refused his invitation to spend a weekend with him at his stud farm in St. Créspin near Deauville, it was only because she had professional commitments she would not break. They were no longer in doubt about each other. Obviously they were bound to end up in each other's arms. Aly was not yet aware of it, but Bettina had resolved to be more than one of Aly's passing fancies.

She had qualities of temperament and character that augured well for their association, quite apart from her captivating elfin figure, glowing red hair, wistfully smiling eyes, and handsome face with the freckles that often defied makeup. A daughter of the solid Breton soil, little Simone Bodin, as she was christened, and her sister were still babies when their mother took them to Elbeuf, in Normandy, after their father deserted both the family and his job with the railway. She went to school at Elbeuf and grew into an enchanting girl whom Paris lured, although her elder sister, after a none too successful foray into the postliberation capital, had returned home and married a local lad. Simone's animal grace and charm assured her a better reception in the glamour-starved big city and soon earned her a job as a mannequin with a minor fashion house. There she was discovered by Jacques Fath. The young couturier liked to give his models new names. Simone Bodin became Bettina. After her first uncertain steps along the catwalk she soon found her feet. Early marriage to Benno Graziani, an Italian photographer, was not successful and did not last long, but she still bears his name. She showed Jacques Fath's clothes in many parts of the world and after his death joined Givenchy. Famous photographers, like the late Bob Capa, sought her out as model and friend, and some quiet remarkable people responded to her attractive personality. Picasso agreed to become a prop in a set of fashion photographs that featured her as the star. She captured Jean Cocteau's imagination, and Guy Schoeller introduced her to the world of publishing—and to Françoise Sagan, whom he later married. After Schoeller came Peter Viertel, the American writer who has since become Deborah Kerr's husband.

Bettina had been with Peter for two or three years when Aly drew her into his social orbit. He asked her to give up her job and without much ado had her things transferred from her place at Garches, on the outskirts of Paris, to his house in the Boulevard Maurice-Barrès. But for her the great moment came in Cannes, at the Château de l'Horizon, one evening when Gany, the butler, had laid the table on the terrace. The cicadas were chirping, the waves sighing, the stars shining. So were Bettina's eyes. "I thought I must be dreaming," she said. "It all seemed too beautiful to be true." After the meal Aly took her by the hand. "This is your home, Zinette," he told her gently —"Zinette" or "Zine" were his pet names for her. "One day," he said later, "we are going to be married." Bettina brought order into his homes, which had lacked a woman's touch, and chased away "the women in slippers," as she called the female hangers-on she had encountered on previous visits.

For once the family was delighted with the woman of his choice, who was so different from her flamboyant predecessors.

They received the pleasant and modest girl with open arms.
That year Rita Hayworth at long last agreed to let Yasmin spend
some time with her father in Europe. Bettina looked after the
child, who became very attached to her. "Dear Bettina," she wrote
on one occasion as the aircraft carried her back to the United
States at the end of her visit, "I have a good flight in the plane;
I will miss you very much. I hope I will see you soon. Love,
Yasmin." Aly, who was with his daughter, wrote a postscript in
French: "*Ma Zinette adorée: Tu nous manque. Nous pensons à
toi. Je t'embrasse mille fois.*" At one of Aly's parties the aloof
Begum playfully bombarded Bettina with colored paper pellets,
a mark of fellow feeling for a girl whose background was not
unlike her own, except for the difference in climate between
Brittany and the Alpes-Maritimes.

To keep up with Aly's perpetual motion required great stamina. Bettina never flagged or complained. On race courses, at
Chantilly or Gilltown, at social gatherings, she made an even-
tempered, strikingly handsome companion. When Aly gambled
at a casino, Bettina waited up for him. When he danced with
another woman, she sat the dance out with friends, refusing to
take the floor with anyone but him. When he traveled without
her, she was there to greet him on his return. Nobody was
allowed to guess that gossip about him disturbed her. Kim
Novak came to Europe to attend the Cannes Film Festival and
caught Aly's eye. She later told the story of their courtship, or
infatuation, in an American magazine, adding a few details that
cast doubt on her memory. Her first glimpse of Aly, she said,
was at Yakimour, where he was tending the roses and came up
to her holding an earth-covered hand out to her. It does not
tally with the image of Aly as his friends knew him. Bettina
made no scenes, did not seem to take these things too tragi-
cally, and loved Aly for qualities of the heart which were less
obvious to outsiders and would have made less-interesting magazine material.

So as to share his sporting interests, Bettina began to unravel the mysteries of French and English race cards and loyally ran through the pages of *Le Figaro*, the Paris *Herald, Sport Complet*, and the racing news in English newspapers when he had finished with them. He spoke to her about his favorite horses as one might about dear members of the family and showed her the beautifully kept graves with white tombstones where some of them lay buried on his stud farms. Patiently she suffered his "jockey regime" of Turkish baths, massages, and dieting, and watched him racing.

Aly was finding it increasingly difficult to make the required weight. At times he kept looking frantically for his glasses and complained bitterly that his eyesight was deteriorating, his hair thinning, and that he was getting old. He could be irritable, too. With Bettina standing by, he would examine the daily ration of press cuttings about him and fume about "inaccurate stories," screw the paper into a ball, and fling it away. Harvey, his dog, was always lying in wait to catch it.

Bettina came to know the Aga Khan better while he was still convalescing at Yakimour, and she thought he approved of her. Seeing him and Aly together, she began to understand their complicated relationship. As a boy Aly had seen little of his father, whom he loved and feared at the same time. "And yet," she remarked, "he, who had suffered so much from his separation from his parents, did not manage to bring up his own children in their family surroundings."

Karim and Amyn spent August at l'Horizon with their mother, while Aly stayed at Deauville. But if he was not close to his boys, the prospect of seeing Yasmin always excited him. Unlike Karim, whose interest in horses was still nonexistent and who felt inhibited when talking about them to his knowledgable father, Yasmin loved them and had a good eye for them on race tracks or stud farms. With "Yassy" around, Aly created a children's world with games and parties that he enjoyed as much as she did. He was a real-life fairy-tale prince, who had, perhaps, never fully grown up.

For Bettina, traveling in his wake, it was also a fairy-tale magic-carpet passage through life. Aly took her with him on the first stage of a tour of Ismaili centers. They lingered for a few days in Cairo, where he met friends and played bridge, then flew on to Beirut and Salamiyya. He warned her what to expect, but she was overwhelmed by the roaring reception from excited Ismaili crowds mobbing her prince, who looked striking in a burnoose and the local headgear, an Arab among his Arab brothers. The change of scene and attitude was bewildering.

Back in France there was no respite. While he was dressing, telephone calls from New York, Buenos Aires, Karachi, or Nairobi would pursue him. If Bettina hoped for a private chat, she was liable to be disappointed. In his own room Eric Bigio, his secretary, would be taking dictation—letters, messages—Aly's voice rising above the buzz of his electric razor. The corridor would be full of people waiting to catch his ear, among them, more often than not, Alec Head, trainer and friend, Robert Muller, Ismaili visitors. While putting on his trousers, he would already be giving instructions for Lucien, the chauffeur, to warm up the engine of the car. His progress past all these people was slow as he shook hands all around, exchanged views, listened, looked at documents, and had a word and a smile for all before letting himself out of the front door.

He would not be gone for long before he was telephoning Bettina to warn her that a number of people would be dropping in for dinner that night ("Talk it over with the chef, *ma chérie*"). Guests arrived frequently long before he himself had returned home. At l'Horizon people kept turning up whom Aly had casually invited months earlier in the course of his travels. They were well received, but Aly himself was unlikely to be there. Among those who always enjoyed his hospitality was the telephone operator of the London Ritz Hotel who conducted a clearinghouse for the Aga's and Aly's messages throughout the year and was rewarded with a summer holiday at the château.

Aly was not there either when Sadruddin and Karim came

from Harvard to spend their vacation in the south of France. That summer Sadruddin, twenty-three, more studious than his elder half-brother but not averse to a lighthearted adventure, met the strange, exotic Nina Dyer, Ceylon-born daughter of an English planter. Nina had been a leading model in Paris and London and briefly married to the immensely wealthy Heinrich von Thyssen, heir to a German industrial empire, who gave her a Caribbean island and a panther, both curiously appropriate to her personality. When they were divorced he settled half a million pounds on her. She was twenty-six with a reputation for eccentricity—apart from the black panther, Nina shared her fifteen-room villa in Versailles with two hundred parrots, eight Pekinese, and two borzois—and her marriage was already on the rocks when she and Sadruddin began a holiday romance that seemed unlikely to last much longer than the hot Riviera summer but swiftly led to an engagement. The Aga Khan gave his blessing and the wedding date was eventually fixed for July 15, 1957.

Karim spent most of his time with Grandfather or one of his secretaries, Gaetane Beguel, researching and acquainting himself with the Imam's affairs, both personal and religious. It looked as if the grandson was being groomed for a place in the Ismaili hierarchy, but though Karim himself was not aware of it, this summer school in Ismaili affairs had a much more immediate significance. Since he was not staying at his father's château, Karim did not notice the changes in some of the familiar rooms, the empty walls where most of Aly's treasured paintings used to hang. The Degas, Utrillos, Renoirs, Rauol Dufys, and works by Vlaminck, Modigliani, and Dunoyer de Ségonzac, which made up half of Aly's collection, were packed and ready for dispatch to Paris. The other half of the collection, at the Boulevard Maurice-Barrès, was also in the process of being taken down.

A few months later the paintings turned up at the Galerie Charpentier in Paris, where they were offered for auction. The

news that Prince Aly Khan was selling his paintings persuaded
many that he was, as someone put it, as broke as a millionaire
can be. In modern parlance, he was suffering from a shortage
of liquid funds. "Everyone was busy saying that Prince Aly Khan
was getting rid of his pictures in order to be able to feed his
horses," Bettina noted, but went on to deny that he was short
of money. "He simply wanted to buy some new paintings," she
insisted. Still she did not deny how sad he was about parting
with his treasures.

When the Dufy painting of Deauville race course which used
to hang in Aly's Paris house came up for sale, the Aga Khan, in
a characteristic gesture, bought it back and gave it to Aly as
a birthday present. Mrs. Mike Todd (Elizabeth Taylor), already embarked upon her celebrated purchasing spree which
was still going strong a dozen years later, bought Aly's Degas,
one of the Utrillos, and most of the Dufys. When Aly saw the
bare walls at l'Horizon with the outlines of the paintings, he
decided to start buying again, acquired a few new Dufys, and
looked out for works with a "horsy" motif by English and Dutch
masters. Bettina says he never mentioned the auction again.

Nearby at Yakimour the Aga Khan was in precarious health.
His temperature was high and erratic, and he felt weak and
tired. One of his great joys was a visit from little Yasmin, who
was in Europe on a six months' visit and growing up into a
delightful girl, much in her father's image. Her exuberant birthday greetings for Grandfather were as great a boon to him as
the felicitations from his followers all over the world, who were
celebrating the anniversary of his birth as a holy day and
praying for him. On Yasmin's birthday, anxious to reciprocate,
he asked her what she would like as a present, and when she
pointed to the glittering chandelier overhead, he had it taken
down. She proudly claimed it as her property but fortunately
did not insist on taking it away with her.

Yasmin got on as well with her big brothers, and Karim in
particular kept a fatherly eye on her. He kept her, the daughter

of a Muslim prince, from eating pork until she learned to draw back when she saw a slice of ham. Occasionally, she accompanied her grandfather on a drive along the Croisette and past the Riviera landmarks, signposts of many stages of his life for the past sixty years.

The subject of racing also roused his flagging spirits. As soon as he was well enough, he insisted on going to Chantilly, where he could watch the racing from his car, drawn up beside the track. Plans for the future of studs and stables occupied his mind. One of his last contributions to the sport was the production of Charlottesville, bred to the Vuillier points formula for hereditary characteristics to which he subscribed to the end. Charlottesville, a worthy symbol of the Aga Khan's acumen, earned £75,000 in stake money in a spectacular racing career and now occupies pride of place as the leading stallion in the Ballymany Stud in the Curragh.

During the second half of the fifties his colors were not as prominent as of yore, but at least Aly won another classic when Charlie Smirke rode Rose Royale to victory in the Two Thousand Guineas. The Aga Khan's public image remained unimpaired. People still saw him as an international *bon viveur* and he responded with good humor. In a radio interview he was asked how he related his good living to his religious position. "I don't know why the gods should reserve the good things in life for bad people," he replied. That spring (1957) he again came to Chantilly but was not well enough to go to the races. He went to lunch with Aly and Bettina. Though he was still interested in good food and very complimentary when the chef produced two of his favorite dishes, calf's head followed by strawberry mousse, he did not eat. His weight was down from 240 to 170 pounds, and the current heat wave aggravated his condition. The Begum was deeply worried. "He should never have come here!" she grumbled. He was anxious to get home, home at the end of a long nomadic life being Switzerland. The end could not be far away and the extraordinary old man who felt a deep responsibility for millions of followers wanted to die in his legal residence so as to leave his and the community's affairs in perfect order.

A Viscount airliner was chartered and an ambulance took the ailing Aga to the airport, where he was carried aboard on a stretcher. The Begum, Sadruddin, and Nina Dyer joined him on the aircraft, and Professor Laporte, the French heart specialist, and two nurses went along. At Geneva an ambulance was waiting to take the Aga to his villa. He was extremely ill and his condition continued to deteriorate. At the end of the first week of July all hope dwindled. The Begum refused to leave her husband's bedside, Karim was summoned from Harvard, but Amyn postponed his journey so as to take a vital examination. Yasmin was already on her way to Europe by sea. Aly rushed to Geneva and telephoned Bettina in Paris, asking her to await Yasmin's arrival and bring her to Versoix without delay. They traveled from Le Bourget, and when they arrived at Geneva airport, Aly took the child straight to the Aga. Yasmin's visit had been a wonderful tonic for his father, he said when they emerged from his room. Ismaili leaders from East Africa and the subcontinent began to arrive to pay their last respects to the Imam who had guided the community's fortunes for seventy-two years, longer than any other.

In the early hours of July 11 the Aga's heart weakened. Aly and Sadruddin were summoned to Barakat, but their dying father could no longer speak. Karim came, and the Begum was still keeping her vigil. Four doctors were in attendance, and nurses left the sick room only to change their clothes or take something to eat. At midday the Aga Khan was sleeping peacefully. Forty minutes later his life slipped quietly away. The Swiss doctor who signed the death certificate in accordance with local regulations gave heart failure and cancer as the cause of death. Aly, Sadruddin, and Karim filed past the bed. They had tears in their eyes and looked strained and tired. The Begum was numb with sorrow. When Yasmin was told that her grandfather had gone forever, she could not quite understand but wept. Nina and Bettina, who had been waiting in an adjacent room, were crying. It did not occur to either of them that Bettina might be destined to become the new Begum. The curtains were drawn, and darkness fell over a great figure of the age.

CHAPTER XIV

THE NEWS OF THE Aga Khan's death spread quickly. Ismaili leaders came from their hotels and gathered on the grounds of the villa. Reporters, press photographers, and newsreel cameramen began to arrive and the road outside was filled with a growing crowd. The drive was jammed with cars and three more policemen reinforced a lone comrade who had been standing guard outside. They were trying to keep a passage for the diplomats and friends who wanted to present their condolences, but by now the crowd was so thick that some of them could hardly make their way to the villa. Aly, visibly wilting in the heat and showing signs of tension, his face drawn and shirt unbuttoned, scanned messages, dictated notes, greeted arrivals, and generally busied himself as if to keep his mind off the question that was on all lips.

The Imam was dead; long live the Imam—but who was he? In spite of the genuine grief among family and followers, the succession was the chief topic of speculation. Would it be Aly, or had Sadruddin superseded his elder brother as the Aga's choice? Karim's name was already being mentioned, and even Amyn, who had arrived too late to see his grandfather alive, seemed to be in the running. Maître Ardoin was on hand to discuss legal and financial points with Aly and Sadruddin, but not until the man from Lloyds Bank brought the will from London would there be a full answer. When the bank official arrived the following morning, he was accompanied by Otto Giesen, a solicitor whose firm, Slaughter and May, had helped to draw up the document.

In the garden some thirty Ismailis and their wives were waiting to pay homage to the forty-ninth Imam. Inside, in the villa's ground-floor sitting room, the family assembled to hear Giesen read the ten-page will and the two-page codicil:

I SULTAN SIR MAHOMED SHAH AGA KHAN V.C.I.E., G.C.S.I., born on the Second day of November One thousand eight hundred and seventy seven at Karachi temporarily residing at the Hotel Ritz London HEREBY REVOKE all Wills and other testamentary dispositions heretofore made by me AND DECLARE this to BE MY LAST WILL which I make this Twenty fifth day of May One thousand nine hundred and fifty five.

1. I DECLARE that I have made my permanent home and am domiciled in the Canton of Geneva, Switzerland, AND THEREFORE I DECLARE that in accordance with Article 32 and Article 22, Section 2 of the Swiss Federal Law of the Twenty fifth day of June One thousand eight hundred and ninety one my estate be governed by Shia Muslim Law which is my personal law in force for all the members of the Shia Muslim Ismailian Community in my country of origin Pakistan.

Lloyds Bank (Foreign) Limited, of 10 Moorgate in the City of London, was named as executors and trustees, and "my relative" Majid Khan, son of Aziz Khan of Poona, India, adviser to the bank in matters concerning the estate in India (a provision revoked in the codicil, as Majid Khan died before the testator). The will proceeded to enumerate the Aga Khan's marriages:

In the year 1897 I was married to Shahzadi Begum daughter of Aga Jangi Shah. I divorced the said Shahzadi Begum on 8 December 1926 in accordance with the requirements of Shia Moslem Law. I have no children by the said Shahzadi Begum who is now dead. In the year 1908 I was married to Cleope Teresa Magliano according to the Muta form of marriage as recognized by Shia Law. The period and dowry were fixed at fifty years and ten thousand francs, respectively. Previously to the said marriage my wife, the said Cleope Teresa Magliano, became a convert to Mahomedanism, adopting the tenets of the Shia sect and thereafter continued to be a Moslem by religion. . . . There were two children born of the said marriage, a Son named Giuseppe Mahdi Khan who died in or about the year 1911 and is buried at Monaco and a Son named Aly Salomone Khan who was born at Turin on or about 13 June 1911. On the 23 day of January 1923 I went through a permanent form of marriage with my said wife Cleope Teresa Magliano in Bombay observing the ceremonials which are customary among Shia Moslems. To the said marriage were several witnesses including Sir Thomas J. Strangman, Knight, Sir Stanley Reed, Knight, K.B.E., LL.D., and my relatives Aga Shah Rook Shah and Aga Aziz Khan. My said wife died in Paris on 1 December 1926 and is buried at Monaco near our elder son Giuseppe Mahdi Khan.

I was married to Andrée Josephine Marie Louise Carron on 7 December 1929 at Aix-Les-Bains in France. In addition to the Civil marriage I was married according to the Moslem permanent form of marriage by the Imams of the Paris Mosque. The Mehr or Dowry was fixed at 10,000 (Ten thousand) French francs. Of this marriage a Son was born to me on 17 January 1933 at the American Hospital, Neuilly-sur-Seine, and was named Sadruddin Aga Khan. This marriage was dissolved by a double divorce process in Geneva in December 1943. The civil marriage was dissolved by a Judgment of the Geneva Court. The religious marriage was dissolved according to Shia Moslem Law in the presence of two Moslem witnesses and a Notary Public at Geneva and the Mehr or Dowry of 10,000 French Francs was paid by me to my former wife and hence there is no dowry due to her. By conventions made at Geneva between my former wife and myself I have made certain engagements for her life. I desire that the Bank shall consider these conventions as a debt contracted by me and that they shall deal with them accordingly. . . . On 9 October 1944 I was married at Vevey according to Swiss Law to Yvette called Yve Blanche Labrousse. Previously to this I had married her according to Moslem Law at Geneva in the presence of several Moslem witnesses and of a Notary Public.

Under Shia Moslem Law his only heirs were his two sons, Aly and Sadruddin, and his wife, Yve. Finally, in paragraph 8 of the will, the mystery of the succession was unveiled:

Ever since the time of my ancestor Ali, the first Imam, that is to say over a period of some thirteen hundred years, it has always been the tradition of our family that each Imam chooses his successor at his absolute and unfettered discretion from amongst any of his descendants whether they be sons or remoter male issue.

The preamble made it clear beyond doubt that the succession on this occasion was not passing from father to son. From that moment Aly knew that he would not be the next Imam. Otto Giesen, a trace of accent betraying his German origin, continued to recite in an unemotional, almost monotonous voice:

. . . and in these circumstances and in view of the
fundamentally altered conditions in the world in very
recent years due to the great changes which have taken
place including the discoveries of atomic science I am
convinced that it is in the best interests of the Shia
Moslem Ismailian Community that I should be succeeded by a young man who has been brought up and
developed during recent years and in the midst of the
new age and who brings a new outlook on life to his
office as Imam.

For these reasons and although he is not now one of
my heirs, I APPOINT my grandson KARIM, the son of
my son ALY SALOMONE KHAN, to succeed to the
title of AGA KHAN and to be the Imam and Pir of
all my Shia Ismailian followers, and should my said
grandson KARIM predecease me then I APPOINT
his brother AMYN MAHOMED, the second son of my
son ALY SALOMONE KHAN, as my successor to the
Imamate. I DESIRE that my successor shall during the
first seven years of his Imamate be guided on questions
of general Imamate policy by my said wife YVETTE
called YVE BLANCHE LABROUSSE, the Begum Aga
Khan, who has been familiar for many years with the
problems facing my followers and in whose wise judgment I place the greatest confidence. . . .

The die was cast; the rest was routine. Out of a sense of duty,
the family listened to the other provisions. The Begum was to
decide the form of his coffin and the fashion of his tomb and the
place of his burial. The sum of £25,000 was to be placed at her
disposal for the purpose (the amount was doubled in the codicil). Yve, Aly, and Sadruddin should share his jewelry. Only
the paragraph dealing with the horses revived flagging attention.
Any race horse belonging solely to the Aga at his death was to
be sold by public auction and the proceeds to form part of his

estate; any race horse in which he had a share was to be offered
to the partner for purchase, which applied chiefly to Aly. His
share of any other property owned jointly with the Begum or
Aly or Sadruddin should go to the partner. Persons in his service
at the time of his death were to get tax-free wages and pensions
for eighteen months. A Norwegian nurse who had been with the
family for a long time received £10,000.

Objets d'art, furniture, and effects in the Begum's villa at Le
Cannet (Yakimour) became her absolute property, and a similar
provision in respect of the Versoix villa was made in the codicil.
Art, furniture, and effects in Princess Andrée's villa at Antibes
(Villa Jane-Andrée) became her absolute property. The Aga
Khan solemnly requested Aly always to be kind and devoted to
Sadruddin, to give him good advice, and to treat him with great
affection as if he were his own son; he asked Aly and Sadruddin
to treat his wife, Yve, and his former wife Andrée Joséphine with
great consideration and kindness.

According to Shia Moslem Law, all the Aga Khan's remaining
property was divided into three equal parts. Of the first two
thirds, the Begum was to get an eighth; the other seven-eighths
were to be divided equally between Aly and Sadruddin. The
residue (one third) after payment of legacies and duties was
to be divided between his three heirs in the same proportion.

Religious property, on the other hand, *jamatkhanas* and bury-
ing grounds in India and East Africa, went to Karim, the new
Aga Khan, including premises that were part of *jamatkhanas*
even if used for secular purposes. Without any specific reference
in the will, it was, of course, understood that the new Imam's
income—apart from the proceeds of his grandfather's trust—
would come from his followers, who would now start paying the
traditional *zakat* and *khums* to him. The will was astutely
drafted to reveal as little as possible about the state of the Aga
Khan's finances at the time of his death and gave no hint of the
huge amounts involved in the trusts, corporations, and properties
which now devolved on his heirs. There was nothing about his

oil shares, which had multiplied many times in value, his investments in Indian and African enterprises, his stakes in European corporations, or the proceeds of many advantageous financial operations by a friend of the world's great who had had access to invaluable advance and inside information. The value of his racing interests alone was many millions of pounds. The estate left in England was valued at £709,700 before taxes.

The Aga Khan was much wealthier than was suggested by his standard of living, which compared with that of other Indian princes was positively modest. Even when split among his principal heirs, his estate still gave each of them control over substantial assets and guaranteed them enviable incomes. How much of his followers' contributions the new Aga Khan would retain for his own purposes was left entirely to his discretion, but it soon emerged that he intended to return no less to the community—if not more—than his grandfather had.

Those immediately associated with the final chapter in Versoix have kept tight lips about individual reactions except for Bettina, who wrote, "To Aly it seemed that his father's preference for his son was a kind of public humiliation. He was never quite the same from that day on. His deep sadness took cover beneath a life of still more inhuman activity." But she also said that Aly, as all who knew him fully expected, did not bear the slightest resentment toward Karim; on the contrary, he behaved generously and unselfishly in a difficult situation. About Karim his mother said to me, "He accepted the situation easily and did not regard it as a burden. He had a strong sense of mission, an instinctive thing that works automatically. It is something that some people have."

Still, it took some time for the young Imam to adjust himself to his new responsibilities. Some thought that he looked dazed when he first emerged from the session with the lawyers. Sorrow about the loss of his grandfather to whom he was so close mingled with apprehension about his relationship with his father. In Bettina's words, which reflected Aly's feelings at the time, Karim was now the spiritual father of his own father. His natural humility enabled him to adapt himself to this unnatural posture. Neither too independent nor too solicitous, he continued to act as a loyal, devoted son.

The rush of events carried him along without giving him much time to think. The Ismailis were waiting to greet their new Imam. Some of them, like Sir Eboo Pirbhai, knew Karim well; others were introduced to him by Aly. Reporters and photographers from many parts of the world demanded their rights and Karim girded himself to face them. For their benefit he read out the provisions of the will dealing with the succession and mentioned his grandfather's wish that he be guided by the Begum for the next seven years. Aly stood by silently, but the photographers caught father and son in a picture of perfect harmony.

The next morning a chair was placed on the lawn in the garden to serve as a *gadi* for a simple enthronement ceremony. The forty-ninth Imam appeared before the waiting Ismaili leaders. Looking solemn in his blue suit, pale and seeming younger than his twenty years, Karim took his seat. One after another of the Ismaili nobles approached and pledged his loyalty. Not wanting to steal the limelight, Aly kept away.

At Barakat family, friends, and followers filed past the Aga Khan's body, which was covered with a white silk shroud. As soon as the public was admitted, hundreds of tourists invaded the house, brandishing cameras and allowing their curiosity to get the better of decorum. The doors were hurriedly closed. Instructions went out to Aswan to prepare a temporary resting place on the grounds of the Aga's house, which he had not lived to see. In time a permanent mausoleum would arise behind the villa.

The following morning a hearse carried the heavy oak coffin from Versoix through the center of Geneva. On its slow way to the airport it was escorted by police on motorcycles and followed by more than two dozen limousines, the Begum and Karim occupying the first, Aly and Saddrudin the second. A silent crowd watched the coffin being hoisted into a chartered

DC-6 for Cairo. Karim, the Begum, and Aly traveled with it, while other members of the family and Ismaili leaders went on the next regular flight.

At Aswan airport, some six hundred miles south of Cairo, where no aircraft had landed in many months, a gang of bare-bodied, dark-skinned men cleared the sand from the runway with brooms made of palm leaves. The temperature was in the nineties. The Governor of Aswan, a small group of local officials, and reporters were awaiting the arrival of the funeral party. Photographers shielded their cameras from the blazing sun. As the aircraft appeared on the horizon, descended, and landed in a cloud of dust, a red fire-brigade vehicle emerged from a wooden shed and made toward the runway. The aircraft's doors swung open and the Begum appeared in an ample pitch-black sari that covered her head. She wiped the tears from her eyes, which were blinded by the piercing light. Behind her came Karim Aga Khan, looking tired but completely composed. Aly was last to emerge.

So far everything had gone according to plan. But the soldiers who were transferring the heavy coffin from the aircraft to the red vehicle got into a tangle. Amid conflicting instructions they jostled in the narrow space. President Nasser's big wreath was already wilting in the heat. "No funeral march, no flags at half-mast, no guard of honor," one German newspaper correspondent noted. "On the Aswan runway the coffin of the Aga Khan was unloaded like a packing case."

Especially opened for the occasion, the Cataract Hotel was expecting big business. So were the taxi drivers, souvenir ped-dlers, and owners of motorboats. Visions of a Pharaoh's funeral procession across the Nile faded as soon as the coffin went on its way to the white villa on the other bank. An arguing, gestic-ulating horde of luggage porters got hold of it, dragging rather than carrying it. More than once it looked as if the coffin would slip into the water as they laboriously maneuvered it onto a boat. Owing to a misunderstanding, the family was waiting for transport at the Cataract Hotel and it took half an hour to get them to the starting point. By this time the Nile was thick with boats carrying mourners and sightseers. At the villa the tiny landing stage could not accommodate the approaching flotilla. The Begum was distressed; Karim, Aly, and Sadruddin were unhappy and soaked in perspiration, their black silk suits crumpled. With difficulty the coffin was placed in position and Sheikh Mohammed Mahmud intoned a recital from the Koran. After the brief service all but the Begum returned to the mainland and the Cataract Hotel. First to reach the terrace, Aly rushed straight into the dining room and buried his glowing face in an ice-cold watermelon. Sadruddin asked for a telegram form. A reporter, looking over his shoulder, read his message, addressed to Nina Dyer in Paris: "Aswan glowing heat—complete chaos—impatient to return to you." But that evening the new Aga Khan, his brother, and his uncles presented themselves to the community leaders in immaculate silk suits. Conscious of his new duties, the Aga Khan played host to the Ismailis while Sadruddin talked to journalists.

The service in the small Abu-Shok mosque the next morning was a more dignified affair. Having discarded their shoes, the late Aga's four closest male relatives led the congregation in prayer. In devotion they touched the ground with their foreheads. To emphasize the universality of the Ismaili faith, Aly wore a Pakistani Persian-lamb hat, Sadruddin a Burmese skull-cap, Karim and Amyn Arab tarbooshes. At the villa they carried the heavy coffin on their shoulders through the crowd of praying Ismailis to the inner court and the small vault. It had only just been made by the local builder, was found to be too small, and had to be widened by hammer and chisel.

Before night fell, the three principal characters in the succession drama were off on their separate ways, Sadruddin to rejoin his fiancée (their marriage had been postponed until the end of the forty-day mourning period), the new Imam to see his mother in London, and Aly Khan on a mission to avert the first threat to the Imamate of his son.

CHAPTER XV

ALY's DESTINATION WAS Syria, where the community was in an uproar. Syria's Ismailis had always taken it for granted that Aly would succeed his father as Imam. He was the only leader they knew well because the Aga Khan and other members of the family had only rarely visited their country. His courage, his panache, his manly virtues, counted so highly among these hardy mountain men that the choice of Karim was not as loyally received in Salamiyya as in other Ismaili centers. There was talk of choosing Aly by acclamation as Imam, which could only lead to a schism in the Ismaili world.

Aly was the last person to encourage heresy or to expose the community to another split. To greet him on arrival, Ismailis came out in the thousands, surrounded his jeep, and pressed on it so hard that it broke down under the weight. By horse and mule he made his way to remote villages, where he talked to the elders and addressed the rank and file, proclaiming that his father had chosen his son Karim al-Huseini as Imam and that he himself accepted the choice. Karim had asked him to say that he would come to visit Syria as soon as possible. Aly's charm and powers of persuasion saved the situation. It was an act of splendid generosity in which he rose above his disappointment about his own exclusion. Syria's Ismailis rallied behind the new Imam.

There were similar rumblings at Sargodha and Kasur in the Punjab, home of some fifteen hundred Ismailis, mostly owners of small businesses. One group led by Dr. Aziz Ali "went into opposition," refused to acknowledge Karim, and claimed Aly as the new Imam. As soon as he heard of the trouble, Amirali Fancy, head of Pakistan's Ismailis, traveled to the Punjab to put things right but was not wholly successful. A few weeks later, when Aly arrived in Karachi, Fancy informed him of the incident. "Let me talk to these people," Aly volunteered at once. Fancy arranged a meeting between Aziz and Aly, who was staying at the President's house. Once more, Aly made his position perfectly clear. "My son is the rightful Imam," he insisted.

Outside in the street supporters of Dr. Aziz staged a small demonstration and shouted "Shah Aly Khan Hazar Imam Zindabad!" (Long live Imam Prince Aly). Aziz emerged from the interview brandishing a signed photograph of Aly from which it was deduced that Aly had not seriously discouraged the dissidents. But he had certainly not encouraged them, and the revolt fizzled out except for a few families who were temporarily excluded from the community and banned from the *jamatkhana*. The rest remained firmly loyal and when a year or so later Prince Karim visited Sargodha, put up a considerable sum toward a new hospital, and awarded fifty scholarships for higher education, he was roundly cheered and there was no sign of any opposition.

In the meantime the new Imam was immersed in work and confronted with a series of difficult decisions. Not that he suffered from any shortage of help and advice. The shadow of the Begum loomed large. The Aga's idea that she should advise his grandson for seven years was obviously rooted in the memory of his own mother, who virtually acted as Imam after his own enthronement; but this stipulation was difficult to reconcile with his wish that the community should be guided by a modern young man. Another problem for Prince Karim was finding common ground with the elderly leaders of the community, who while offering advice, still expected to be guided by the Imam, however young. As these subtle pressures came to bear on him at the very moment he assumed supreme authority, he soon developed an iron will beneath a gentle manner. This became his outstanding characteristic.

All sorts of problems in Africa and Asia that he had encountered in history books suddenly became realities demanding his personal attention. Before he could cope with the new world into which he was plunged, however, he needed time to think and relax with his own family. At the end of a momentous month he reached London and joined his mother, whose natural protective instincts drew her close to him. In the privacy of her Eaton Square duplex flat, in his own room among his books, drawings, and sculptures, he found the first respite since the historic date of July 11, which would henceforth, as long as he lived, be celebrated by millions as the Day of Imamate.

Preparations for a quick tour of Ismaili centers went ahead at once, setting the tone and determining the rhythm of the Imam's future travels. In consultation with Ismaili leaders a timetable was worked out with almost contemptuous disregard of distances. It was firmly of the jet age: August 4, visit to Karachi, Pakistan; civil and religious functions. August 9, visit to Bombay, India; civic and religious functions and conferences with Ismaili leaders. August 12, visit to Nairobi, Kenya, beginning a week's tour of the principal East African Ismaili centers including Zanzibar.

Cables went to every corner of the world where Ismailis resided; replies came back with suggestions and requests for approval of local plans. Karim's grandfather's secretaries, Mme. Beguel and Miss Blain, dealt with the alarmingly swelling files and dug up relevant precedents. Requests for the Imam's appearance here, there, everywhere, were weighed and balanced until a program emerged in which every hour, indeed, every minute, was allocated to a specific task. Reports about communities he was about to visit, personalities he would meet, and schools, hospitals, and *jamatkhanas* he would inspect mounted on his desk. One of his first official functions as Imam was to meet the London *jamat* (community), which would soon be moving into new and bigger community quarters.

Although, in his own words, his life was now dedicated to the community, he was anxious to complete his studies. This was clearly in the interests of his followers. His mother also thought he ought to return to Harvard, but his new responsibilities and ceremonial duties were likely to keep him away from the university for the better part of a year. Ahead of him loomed the elaborate ceremonies of the *Takht Nishinis,* the formal installations as Hazar Imam in East Africa, India, and Pakistan, which were scheduled for the end of the year and the beginning of the next, each an occasion for a big speech. Neither would it be a matter of a few polite formal phrases. To his European and American friends Karim might remain the charming, natural, and cheerful companion they knew. His followers took a different view of him. "We all hope," said Ataur Rahman Khan, Chief Minister of East Pakistan, "that from his leadership the Muslim world will be as greatly benefited as from his predecessor's." With the duties came the honors. The Queen of England conferred on Karim Aga Khan the title of Highness, which his grandfather had held by the grace of Queen Victoria.

The other side of the medal was less glittering. As the new Aga Khan, the twenty-year-old prince and religious leader became public property, a prime target for insidious commentaries. An early report claimed to reveal a second secret will of the Aga Khan and talked of frantic attempts to compose a violent quarrel between Prince Karim and the Begum involving millions before it came before the courts. There was no truth in the story. With as much gusto Prince Karim's private life was examined in an Arabian Nights aura that turned him overnight from a boyish,

sports-loving Harvard man into an Eastern Romeo. Presenting
him as a worthy son of the amorous Aly, gossip columns described a veritable world war in which young ladies of every
nationality seemed to fight for the heart and the hand of the
young Aga Khan.

Those mentioned were a handsome lot. Pride of place was
allotted to Sylvia Casablanca, whose friendship with Karim had
survived their separation. Bunny Esterhazy figured next on the
list of potential brides. "Bunny met Prince Karim shortly before
his grandfather's death," the newspapers reported quite wrongly.
Andrea Milos von Vangel, another Hungarian girl, was said to
have become secretly engaged to Karim when they were still
at school, and an Egyptian newspaper told romance-hungry
readers that Karim and Mona el Badrawi, seventeen-year-old
daughter of an Egyptian financier, were promised to each other.
A French starlet, Annemarie Mersen, completed Karim's harem
—except for Kim Novak, whose inclusion indicated a certain
confusion among reporters about which glamour girl was Aly's
and which Karim's. Karim's cup was overflowing when girls
started writing to newspapers to offer themselves to him. A
Swiss girl's only condition was that she should remain his only
wife, a French girl claimed him by rights because his grandfather had chosen two Frenchwomen as his wives, and a third
said she was willing to adopt the Muslim faith if he would marry
her.

These frivolous stories in the daily press could not have been
more remote from the young Aga Khan's preoccupations on the
eve of his trip to Pakistan, the first big test of his career as Imam.
It was a daunting prospect. Karim's face did not show the
tension, and the upsurge of warmth and adulation that greeted
him on arrival in Karachi was such as to dissolve all apprehension. Headed by their leaders in traditional cloaks and gold-
threaded turbans, the community turned out in strength. Aged
men knelt before him and kissed his hand; many prostrated
themselves and tried to touch his clothes. A little shy and self-

conscious but deeply moved, he accepted the homage and made a short speech that reflected genuine feeling. "I shall cherish the memory of your love and affection," he said, and assured his followers that they were near to him and ever present in his heart and thoughts. "I have dedicated my life to the uplift and progress of Ismailis all over the world and I pray for all your happiness and success."

At the *jamatkhana* the ceremony of *bayat* (allegiance) was performed wherein followers pledged their loyalty by kissing the new Imam's hand. He sat on an elevated chair, a slim, handsome, embarrassed youth whom they regarded as near-divine and infallible. The community leaders sat by his side, knelt by him, and made their reports about health, youth, housing, religious affairs—each about the department of which he was in charge. They discussed the long tour for which he would return later in the year. They asked him to visit their homes. "Every Ismaili house is a shrine to the Aga Khan," as one of them told me.

The only noncommunity function he undertook was to donate an Aga Khan Gold Cup to the Karachi Racing Club in honor of his grandfather. After a brief visit to Bombay he traveled to East Africa, reaching Nairobi on August 12. Chaperoned by Sir Eboo Pirbhai, he went on to Kampala, Dar-es-Salaam, and Zanzibar (where he was awarded a decoration, the "Brilliant Star of Zanzibar"). He was shown over the grounds chosen for his formal installation in October. The tour was a trial run for the *Takht Nishinis.*

Returning from Africa, his first stop was at the Côte d'Azur, where he joined his father at the Château de l'Horizon. "Nothing seemed to have changed between them, at least not that one could see," Bettina noted. "Come on, Father, let's play some tennis!" Karim would call out. According to Bettina, he was a better player than his father and had Aly running all over the court. They went swimming and often talked together late into the evening. The atmosphere was relaxed. Karim talked about his school and the exams he still had to take. Although Aly was somber on occasions and the situation undoubtedly was delicate, father and son seemed closer than ever.

Together they traveled to Geneva, where at the end of the mourning period Sadruddin and Nina were to be married. The press made a lot of fuss about the costly engagement ring and car which were Sadruddin's wedding presents to his bride. Rumor had it that the late Aga Khan had disapproved of the marriage, and that Nina was disappointed not to be the next Begum. Sadruddin skillfully disabused reporters of these notions, all far from the mark. The obligatory civil wedding at the town hall was followed by the traditional Muslim ceremony over which the young Aga Khan presided in the privacy of Château Bellerive. Nina became Princess Shirin, which is Arabic for "Sweetness." One photograph on the occasion shows Sadruddin carrying his bride across the threshold of the château with Aly, Karim, and Amyn watching. "This was the shot photographer Tony Armstrong-Jones had been waiting for," reported the *Daily Express*, which published the picture.

Presently the Aga Khan went back to London and immersed himself in the preparations for the enthronement ceremonies in Africa and Asia. These were not easy to plan from Europe, where the unique status of the Imam among his followers was not readily understood. His first tour had convinced Karim that he ought not to enter the maze of African affairs with its many racial, religious, social, and political hazards without a professional expert by his side. The need was for an aide-de-camp experienced in political and public relations to cushion him against day-to-day pressures and interpret him to a world audience attracted by the glamour of the occasion.

One of the friends Princess Joan Aly Khan consulted in her search for a suitable person was Denis C. Hamilton (now editor-in-chief of the London *Times* and *Sunday Times*), who suggested Michael Curtis, a former editor of the liberal *News Chronicle*, as the man best equipped to fill such a post. Curtis was invited to meet Prince Karim at his mother's house, where they discussed the tour over lunch. Press relations, the drafting of speeches, the program, all that would fall into the aide's province was covered. The Aga Khan was impressed and arrangements for Curtis to join him were quickly completed.

Traveling in a chartered aircraft, the party, including Aly and Joan, left London on October 16, 1957. After a brief stop in Nairobi they went on to Dar-es-Salaam, where a tremendous reception awaited them. Official Tanganyika, including a strong British contingent, was at the airport, and there were humble addresses and loyal greetings from Ismaili leaders. A troop of Aga Khan Boy Scouts and Girl Guides formed a guard of honor which the Imam inspected. His car, accompanied by the usual procession of motorcycles and limousines, went along densely lined streets to Government House, where he was staying as an official guest. The evening was spent preparing the next day's elaborate program: flag march of Ismailis from *jamatkhana* to Upanga ceremonial area, informal drive through the city, procession of decorated floats, meeting with Ismaili Council to discuss enthronement ceremony.

Members of the Council could not agree on the introductory prayer, some plumping for one set of verses, others for a different set, both looking to the Aga Khan for a decision. Though it seemed a small matter, how could he avoid offending half his Council? After listening to the rival arguments, Prince Karim thought for a while, then asked who would do the recitation and was told that a young choir boy from Zanzibar with an excellent voice and bearing had been chosen. After a brief silence while everybody wondered on whose side the Imam would come down, he announced his verdict, which would have done honor to King Solomon. "Let the choir boy decide what he will sing," he said amid sighs of relief that he had so deftly avoided giving offence to either side. A buffet supper in his honor at the Mayor's residence concluded the day's proceedings.

The following morning brought a more intractable problem.

From Kampala Sir Frederick Crawford, the British High Commissioner in Uganda, sent word that the Kabaka of Buganda ("King Freddie") had reservations about a ceremony on the same scale as that at Dar-es-Salaam. The Kabaka, who was later driven from his country and died in London in 1969 after a miserable existence as a refugee, was still all-powerful then and thought that an enthronement at the big Nakivubo Stadium, as envisaged by Ismaili leaders, might be too grandiose an affair and detract from his own dignity. The Kabaka believed he should be the only one to be crowned in Uganda. Ismaili custom and tradition, however, clearly demanded that the ceremony be attended by the whole community and that the new Aga Khan should literally be seen to succeed.

Anxious to avoid a conflict, the Aga Khan sent Michael Curtis to Uganda to consult the Governor. At Kampala Curtis saw Sir Frederick Crawford and the head of the Ismaili community and arranged for the three of them to see the Kabaka. It was dark when they arrived at the Winter Palace, where they were received with a roll of drums and offered whiskys before being taken into the Kabaka's presence. Aping the aristocratic stutter cultivated by upper-class Englishmen, the Kabaka was friendly and apologetic and pretended that the problem was not of his making, that he had been a friend of the late Aga Khan and was on the best of terms with Prince Aly Khan. But as a constitutional monarch he had to submit to the decisions of his cabinet. The best thing would be for Curtis to meet with the members of his government.

Prime Minister Michael Kintu was in the chair at the cabinet meeting to which Curtis put his case the following morning. He explained the significance of the ceremony and the importance of its public character and answered questions put to him by several ministers. The Prime Minister concluded that there would be no objection to an enthronement in a place of worship and suggested that it should be held at the Aga Khan Mosque, which, since the large grounds could comfortably accommodate the Aga Khan's followers in Kampala, seemed a satisfactory compromise. Curtis was about to rejoin the Aga Khan when confidential information reached him that the cabinet expected the ceremony to take place inside the mosque. Attendance would be restricted to those who could find room within its walls. He put through a call to the Aga Khan in Dar-es-Salaam and had just finished the conversation when the hotel telephone broke down. To talk to the Prime Minister he had to use a public telephone booth. Uganda was the only country, apart from South Africa, he told the Prime Minister angrily, where such a restriction was imposed on the Aga Khan. After a long and heated discussion, the Prime Minister agreed that the enthronement could take place on the grounds of the mosque after all.

At Dar-es-Salaam Curtis found the Aga Khan up to his eyes in work—discussions with the Supreme Council, conferences with the British authorities, conversations with envoys from many parts of the world. He was visibly rising to the occasion. The family was with him, including the Begum Aga Khan, who was the last to arrive. She had stopped off at Mombasa, Tanga, and Zanzibar to discuss arrangements for the funeral of her late husband, whose final resting place at Aswan was nearing completion.

The Dar-es-Salaam *Takht Nishini* did credit to the devotion and discipline of the Ismailis and established the young Aga Khan as a personality in his own right. His final address, ranging over many subjects beyond religion (because Islam embraces the whole life of the believer), was well presented. In the spirit of his grandfather, he referred to the new and unbound source of energy—atomic energy—which when released for the use of mankind would benefit countries like Tanganyika and help to create new towns, railways, and factories and to promote industrial progress. Once more he promised to devote his life to the community.

The following morning at the *jamatkhana* the Aga Khan conducted the religious ceremony of *bayat* during which nine hundred Ismailis pledged their loyalty. Ten times that number watched his *durbar* when East Africa's leading personalities were presented to him. The leisurely pace of the ancient rites gave way to a burst of speed typical of the Aga Khan's youthful zest. Having taken leave of his followers, a car took him to the airport at over sixty miles an hour. Princess Joan and Michael Curtis joined him for the flight to Nairobi.

The Nairobi *Takht Nishini* was a repetition of the Dar-es-Salaam ceremony on a smaller scale. On the grounds of the Aga Khan Club the lone figure of the young new leader seated on the throne set high amid his people was strangely appealing. The red robes and gold turbans of the Ismaili dignitaries who invested him with robe, *pagri*, sword, chain, and ring made a vivid picture such as Kenya had not seen before. The dais, a mass of red, blue, white, and yellow flowers, and the throne, flanked by great vases of roses, stood out against the background of flags fluttering gently in the slight breeze. A thousand people of all races gathered that evening to greet the Aga Khan, who arrived with the Governor of Kenya, Sir Evelyn Baring. There was dancing to a regimental band and a sumptuous dinner. The Aga Khan thoroughly enjoyed it and the local society reporters had a field day. They noted that the Kenya establishment was all present and correct.

After the untroubled days in Kenya, the Aga Khan arrived in Uganda in an almost symbolic downpour from dark skies. It did not deter large crowds of Ismailis from greeting him, but formalities at the airport were cut short because of the atrocious weather, and the Aga Khan, sheltered under an umbrella, quickly walked past the long line of well-wishers, followed by three leading Ismailis in his entourage—dapper Sir Eboo Pirbhai, Count Fatehali Dhala, of Mombasa, and T. E. Nathoo, Kenya's Minister of Works.

The last-minute switch from Nakivubo Stadium to the Aga Khan Mosque complicated technical arrangements, but there was no question of curtailing the big program for the Aga Khan's first day in Uganda, which was fairly typical of his schedule throughout:

9:00 A.M.	Leave Government House, Entebbe
9:30 A.M.	Arrive at Aga Khan Mosque, Namirembe Road
10:30 A.M.	Meeting with Celebration Committee
11:00 A.M.	Visit Aga Khan School, Old Kampala
12:30 P.M.	Lunch at Imperial Hotel
2:00 P.M.	Governor's Lodge, Makindye (Rest)
4:30 P.M.	Civic Garden Party, Jubilee Gardens
6:30 P.M.	Celebration procession
7:20 P.M.	Watch procession from Imperial Hotel
8:00 P.M.	Return to Entebbe with Governor
9:00 P.M.	Dinner at Government House

Thousands of Ismailis thronged the area around the mosque in Namirembe Road the following day when the Aga Khan conducted a religious service. During an extensive tour of inspection afterwards he was garlanded and greeted enthusiastically everywhere. Kampala, Ismailis and non-Ismailis alike, was taking the personable young man to its heart. So strong was his personal appeal that the Kabaka decided to attend the enthronement ceremony. For the third time the Imam was invested with the symbols of his office, and once more he rose to make a speech, treating a delicate subject without losing his human touch. Obliquely referring to the racial tensions between Africans and Asians in East Africa, he talked about a boxing match between an African and an Asian boy he had been watching at the Aga Khan School the previous day. "At the end of this sporting event," he recounted, "the two boys shook hands and stood together to be photographed. To me this symbolized the partnership between different races which I am convinced is the only condition of peace and prosperity."

Racial tolerance was his main theme. If the different races in

Uganda, or anywhere else, fell out and quarreled, foreigners would lose confidence in the country's stability, capital would stop coming in, and industrial development and the country's progress would slow down. "That is why I most strongly urge the Ismaili community to work hand in hand with all other citizens!" Shouts of "Zindabad" (Long live the Aga Khan) greeted his words. The amount of goodwill he generated was surprising. The little argument of a few days earlier was forgotten and the Kabaka gave a cocktail party in his honor. In a truly ecumenical spirit, the Imam of the Shia Ismailis walked under an archway erected by the Sunni Muslim Association. To Muslims of all sects his elevation was a great occasion.

As the tour neared its end, the pace quickened. So many people wanted to see him; there was so much he wanted to see and hear. Aly worried whether the pace was not becoming too much for this slender young man. "He saw it through magnificently," Princess Joan recalled. The presence of his parents was a help, no doubt, although Aly's position became a bit awkward at times. As for Princess Joan, she did not have the slightest anxiety about her son. "Listening to him making his speeches with knowledge, grace, and calm," she said, "not once were my palms moist. He has a great faculty for acquiring facts, can learn anything, is mad to learn." His East African speeches were knowledgeable, graceful, and confident. He stressed Ismaili interests, bolstered Muslim morale, made donations to many causes —schools, hospitals, mosques. In the words of a Sunni leader (no compliment is more welcome than a rival's), the tour "filled the minds of Muslims all over the world with fresh hopes and renewed strength to face with confidence the struggles that lie ahead."

Back in London for a brief rest, the Aga Khan celebrated his twenty-first birthday on December 13, 1957, a family affair but also a holiday for every Ismaili. A delegation representing the Pakistan community came to extend a formal invitation for his Far Eastern tour, and he graciously approved the "Program for the Visit of His Royal Highness," submitted by *wazir* Ebrahim Manji. The new tour started on January 20, 1958, and the party again included Princess Joan, Michael Curtis and his wife, Mme. Beguel, and the old Aga's faithful valet, who was steeped in the technicalities of Ismaili tradition. Prince Sadruddin and Princess Shirin were also coming, but Aly Khan was "unable to leave Paris at this time."

The first stop and only possible cause for anxiety—though the Aga Khan showed no sign of it—was a brief visit to Damascus to meet Syria's fiery Ismailis. Would they acclaim the young Imam? Would the "Aly faction" protest? Curtis' instructions were to keep close to the Aga Khan at all times. As soon as the aircraft landed, it was surrounded by the bearded, colorful, strong men of the mountains, who pressed forward toward the Imam with a crowd of at least fifteen thousand closing in behind them. The Aga Khan and Michael Curtis were bodily lifted up and carried shoulder high. "It was a great emotional upsurge," Curtis recalled. For a few moments the situation was completely out of hand. "I had a feeling anything could happen." But the crowd, though excited and uninhibited, was wholly friendly. In their own exuberant way they showed that they accepted Karim as their leader. When he managed to climb into a car, he stood up and addressed his followers in Arabic. They cheered but calmed down.

The Aga Khan was composed throughout, but, said Curtis, it was a great relief to get him back into the aircraft. He was his thoughtful, considerate self. Seeing Curtis hot, battered, and disheveled, he leaned over and whispered, "You know I don't take alcohol myself, but I think you have earned a double Scotch!" Karachi offered a quieter prospect. There was certainly nothing to worry about. Pakistan was a Muslim country which remembered the old Aga as one of its founders and was happy to receive his grandson.

The full-dress reception reflected the regard in which the Ismaili leader was held. President Iskander Mirza's military

secretary greeted the Aga Khan, and the official welcome party
included several members of the Pakistani cabinet. Personal
exchanges were drowned in a joyous and exuberant public ovation. Addressing his "spiritual children" so solemnly that the
contrast between the appellation and his great youth was hardly
apparent, the Imam extended his traditional greeting to the
community and pledged himself to help Pakistan to the best of
his ability to achieve prosperity and happiness.

Almost buried under a mountain of garlands, the celebrated
visitor was then driven to the President's house along a route
decorated with "Long Live the Aga Khan" streamers and deli-
cately-designed gateways and portals. Large-scale illuminations
turned night into day. *Jamatkhanas*, particularly those in the
Ismaili districts of Kharadar and Garden where the Aga Khan
was expected, were brightly festooned. Ten years later at the
headquarters of the Ismailia Association, the research and ideo-
logical center, I saw proudly displayed on the wall the telegram
that Imam-e-Zaman had sent "on the auspicious occasion of
the *Takht Nishini* celebrations in Karachi": "BEST PATERNAL MA-
TERNAL BLESSINGS ALL SPIRITUAL CHILDREN PAKISTAN OCCASION MY
INSTALLATION STOP ASSOCIATION MUST CONTINUE KINDLE FLAMES
OF FAITH IN HEARTS OF FUTURE GENERATION—AGA KHAN."

During these days Karachi belonged to the Ismailis. Nearly
twenty thousand of them who came in from out of town were
accommodated in tents in the former Haji Camp, which was
bursting at the seams. Some found room in Ismaili schools or
were put up by private families. Their numbers were swelled
by a never-ending stream of delegations from twenty countries,
among them the United Kingdom, France, Iran, East Africa,
Syria, Burma, Ceylon, Goa, Kuwait, Bahrein, in the Persian
Gulf, Gwadar, South Africa, and Lebanon.

Elaborate plans provided for a hundred thousand people to
enter the stadium by ceremonial gateways over which the Pakistan flag fluttered by the side of the Aga Khan's, green for peace,
with a diagonal red stripe recalling Huseyn's sacrifice at Kerbela.

A seven-foot-high dais with a revolving stage had been built under a velvet canopy of sky blue and gold. The special *takht* (throne) was upholstered in maroon and gold velvet with Persian and Mogul motifs. Big enclosures were reserved for ministers, heads of diplomatic missions, rulers of state, high civil and military officers. A small army of international reporters, photographers, and broadcasters was on hand. For those unable to find a place in the stadium, there would be commentaries in Urdu and English. The day of the ceremony was declared an official half-holiday.

The sound of trumpets heralded the arrival of the Aga Khan at the side of Pakistan's President. Prime Minister Malik Firoz Khan Noon and his cabinet were already in their seats. The brief act of installation was no different from the East African ritual except for the three-hundred-year-old copy of the Holy Koran that was presented to the Aga Khan, a rare example of Arab calligraphy written in Medina by a *haji* from Bokhara.

In his *irshad* the Aga Khan asked his followers to use their great influence for the benefit of Pakistan. Pakistan's task was to adapt modern values and the pressures of a changing society to the basic ideals of Islam, putting modern democracy into Islamic form. "There is no reason," he said, "why our traditions and our faith should stop us from moving with the times, nor why we should not lead our fellow men to new spheres of knowledge and learning." At the end of his speech he was showered with rose petals.

A relentless program kept him busy for the next three weeks. He gave talks on religion and on Africa, visited Peshawar and the Khyber Pass, and was ceremonially enthroned for a second time at Dacca, capital of Pakistan's underprivileged eastern wing. On February 15 he returned to Europe. "You look thinner," a friend remarked when he saw him in Geneva. "It was a pretty strenuous tour," Karim replied. "Since my grandfather's death I have lost twelve pounds."

His travels were far from over. Within a month he was back

on the subcontinent for his enthronement in Bombay, birthplace
of the modern Ismaili community. "Every able-bodied Ismaili
in Bombay," said the *Times of India,* "attended the Takht
Nishini at the Vallabhbhai Stadium." Many of them had traveled
long distances. They cheered when the new Aga Khan, in white
achkan, black trousers, and high black cap, mounted the dais,
which was decorated with white and pink asters and roses. With
the setting sun lighting his face, he made an impressive figure
as the congregation looked up to him. The burden of his speech
was that in secular matters his Indian followers owed loyalty
only to India and its elected government. The speech was well
received—and not only by Ismailis. The *Times* thought the occasion lacked the glitter of the late Aga Khan's Diamond Jubilee
but that "the sense of loyalty and reverence of the huge crowd
was by no means less." At Delhi the new Imam met Prime
Minister Nehru, who recalled his encounters with the old Aga
and wished him well.

The new Aga's next destination was the Congo and South
Africa—not an easy mission. South Africa was already in the
grip of apartheid, but the Anglo-Indian prince was given V.I.P.
treatment by the government, which lifted all color restrictions
for him. Black or white, the crowds loved him and cheered
him as if he were a teen-age idol. The situation of the Ismaili
community in South Africa, however, gave little cause for cheers.
He discussed it with the Minister of Home Affairs, Dr. T. E.
Donges, but the new laws on segregation of nonwhite businesses
dealt a heavy blow to Ismaili traders, who were being forced
back to the colored areas. The Aga Khan put the case for his
followers forcefully, but it was a lost cause. Fortunately, their
number was not large and they soon drifted away—to the Congo,
to Tanzania, and to Kenya, where fellow Ismailis helped them
make a new start. Only a few Ismailis remain in South Africa
today.

Soon after Karim's stay in Karachi as the personal guest of
President Mirza, Prince Aly Khan returned the hospitality of-

fered to his son. When President Mirza visited Paris at the invitation of President Coty of France, he wanted to stay on privately for a few days and asked Aly to put him up. The President and Madame Mirza, two secretaries, two aides-de-camp, a valet, a lady's maid, a cook, a laundryman, and various others moved into the house in the Boulevard Maurice-Barrès and were soon joined by security men, couriers, chauffeurs, and French police permanently on duty. There was nothing for Aly and Bettina to do but move out. As Aly's other houses were also full of people ("as usual," Bettina said), they sought refuge in a friend's apartment.

On the day of Mirza's departure he and Aly lunched with the French President. Leaving the Elysée, Mirza, rather than travel in the official limousine, squeezed into Aly's small car. Escorted by a bevy of motorcycle outriders, Aly drove the President and his wife to the airport. That evening, when he and Bettina were leaving for England and were, as usual, late setting out for the airport, the police motorcycle escort came to their rescue. With sirens screaming, they raced through the crowded streets of Paris at eighty miles an hour to clear the way for Aly's car. They ought to have known better. Aly drove so fast he beat all but two of the police motorcyclists to the airport.

This Paris interlude gave birth to an arrangement that helped fill the void in Aly's life. The horses and the studs (he had bought more studs and horses from his father's estate) no longer satisfied his restless search for fulfillment. It was as if the time he had subconsciously expected to devote to the duties of the Imam hung heavily on his hands. Mirza realized that Aly was not his former self and seemed to discover signs of acute depression. He needed something to do. "You could help my country—our country!" the President suggested. What he had in mind could indeed be useful to Pakistan as well as to Aly. The President offered to appoint him as head of the Pakistan delegation to the United Nations and he accepted with alacrity.

Aly's appointment as Pakistan's Ambassador and Envoy Plenipotentiary was announced early in 1958. Inevitably there were a few snide comments. The *Pakistan Times* remarked that diplomatic assignments were too often regarded as sinecures to be distributed among favored officials, friends, and relations, but Prime Minister Malik Firoz Khan Noon assured reporters that Aly would make an ideal diplomat. After a briefing in Karachi, Ambassador Prince Aly Khan traveled to New York. He took an apartment for himself and offices on Sixty-fifth Street, off Fifth Avenue; and an American public-relations adviser and a Pakistani career diplomat from the Washington Embassy, Agha Shahi, joined his staff. Mr. Shahi soon corrected some preconceived notions about his famous chief. "He sometimes works till ten or twelve at night," he said, "and has a very quick grasp of the most complicated subjects. He does not smoke and drinks only tomato juice."

But it was not easy for Aly to live down his past. When he went to the United Nations to present his credentials to Secretary General Dag Hammarskjöld, work in the tall skyscraper almost came to a halt because every female secretary in the building—and not a few of the delegates—posted themselves at vantage points to watch him arrive. They saw an alert and handsome man in a sober dark suit looking sternly ahead of him. The accreditation formalities completed, Aly returned to his office and started work. His first public duty was to give a party on Pakistan's Constitution Day. He invited a thousand people; twice as many turned up. Invitations were sold on the black market and there were many forgeries. But he resisted the blandishments of the New York social set. Anxious to get on with the job and oblivious of the good-humored wisecracks about "Aly's forthcoming *maiden* speech," he spent weeks working on the draft of his first address. Over transatlantic telephone he told Bettina how much he wanted it to be a success. "It was so important to him to convince people that he could do something serious," Bettina said to me. "He had to prove himself to the world, but also he loved this kind of work, liked working with his fellow delegates. As always, he was doing things deeply, properly, completely."

For my benefit, Bettina put on a record of his speech and presently Aly's voice filled her Paris apartment. "Some of the new nations are small," he was saying with an English upper-class intonation only slightly marred by a foreign accent. "All of them, in relation to the Great Powers, are weak—geographically, politically, and economically. But there is one way in which they are not weak. They are not weak spiritually. They possess the God-given, inexhaustible spiritual resources of the individual human soul. . . . They are strong in their determination to survive and to succeed."

What he said about spiritual resources also seemed to apply to him. For a few minutes Aly lived in Bettina's living room exactly as he had been on that Tuesday, August 19, 1958, when addressing the Third Emergency Special Session of the General Assembly. The impression of his vibrant, captivating personality was so strong that Bettina had tears in her eyes. "Immediately after making the speech he called me," she mused. "He was pleased with the reaction." Strong applause had greeted his words. He was speaking not only for Pakistan but also for every small nation. Traditional Ismaili concern for the underdog broke through. Delegates, irrespective of their affiliations, congratulated him. It was on merit that the following month he was elected Vice President of the General Assembly.

His tenure of office coincided with difficult problems. The political situation in the country he represented was rapidly deteriorating. The quarrel over Kashmir divided India and Pakistan, but he spoke up courageously, completely disregarding the big stakes his family had in India. The administration he served was under bitter attack in Karachi, accused of corruption and inefficiency. To avoid bloodshed the army's commander-in-chief, General Ayub Khan, assumed control. President Mirza resigned and left for London, where he lived in retirement until his death at the end of 1969.

Ayub made a clean sweep of Pakistan's public life, but Aly, who had shown his dexterity on the diplomatic parquet, was retained in office. His stature was visibly growing. Speaking on disarmament to the Political Committee of the Assembly, he quoted his father's speech of 1932: "There is a cry going up from the heart of all peace-loving citizens . . . for the security of civil populations against indiscriminate methods of warfare and, above all, for security against the very idea of war." He was strong on the racial issue, and when the Security Council discussed South Africa, he gave his listeners an example of Islamic philosophy: "To hear and to obey is binding so long as one is not commanded to disobey God; when one is commanded to disobey God, one should not hear or obey."

At this time emissaries of the Algerian rebels thought Aly might be able to mediate in the conflict with France. They asked to see him and talked with him over lunch. He was European and oriental at the same time, a Muslim, yet steeped in Western culture, one of the few men capable of truly understanding both sides. "They want me to go and see General de Gaulle as soon as I get back to Paris," he confided to Bettina. Contact was made through General Catroux, but the French President, who had returned to office on the issue of *Algérie française,* thought the time was not ripe. Not until Bettina joined Aly in New York did she realize how hard, almost frenziedly, he was working. But he was happy in his new milieu and she thought, "The nomad has pitched his tent."

CHAPTER XVI

AFTER THE BURST of publicity about his succession and enthronements Prince Karim's name began to fade from the news and gossip columns of the press to which he had been such a regular but reluctant contributor. Instead, Ismaili scholars in Pakistan and East Africa began to chronicle the forty-ninth Imam's every move. His own record of his activities recounted his journeys from the Congo, South Africa, and Portuguese East Africa to Geneva, the Château de l'Horizon, London, and Ireland in quick succession. The entry under September 9, 1958, said, "Arrived for 36 hours visit in Nairobi and performed the opening ceremony of the Aga Khan Platinum Jubilee Hospital, considered to be among the best hospitals in the world."

On September 16, 1958, the Aga Khan returned to America to resume his studies at Harvard. Virtually the whole family was in the United States. Aly was firmly installed as Pakistan's UN envoy; Sadruddin was back at Harvard, where Amyn also returned to continue his studies after summer vacation. "Coming back to school, with a year of travel behind me," Karim said, referring to his enthronement tour with a British sense of understatement, "I'm driven by a desire to know more. This is a warm and happy place when it is your last year and you know what you want." He was considered a first-class student ("I work until around midnight, take a coffee break, then go back and hit the books until two or three") and a sportsman with a will to win ("I can't imagine myself without athletics"). While the newspapers reported Aly's speeches, the Ismaili record of the Aga Khan's progress under October 22, 1958, reads as follows: "In a soccer game brought Harvard victory by scoring two goals, the only player on either side to do so."

Even so, the Aga Khan's football—and sometimes his studies— often took second place to his community work. Mme. Beguel was helping him to deal with the correspondence which was quite as voluminous as his grandfather's had ever been. Michael Curtis was with him to deal with the press. *Life* photographed him for a cover story and he gave his first television interview to the British Broadcasting Corporation. Although none too enamored of reporters, the idea of having his own newspaper began to germinate in his mind. "Grandfather once considered starting a newspaper in East Africa," he told Curtis. What Karim had in mind was not an exclusively Ismaili newspaper—that would not work. He had been studying East African newspapers, products of colonial rule. "He thought they were pretty lousy," Curtis said. What he wanted was a newspaper that was independent, run and operated by Europeans until Ismailis and Africans could be trained. As a newspaper, it should be capable of standing on its own feet, backed by its own printing works. The plans took on a more definite shape the nearer the Aga Khan approached graduation.

One emotion-charged function lay immediately ahead—the interment of Karim's grandfather at Aswan Mausoleum. The Begum was at Aswan to supervise the completion of her husband's resting place, but responsibility for the religious burial rested with Hazar Imam, the Aga Khan. To look after arrangements on the spot, he appointed three leading Ismailis: Zulfikarali C. Valiani, brother of Captain Currim, the family's estate agent in Pakistan; Mohammed Ali Kara, an Indian; and a Mr. Lateka, an East African from Kampala. In January, 1959, these three traveled to Egypt and began arrangements for the transport and accommodation of some five hundred special guests and thousands of others who were expected to attend the burial at Aswan. Egyptian authorities waived formalities for visitors and dealt sympathetically with the requirements of a family whose ancestors had ruled their country when it was at the peak of its power. To be closer at hand, Prince Karim interrupted his studies, flew to Europe, and watched the progress from Geneva.

Questions of etiquette complicated transport to such a remote place. The Aga Khan's emissaries watched the water of the Nile with hawk eyes. If it started to fall, there was a danger that the flotilla that had been brought from Port Said would be unable to ply between the two banks. A unit of army engineers stood by to throw a bridge across the river in an emergency, but the water remained at an adequate level. Accommodations were scarce. The Cataract Hotel's three hundred rooms were reserved for the most eminent mourners, including the Aga Khan. The Grand Hotel's fifty rooms were unfinished and furniture had to be ordered from Cairo. Some of the delegations arriving from the Far East went straight to Aswan; those from East African countries were flying to Luxor, where a special train was waiting to take them on the last stage of their journey. On his way to the funeral the Aga Khan, coming from Geneva, spent the night at Shepheard's Hotel in Cairo, where he found an invitation to see President Nasser the following morning.

The meeting was scheduled to last fifteen minutes, but instead of shaking hands formally and exchanging a few polite words, President Nasser drew his visitor into a political discussion that went on for over an hour and a half. The aircraft standing by to take the Aga Khan to Luxor would have missed the special train had the President not sent out instructions for it to wait.

At Aswan Prince Karim first went to the Begum's house, where the body of his grandfather was lying in state, and discussed with her the next day's funeral arrangements and the part of the mourners in the ceremony. Muslim tradition required it to be an

all-male affair, with the ladies remaining in the background.
"According to our customs," Mr. Valiani told me, "the men
would assemble in one tent until it was time for the body to be
taken to the mausoleum, while the ladies would be in another
tent. . . ."

At twelve-thirty on the afternoon of the funeral Prince Karim,
accompanied by the Mir of Hunza, Sir Eboo Pirbhai, Amirali
Fancy, and other Ismaili dignitaries, went to the local mosque
for Friday prayers. The funeral procession formed at 3 P.M. In
Aly's absence, the three nearest male relatives—Karim, Amyn,
Sadruddin—and the late Aga's old valet, Solomon Bandely,
carried the coffin on the last stage to the fortresslike mausoleum
on the hill overlooking the Nile. As the procession passed the
ladies' tent, the Begum emerged. Dressed in a white sari and accompanied by a friend and a maid, she followed the cortege, a
break with Muslim custom. The young Imam showed no sign of
his disapproval and did not utter a word. But when the funeral
was over, the coolness between him and the Begum was evident.
The Imam of the time had been publicly defied by the widow
of his predecessor. The incident caused a rift which was not
healed for several years. It certainly put an end to any notion
of Prince Karim accepting guidance from the Begum—or anyone else for that matter. He felt he must be Imam in his own
right.

As if to underline her own rights, the Begum at the head of
a large retinue of women paid another visit to the mausoleum
a few weeks later. To reporters she talked with some bitterness
about the Aswan incident. "Prince Karim did not want me to
follow the procession on the grounds of Ismaili rites," she said.
"If I went to the mausoleum contrary to his wishes, it was only
because I was tired and did not want to wait for hours in the
gilded armchair in which I was to sit." Members of her late
husband's family, she added, did not speak to her and left the
day after the ceremony. "I know that Prince Karim does not have
the slightest intention of following his grandfather's wishes so far
as I am concerned. . . ." Ten years later, when I mentioned the

incident, the Aga Khan dismissed it as a minor misunderstanding about religious etiquette which was best forgotten. "The Begum is European," was all he said by way of explanation.

Whether in the United States or in Europe Karim kept in close touch with his father, followed his diplomatic career with filial loyalty, but still could not share his abiding interest in racing. "I do not like to talk about horses with you," Bettina once heard him tell Aly; he did not want to talk about a subject of which he knew so little. It was a subject on which Aly had much to say just then. After months of absorbing diplomatic work, his racing interests were given a strong fillip by the spectacular success of a typical product of his stable's breeding theories: Petite Etoile, the brilliant daughter (1956) of Star of India and Petition, who, after a very good season as a two-year-old, went on to even greater things in 1959, winning the Thousand Guineas at Newmarket. When Taboun won the Two-Thousand Guineas, Aly completed a rare double, following it up with other successes.

Presiding over the annual racing conference with his stud managers at l'Horizon toward the end of the year, Aly proved his instinct when he made the mating that produced Daranoor (House of Light), the name given to the chalet at Gstaad, which became Karim's favorite holiday home. Daranoor grew up to be the best stallion of 1962 and was sold to Japan, where he became a phenomenally successful sire.

To mark the end of his studies and his impending graduation, "K. Khan" donated $50,000 to Harvard University for scholarships for Muslim students. Leaving Harvard meant an instant transference from youth to heavy responsibility. Age would not wither him for many a decade, but the life that awaited him demanded a very mature approach. The formal award of his Bachelor of Arts degree with honors in history reached him on July 11, the second anniversary of his Imamate, which he celebrated with the London *jamat*. Without giving himself much respite, he traveled to the only corner of his worldwide parish where he was still vulnerable as a religious leader and where his rule as Imam had been seriously challenged. In Syria he found an involved situation in which one section of Ismailis were still at odds with the other, but he was well received and his donation of £10,000 to Damascus University was much appreciated.

In August he enjoyed his father's hospitality at the Château de l'Horizon for a pleasant, uninhibited holiday. It looked as if Aly and Bettina might get married before long (Bettina certainly hoped they would), but Aly was still on the move and Karim had the château much to himself. It was there that the prying long-focus lenses of magazine photographers—French, Italian, American—discovered him lazing on the beach, his head in the lap of a pretty girl who was soon identified as Annouchka von Meks, daughter of a German-born father with business interests in Paris. It was the beginning of a relentless pursuit, with Karim and Annouchka, sometimes protected by bodyguards, just one step ahead of the reporters. It went on for years. Somehow the press was convinced that Annouchka would be the next Begum. "Such is the power of the popular press," Karim said in an address to the Royal Commonwealth Society at Oxford, England, a little later, "that few people know very much about the Ismailis today, except that the Aga Khan is their leader, is weighed in diamonds from time to time, owns a number of race horses, and (so far as I am concerned, at any rate) appears to be perpetually on the brink of matrimony."

The tour on which he set out in mid-September enabled him to become more intimately acquainted with his community. He went to East Africa for a whole month and was received with great ceremony and genuine warmth. He opened a mosque on the outskirts of Kampala and laid several foundation stones, one for a housing scheme in Nairobi, another for a nursery school in Mombasa. His meetings with the leaders were the most significant of his tenure so far. Imposing figures, venerable men with great authority among their people, they were rooted in his grandfather's reign. Among them were Count Verjee, from

Uganda, Count Abdullah, from Dar-es-Salaam (both of whom have since died), Count Lakha, Count Fatehali Dhala, and Sir Eboo Pirbhai. Attuned to the old Aga's way of thinking and conducting the affairs of the community like a monarch (running it with his nose, as someone said, but without organization), they were not automatic supporters of the modernization measures that the new Imam came to introduce.

His grandfather's spirit pervaded everything. What he had done, how he had done it, was Ismaili legend. But while the previous Aga Khan had been able to set up an Ismaili dressmaker in business with a few private recommendations, 1960 demanded a more sophisticated approach to the community's economic problems. The institutions around which Ismaili business life revolved, the Diamond Jubilee Trust and the Jubilee Insurance Company, were obviously in need of reorganization.

Though perfectly sound financially, the Diamond Jubilee Investment Trust was just then in need of additional capital, and the Ismaili managers, as was the custom in his grandfather's time, looked to the Aga Khan for a remedy. Groping in the jungle of his new responsibilities, uncertain where to find sound advice on so complicated a matter, Karim was suddenly faced with a request for £300,000. It was a big decision for him to make, but he provided the money from his own funds, which were ample. Continuing on the well-trodden path of traditional Aga Khan munificence, he gave £50,000 to Teheran University and £1,500 to the Kenya Olympic Association—to mention only two of many donations. Opportunities to talk publicly about Africa and Islam frequently came his way. He lectured in New York and California and within a few months was at the other end of the world, touring Burma.

Aly, too, was busy and mobile. At Karachi he saw President Ayub Khan, who appointed him Ambassador to Buenos Aires, an exciting prospect. He looked forward to taking up his duties in mid-May, made a hurried trip to New York to wind up his affairs, and flew on to London before returning to Paris. His house was a beehive of activity. The racing season was at hand and stud managers, trainers, and racing friends were in and out. Aly was dashing from Chantilly to St. Créspin, from one stable to the other, talking to Alec Head, to jockeys, lads, and weathermen. Having seen so little of him since his UN appointment, Bettina tried to coax him into a more sociable life, but it was hard going.

In the early morning of May 12, 1960, he still had not made up his mind whether to accept a long-standing invitation to dinner at Marnes-la-Coquette, at the house of André Dubonnet's daughter Lorraine Bonnet and her husband. Stavros and Genie Niarchos and two of the French Rothschilds and their wives would be among the guests. All right, Aly told Bettina, they would be going too. She spent the day as usual: saw to the house and the dogs in the morning, walked in the garden, and went to the hairdresser, where she had her hair done in a new pageboy style. Aly went racing at Longchamp, stopped over at his club to play a few rubbers of bridge, and, as usual, was late arriving home, by which time Bettina was dressed and ready to go.

Several people were still waiting to talk to Aly. He wanted to make a few telephone calls and dictate letters to Felix Bigio. When Bettina put her head around the door he was discussing the Grand Prix dinner several weeks hence. By ten the Bonnets phoned to inquire whether he would be coming at all and he sent word that he would be there presently. He was still in his study, just beginning to shave and change, but told Lucien, the chauffeur, to get the car ready. Fixing his tie as he went, he rushed downstairs and out into the street so fast that Bettina had difficulty keeping up with him.

The Lancia car was on approval, and Aly took the wheel for the first time. Bettina slipped into the seat beside him and Lucien sat behind them. The car drove beautifully. Aly was enjoying it and told Lucien that he had decided to buy it. Approaching St.-Cloud, they turned into the wide Carrefour du Val d'Or and were going up a hill when they were blinded by the headlights of an oncoming car. "Mind," Bettina shouted, but she remembers nothing of what happened next until she found herself standing in the road without shoes, "the terrible sound of shattering glass and rending steel, that excruciating whistle," still in her ears. Aly had been overtaking a little Renault when a yellow car coming from the opposite direction crashed head-on into the Lancia. The other car's driver, Lucien, and Bettina were only slightly injured. Bettina could see Aly, motionless, his head over the steering wheel, with a few drops of blood on his forehead. She was only half-conscious. "What about Aly!" she shrieked, but in her heart she knew that he was dead.

A police van took her to the hospital, where a cut on her forehead was stitched. She was suffering from severe shock. The Bonnets were informed, their dinner party broke up, and Baron Elie de Rothschild came to look after Bettina, who was given sedatives before being taken to the Boulevard Maurice-Barrès. She remembers waking up in her own bed, but had no idea whether she had been asleep for three hours or three days. Her mother, her sister, and the Begum Aga Khan were with her, but the one person she wanted to see was Karim. His arrival brought her comfort. "It was a bit like having Aly there," she said.

Karim was deeply shaken. Remarkable though his composure was under the stress of his official duties, he kept it only with difficulty. "What a terrible thing," he said gravely. "Terrible for you, and terrible for me. I have lost my grandfather and my father in so brief a space. . . . I am alone now." Gently, he took Bettina's hand and she, in her own grief, wanted to console him. Aly's body was brought to the house and Bettina spent the night beside him, her hand on his arm. He looked relaxed, almost smiling. The next morning, Ismaili ritual took over. The body was embalmed, imams from the Paris mosque came to say their prayers, flowers arrived, and the house was filled with mourners.

Aly had expressed the wish to be buried at Salamiyya among

the Syrian Ismailis he knew and loved so well. In the meantime
he was to be interred in the grounds of the Château de l'Horizon, where a grave was dug in the lawn next to his study. Starting on the sad journey to the south of France, chanting and
praying Ismailis carried the coffin, which was covered with the
red and green Ismaili flag, and put it on a special train. In the
coach ahead, Bettina joined Karim, Amyn, and Sadruddin in
their compartment. Regular trains taking precedence, the trip
took twelve hours and it was midnight before they arrived. The
next day the body lay in state, crowds gathered outside the
château, and a policeman trying to keep them at a distance
was killed by a passing train.

At the open grave Karim, palms turned skywards, recited the
funeral prayers. Then Aly was put to rest in the temporary
grave. It has turned out that he still remains there. The Joundas,
who held power in Syria (one Jounda was head of the trade
unions, another ambassador in Paris, though he later fell from
grace), are descendants of a family that seceded from the
Ismaili sect at the turn of the century. Arab quarrels being "hereditary," permission for Aly's body to be buried in Syria was
withheld, and ten years after his death it was still in the grounds
of l'Horizon. Recognition of his ability, given so grudgingly in
his lifetime, was general and genuine. "Pakistan has lost a
diplomat of the highest caliber and value," said President Ayub
Khan, and Britain's UN envoy, Sir Pierson Dixon, was one of
many prominent people who paid tribute to him. Racing men
all over the world were shocked by the tragic death of this
flamboyant and generous sportsman. Years later I talked to
Bettina about him. "I'll never find another Aly," she said.

Bettina was amply provided for in Aly's will, the provisions
of which were carried out by Maître André Ardoin, the family's
legal adviser. Friends and associates received legacies, but the
bulk of Aly's property, much of it inherited from his own father,
was left to Karim, with Amyn and Yasmin sharing in the estate.

Land in Pakistan, shares in American oil companies, houses in Paris, Cannes, Deauville, and Chantilly, residences in the Far East (such as Yarovda Palace in Poona), the bungalow in Nairobi where Karim spent the first few years of his life, were now his own. Geneva was the capital of his industrial empire. In place of Villa Barakat, which was bought by Baron Edouard de Rothschild (but has since passed into other hands), the Aga Khan acquired Mirémont, a fine house on the outskirts of Geneva, as a residence and office. Daranoor, the chalet standing on its own grounds in Gstaad, became Karim's winter headquarters until he sold it to the German publisher Axel Springer in 1968 and moved to St. Moritz. Tekri (Honeymoon Lodge), in Karachi, also became his property.

Prince Karim inherited another important asset: the stud farms and stables in France and Ireland and the famous string of horses carrying the Aga Khan's colors. "What am I going to do with the horses?" he asked Maître Ardoin. "You may not be interested now," Ardoin suggested, "because you are not an expert, but one day, who knows?" There was no need to remind him of the unique racing tradition associated with his name. He was still pondering the matter when the stables came up with a series of spectacular successes. Having won the previous year's Prix Saint Patrick and two Longchamp races as a three-year-old, Charlottesville ran away with the Prix du Jockey Club, the French Derby (and 341,958 F), won the Grand Prix de Paris (404,814 F), and the Prix du Prince d'Orange (31,075 F), bringing his total winnings to over £74,000. The colt was still full of running and had a great career at stud ahead of him. Sheshoon won the Gold Cup at Ascot, the Grand Prix at Baden Baden, and the Grand Prix at St.-Cloud.

The Aga Khan's interest was aroused. He went to visit the stables and stud farms—Marly-la-Ville, where Mme. Vuillier was in residence, Lassy, which became the headquarters of Robert Muller, and St. Créspin, with Shaumiers, the charming Norman-style cottage (no telephone) to which he later oc-

casionally retreated for a few days. The seven Irish stud farms
were not doing badly either. "I shall carry on," Prince Karim
decided. He asked Ardoin to look after the establishment until
he could learn a little more about racing. Eventually, he ra-
tionalized, he could sell some horses and studs and, if necessary, buy others. He at once bought the share of the studs
and horses that had come to Amyn, Yasmin, and Bettina in
his father's estate. Studs and stables would have to be run as a
business. He called Mme. Vuillier, Robert Muller, and Major
Hall to a conference with Maître Ardoin to tell them of his
decision.

Later in the year they met again at Gstaad for Prince Karim's
first regular racing conference. He listened attentively to the
involved discussions on inbreeding, conformation, and temperament of individual horses, made mental notes, and began to
learn. With greater knowledge his interest increased and his
pleasure grew until today he enjoys racing almost as much as his
father and grandfather. "Prince Aly knew every horse in the
stable and its history. He had a great instinct for the game,"
Robert Muller said. "His Highness, Prince Karim, started from
scratch, but it did not take him very long to catch up."

He has learned about all sorts of thing. When talking to his
half-brother Patrick Guinness, the subject of the Italian island
of Sardinia cropped up. Patrick was enthusiastic, describing it
as a Mediterranean paradise virtually untouched by the crowds
of holiday-makers who invaded every coastline in Europe, a
haven of privacy, and if minor improvements were made, an ideal
refuge for private yachts. Karim, who had inherited his father's
handsome yacht, *My Love*, pricked up his ears. He went to
see for himself and told Prince Sadruddin and Maître Ardoin
about his excursion. John Duncan Miller, of the World Bank, and
other friends were brought in and began to plan a sanctuary
where they could enjoy sun and solitude in a beautiful natural
setting. They decided to form a consortium to acquire land in
Sardinia, build villas for themselves and a small circle of con-

genial acquaintances, create a harbor, and turn their little corner of the island into a private resort for like-minded people, most of them owners of private yachts.

For the moment, however, the Aga Khan had to concentrate on Pakistan, where he was heading in September, 1960, for a forty-day tour to acquaint himself with the country and the community as thoroughly as he had done in East Africa a few months earlier. His hosts were the provincial governors, but he also stayed with his community leaders. Amirali Fancy's house in Karachi and Sir Eboo Pirbhai's mansion in Nairobi included small flats reserved for the use of the Aga Khan, who felt much at home in both places. A back-breaking official program was mapped out for him, but the crowded record says nothing about the conferences and conversations that went on deep into the night. What he did affected the lives of thousands. He approved plans for Karimabad, the first Ismaili housing project named after him. It was designed to give eight hundred families two-room apartments costing ten thousand rupees each, to be paid in monthly installments of thirty-five rupees, less than a tenth of the average income in Pakistan. When completed, it provided comfortable homes for people who had been living in mud huts, if not in the streets.

At Malik, in the suburbs, he laid the foundation stone of another typical Ismaili enterprise and met the woman who had made it possible, a Mrs. Puranbhai, a widow, who had given the community a piece of land worth £20,000 which she had inherited. Work soon started on the Mohammedi Girls' Academy, the most luxurious orphanage in the world, not inferior in living accommodations and teaching facilities to the finest English and American public schools. Mrs. Puranbhai herself preferred to stay on in the hut in which she lived and to continue to pick vegetables at a pay of five shillings a day. "I am happier that way," she told me. As with most similar projects, many patrons, Ismaili and non-Ismaili, contributed generously to the cost. In the case of the Academy, they raised 1.2 million rupees.

For Prince Karim this was only a beginning. So impatient was he to launch other new schemes that he pressed the Ismaili Council to submit suggestions. "Can't we set up an industry?" he asked Amirali Fancy. The difficulty, Fancy countered, was foreign exchange, of which Pakistan was desperately short. "I shall provide £200,000 in foreign exchange," the Aga Khan said. "I want to use as much as possible of my money for the benefit of the community." He was not as yet married, he remarked, and his expenses were much smaller than his grandfather's. Prince Karim's foreign-exchange gift made it possible to import machinery for two textile factories and to buy fifty auto-rickshaws to be leased to Ismailis. The rest went toward equipment for a canvas factory, the profits of which were used to maintain the Girls' Academy.

The Aga Khan's spending spree continued. At a formal ceremony Pakistan's Education Minister took over the new Aga Khan School, built by the community at a cost of 600,000 rupees. He laid the foundation stone of a technical high school and opened the Prince Aly Khan Boys Academy. A donation from him enabled Karachi University to start a Prince Aly Khan Library.

He made speeches, opened *jamatkhanas,* blessed the faithful who swarmed around him. Three secretaries were kept busy typing his messages that helped followers solve some of their problems. He could be stern, too. Visiting an Ismaili family in their home, he sensed that the woman was reluctant to show him one of the rooms, but he insisted on seeing it. Seeing four children sleeping on the floor, he reproved the woman and gave her a lecture on hygiene—it was unhealthy to sleep on the floor whether or not it had been the community's practice for generations.

His ambition was a house for every Ismaili family. In East Africa Ismaili schools and hospitals were open to all and he urged the community in Pakistan "to open up a bit." He traveled north as far as Gilgit, then switched to a jeep for the last seventy miles of mule track to Hunza, the first Imam to visit the remote Ismaili Shangri-la in the fourteen-hundred-year history of the sect.

Conditions in East Pakistan were far from idyllic. In Khulna there was poverty and starvation. "My spiritual children in Khulna are in great difficulty," he told Amirali Fancy. "Something must be done for them." Fancy went to Khulna and arranged for the Jubilee Finance Corporation to provide funds to launch a cooperative society. When he paid them another visit two years later, they were already much better off.

Toward the end of the fifteen-thousand-mile tour (the total mileage Karim covered in the first three years of his Imamate was 260,000) even the athletic young Harvard man's energies were beginning to flag. He still allowed himself no rest. Back in London, he discussed the East African newspaper project with Michael Curtis, whom he recalled to launch it. Referring to the famous speech by British Prime Minister Harold Macmillan which set the African continent alight, Curtis said, "We blew in with the wind of change. The Aga Khan felt that this was something that should not be resisted—on the contrary, should be helped along." Unlike the colonial newspapers, the Aga Khan's would devote space to African politics and print what African politicians had to say—and not, as hitherto, at the bottom of the page. He was prepared to invest £1 million, and he wanted the paper to support the British government's progressive move toward independence and to advocate the release of Jomo Kenyatta, who was serving a six-year jail sentence.

Curtis went to Nairobi and prepared to publish the *Sunday Nation*, but it was an uphill struggle with many pitfalls. As a former London editor, he favored an up-to-date slick Fleet Street style, which his African readers did not seem to like. The Sunday paper was followed by the *Daily Nation*, which did not prosper because many Asians, accustomed to offering their wares in the market place, did not believe in advertising. The papers were devouring money at an alarming rate and progress was

slow, a depressing thought for the young Aga Khan, who was
convinced of the importance and the viability of his newspaper
project. He was proved right when they eventually made money
and attained the biggest circulation of any English papers in
East Africa.

At Chalet Daranoor in Gstaad he pondered this problem
and many others. Three times a day he prayed (unlike Sunnis,
who pray five times), seeking guidance from Allah. The community weighed on his mind. The community was his life. "Do
you know what thrills me, what really thrills me?" he asked
Vincent Mulchrone, who interviewed him for the London *Daily
Mail,* and answered his own question. "Well, I believe the community's secondary schools in Dar-es-Salaam and Kampala had
the highest pass rate in school certificates of any Asian school in
East Africa." He followed a strict routine, getting up at seven-
thirty, putting in three hours' work before going out skiing for
a few hours. Then he returned to his desk and to the reports
and personal messages from his followers in East Africa which
only reinforced his view that the community's economic structure was woefully inadequate and that reorganization ought
not to be delayed. Ismaili traders had gone into industry but
could not make a success of their ventures. Some went broke
and asked the Imam for advice and help. It was not a healthy
situation.

What was urgently required was a thorough investigation by
experienced industrial consultants. The choice was not easy. An
American firm would regard the state of the community's economic development as not far enough advanced. English or
French experts might be associated with colonial rule, which
had been discredited and was coming to an end. The Germans
were the best bet because they had themselves started from zero
after the war. The final choice fell on a German firm, Kienbaum,
with offices at Gummersbach, near Cologne.

A meeting with the head of the firm, Herr Gerhard Kienbaum,
was fixed for the earliest date possible after the Aga Khan's

trip to the United States, in the course of which he paid a visit
to the White House. President John F. Kennedy found the young
Ismaili leader with the Harvard background a most congenial
partner. They discussed world affairs, especially Africa's emancipation. Reports of the meeting were just being published when
the Aga Khan was already in Nairobi, addressing one gathering
on the multiracial society and another on the British Commonwealth. He flew to Europe to preside over a conference of the
presidents of Ismailia Associations—Muslim historians, theolo-
gians, scientists—whom he had invited to the Château de
l'Horizon.

His meetings with Gerhard Kienbaum took place in Switzerland not much later. "On September 15, 1961," Kienbaum noted,
"His Highness the Aga Khan Karim al-Huseini entrusted me
with a study of the economic situation of the Ismaili community in East Africa." A fee of £5,000 plus expenses was agreed
upon. The first of Herr Keinbaum's staff to hear of the new assignment was Dr. Peter Hengel, a young German graduate of
the Maxwell School of Economics and Political Science at the
University of Syracuse who had had industrial experience in
the United States. "We rushed to the reference books to see
what it was all about," was how he described the reaction at
Gummersbach. "Of course, we knew the name of the Aga Khan,
but he was less of a public figure in Germany than in Britain
and the United States. We did not even know how to address
him."

At Keinbaum's all available literature about economic conditions in East Africa was closely studied. "The Aga Khan foresaw
considerable changes," Dr. Hengel recalled. "The end of colonial
rule was in sight and he wanted to have a blueprint ready to
integrate his plans into the future economic and political pattern." Sir Eboo Pirbhai was present at the discussions and prepared a schedule for a Kienbaum team to tour East Africa to
investigate the business activities of the community.

CHAPTER XVII

THE AGA KHAN happened to be in Nairobi in December, 1961, when Dr. Hengel and two of his colleagues started their investigation into the economic situation of East Africa's Ismailis. He was the guest of honor at a party in the attractive house of his Education Administrator, Jimmy Verjee, to which Hengel was also invited. Hengel thought his firm's new client was rather solemn, but finally he risked a little joke, which made the Aga Khan laugh, and broke the ice. This informality, he says, has remained a characteristic of their relationship.

The Kienbaum team traveled all over East Africa to meet community leaders and businessmen. "We were struck by the intense religious feeling of the community, which was very well organized as a body," Hengel recounts. His strongest impression was of Ismaili dedication and discipline; their economic committees, education committees, women's committees, youth committees, and health and hospital committees enabled them to be active in many fields.

But economically, seen through the eyes of a West European industrial expert, the community looked extremely vulnerable. It concentrated almost exclusively on small trade. Many were selling the same lines and everybody was in the wholesale business which, once East African states became independent, might well be nationalized. Indigenous Africans might be put in charge and non-African retailers denied licenses to trade—a most unfavorable position to be in. To Hengel the community seemed industrially in the same position as the Germans in 1945—at zero. How to introduce diversification and how to finance it were the two principal problems on which Hengel's study concentrated. "Admirable as they were for an earlier phase of development," he said, "Ismaili institutions were not equipped for the task."

Kienbaum's preliminary report persuaded the Aga Khan to commission further investigations, specifically into the Diamond Jubilee Investment Trust, Jubilee Insurance, and the newspaper group. The trust, started with the old Aga Khan's donation, now had four thousand Ismaili shareholders, dispensed loans at 3 percent interest over twenty years—which was not a commercial proposition—and was run on a personal basis. The Kienbaum study suggested reform of the management and diversion of finance toward industrial ventures; borrowers should be advised on how best to manage their own enterprises.

In the view of the investigators, the Jubilee Trust's management left much to be desired. The company was not looking beyond the community and was not really equipped to handle industrial investment and loans. It supported little lending agencies in small villages which accepted trinkets and all manner of things no bank would regard as security. The newspaper group was losing money, though this was the Aga Khan's personal property and not an Ismaili enterprise. Total assets under review were in the region of £30 million.

The study looked into consumer industries capable of replacing imports and into local products suitable for export. What the findings suggested to the Aga Khan was the need for an entirely new approach. "As you will have heard," he said to me, "when it became essential to go into industry, I founded the

I.P.S. [Industrial Promotion Services]. These institutions in East Africa and elsewhere had to be evolved jointly between the Imam and the leadership of the community." There was no set formula, he said, and the concept had to be flexible because the community was spread through many countries with different conditions and different laws.

To make economic reform palatable to the old guard was not easy because it was bound to reduce their personal influence. Privilege, nepotism, and patronage were liable to be eliminated. Religious and economic life being so closely intertwined in Islam, the Aga Khan could have used his religious authority and imposed the new order with a *firman*. He preferred, however, that his leaders understand what he was doing and accept the changes of their own free will. A younger generation was standing in the wings to take over before long, mostly products of the old Aga Khan's educational program who had been university-educated in Pakistan, the United States, Britain, and France.

In the end economic changes went hand in hand with changes in the community's leadership. To bring the rank and file into the process, Dr. Hengel traveled up and down the country inviting anyone with an industrial idea to come forward and explain what could be done and what was viable. Occasionally the result was a head-on clash with a different age. One man thought his bag of sand was all he needed to start a glass industry; another asked earnestly, "How much does industry cost?" But before long the new ideas took on flesh; the organizations were infused with a life of their own and ceased to be restricted to the community. They became enterprises capable of growth and development independent of religious matters.

For the Aga Khan every single move in this intricate process involved unending conferences. Like his grandfather, he kept on asking questions and analyzed the answers carefully. So many vested interests were involved and not always openly declared. He went to the bottom of every argument and his associates came to respect his ability. As one of them described it, "He read the back of another man's mind."

"He was trained in this way of thinking by his grandfather," was a leading Ismaili's opinion, "and like His Royal Highness, Aga Khan III, Hazar Imam has a faculty for getting to the root of a problem and finding out the ulterior motive behind every proposition." His European business friends echo this assessment. "He is a perfectionist," they say with convincing unanimity, "who checks every angle. It's an intellectual process with an instinct for self-protection. He is naturally suspicious."

Soon he began to rely on a closely knit information system to bring him news from every corner of the world, enabling him to coordinate activities on several continents. Once in possession of all available information, it was his habit to consult his advisers and to toss a project back and forth—"ping-ponging," as he called it—bringing others into the game as required until a decision evolved.

His friends thought he was doing far too much and ought to delegate more responsibility. When work threatened to overwhelm him, some community leaders—Amirali Fancy, of Pakistan, foremost among them—urged him earnestly to take things easier. On Fancy's suggestion it was agreed to make February a closed season as far as the Imam was concerned. No communications from the community, no inquiries, no demands for decisions. The Aga Khan appreciated the thought, but the result was that work piled up and the burden simply doubled in March and April. Throughout, though, he remained even-tempered.

The formidable undertaking ties this young, deceptively humble religious leader and tycoon to his desk for ten hours a day or more. The iron discipline which is a facet of his character alone enables him to pursue his intensely busy life and his sports. For outsiders it is impossible to visualize the extent of his responsibilities when they see him on the snow-covered slopes of Gstaad or on the difficult ski runs of St. Moritz and even less when he presents himself as a competitor in the hotly contested Kandahar Challenge Cup at Davos, the oldest in the world for downhill ski-racing—and wins it.

A few years ago in the course of a quick visit to Paris he inspected an eleventh-century mansion in the narrow rue des Ursins on the Île de la Cité. The mansion was once part of the Nôtre Dame complex and residence of the cathedral's canons. Lavishly restored by a famous Paris architect, it came on the market when the owner became involved in a much publicized affair. The Aga Khan liked it and bought it, but the figure of a million pounds which was mentioned as the price was grossly exaggerated. The house has become his favorite residence in Europe and is conveniently near his racing interests, which gravitate toward France. As for his stud farms, he has recently sold Irish Eyrefield and Ongar, and La Coquenne in France.

Wherever he is, reports about the community's affairs pursue him. He used to dictate his answers on tapes to be transcribed but now rarely travels without two or three secretaries. In line with his policy of giving younger men positions of authority in the community he has appointed Badaruddin Pirbhai, Sir Eboo's son, who is practicing law in London, as president of the Ismailia Council of Great Britain. He is one of the select few who are being drawn into the closest circle around the Imam.

Although never talked about, initiation is still practiced and certain groups inside the Ismaili community are not open to all. In the esoteric Ismaili faith, a man born into the religion does not automatically reach the highest state of religious comprehension but may advance toward it (or be initiated) stage by stage. The Aga Khan was reticent when I asked him about this. It is a degree of involvement, he said. "Those who wish to participate in a more formal manner"—he expressed himself a little mysteriously—"can do so, but the opportunity for such personal spiritual involvement is not always available to all sections of the community."

Initiation does not involve any mystical mumbo jumbo. In fact, at this time, the Imam, in consultation with community leaders, has completed the modernization of the Ismaili Constitution. When sanctioning the new version, he told his followers, "Look to the spirit and not the letter of the Constitution."

The Sardinian project, conceived as a rich man's hobby, has developed into a commercial proposition of some magnitude. With half-brother Patrick (Guinness), his uncle, Sadruddin (whose marriage to Nina Dyer had just been dissolved), lawyer Ardoin, industrialists Miller and Mentasti (an Italian mineral-water tycoon), and some other wealthy businessmen, the Aga Khan first formed a consortium to buy up land in the deserted northeast corner of the island. There was much bargaining, maneuvering, surveying, and patchwork to fit the pieces together. The first few lots went cheaply, but the Sardinian peasants who owned the land soon raised the stakes and prospered beyond their wildest dreams. Bit by bit, thirty-five miles of unspoilt coastline were acquired, including some thirty-two thousand acres of land. Costa Smeralda (Emerald Coast) was the ingenious euphonic name dreamed up for the territory, which also became known as "Agaland" or "the Aga Khan's answer to Spain's Costa del Sol."

The possibilities of this wild, sun-struck, beautiful enclave became more evident with familiarity. Before long there was talk—actually, decisions—about a total investment of £30 million, though the Aga Khan's share has been only a fraction of this amount. Work has begun on a vast infrastructure of roads and drainage, water and power supply, airfields, harbors, hotels, and a colony of villas for wealthy people prepared to conform to the high standard laid down by the consortium. A committee headed by the Aga Khan meets every month and runs the whole scheme. With some difficulty, the Italian government has been persuaded to cooperate in the project from which the country's exchequer profits long before the Aga Khan and his friends can hope to break even.

Charming villages grouped around piazzas with shops, cafés, and discothèques in native style have been conjured up and

Porto Cervo has become the nerve center of Agaland. The consortium's own airline, Alisarda, now flies in visitors throughout a season lasting longer than in most rival resorts. Villas, designed by prominent international architects to many tastes (as long as they blend in with the landscape), have grown up within the strict limits of a population density of five persons per acre. The whole project, nursed by Prince Karim's commercial talent and ingeniously publicized by his Garbo-like craving for privacy, has turned the Costa Smeralda into a major attraction. Most summers Princess Margaret of England and other notable friends, a couple of Rockefellers among them, come to visit him here. Bettina has acquired a charming villa on the island, which is another attraction. Rita Hayworth brought Yasmin and stayed to enjoy the sun. The Aga Khan's mother and her relatives became regulars. International business associates and Ismaili community leaders started flying in and out.

The Aga Khan's own white villa, perched on a cliff, became the center of much activity—in and out of season he spends a week or so on the island as often as possible. Maître Ardoin has bought a villa near Porto Cervo, an investment as profitable as it is pleasurable. So has Dr. Peter Hengel, who, predictably, left Kienbaum by friendly arrangement and joined the Aga Khan's organization. While the chief objective is to promote Sardinia as a luxury resort for a largely villa-owning clientele, the consortium has launched a number of other enterprises, a supermarket and a ceramics factory among them.

Riding high in the harbor is the Aga Khan's new yacht, *Amaloun*. To commute between Sardinia and his other homes he has acquired a Mystère Falcon jet at a price of £400,000, a private pilot, and a copilot. He added a helicopter to his air fleet to take him to and from a Corsican airfield until Sardinia's landing facilities were adequate for the jet. Soon Sardinia became to him what Monte Carlo used to be to Aristotle Onassis, except that he has never been beset by troubles with the ruling prince. In Sardinia the only prince who counts is Karim, and even the island's notorious bandits keep away from the Costa

Smeralda because they think that the Aga Khan is good for Sardinia.

In India he was generously welcomed as few other Muslims. After visits to Calcutta and Poona he flew to East Africa for a ceremonial program that disguised the chief purpose of his visit —to put the final touches to the reorganization of the community. In January, 1963, East Africa's leading Ismailis, some twenty of them, who were on the boards of the Jubilee Trust and the Jubilee Insurance attended a conference with the Imam at Val d'Isère in the French Alps. The slow process of persuasion was at an end. The grand old men of his grandfather's reign gathered around the young leader, some of them clearly feeling that they were ushering in the end of their own epoch. Something of a fairytale patriarch and wise man, Count Lakha, though a very wealthy man, was not really attuned to the language of the Keinbaum report, which was dotted with "concepts," "forecasts," "evaluations," and many statistics. Count Abdullah's flashing eyes signaled disapproval, but total deference to the Imam superseded all other considerations. Count Verjee, like Sir Eboo Pirbhai a member of his country's legislature, was less antagonistic.

Dr. Hengel was called in to give a final summing up of the new shape of things. I.P.S. would seek out new business opportunities and would be staffed with experts (management consultants) to advise the average businessman, maintain liaison with other Ismaili communities, and disseminate information about technological progress in the Western world. The amount needed to launch three East African I.P.S. companies—in Kenya, Uganda, and Tanganyika—was £1 million, but when, even at this late stage, doubts were raised, the Aga Khan simply said, "I will finance it!" I.P.S. was destined to expand into an international organization.

It took years for the community to match the Aga Khan's investment, but governments of the countries where I.P.S. came into being quickly took up a share. When I.P.S. Pakistan eventually launched 60 percent of its capital on the stock market, the issue was oversubscribed, a rare token of public faith in a new venture of this kind. I.P.S. Geneva became a technical clearinghouse to coordinate activities, isolate problems, suggest solutions, and prepare agenda. The total investment amounted to about $10 million, of which 50 percent was the Aga Khan's.

For the Ismaili community it was a historic turning point, a practical application of the Prophet's exhortation: "Have enterprise, expand, spread out!" By taking Ismaili businessmen boldly into the modern age, the young Aga Khan had managed to link the underdeveloped societies in which he had one foot with the highly developed countries in which he had the other. But the going was often hard and there were many setbacks. Sometimes his experts were despondent, lost hope, and wanted to give up. "Had it not been for His Highness's strength," one of them has said, "the whole thing might have collapsed."

His aim was to turn I.P.S. into a public company when the time was ripe, making it independent from the community and from himself. In the meantime this novel kind of organization, privately run with government participation, appealed to foreign investors and accomplished more than a government agency could have. "We can move faster," Dr. Hengel said. "We are not bound by red tape!"

The Aga Khan's associates bubble over with enthusiastic accounts of how I.P.S. works. In Karachi Shamsh Kassim-Lakha, the youthful managing director of I.P.S. Pakistan, told me how the government of the Ivory Coast asked the Aga Khan to help them with the establishment of a sack factory. The result was positive and the Ivory Coast invested handsomely in I.P.S. The plant was built and was opened by President Félix Houphouet-Boigny in 1967. The I.P.S. manager praises the welfare work that goes hand in hand with the Aga Khan's industrial activities. Of the fifteen thousand workers employed by the Peoples and Crescent Jute Mills in East Pakistan, over 40 percent are housed by the company. All have the advantage of primary and high schools for their children, dispensaries, maternity homes, workers clubs, and cooperative stores.

The schools, in particular, were planned in close cooperation with the Aga Khan, who asked to see the plans and discussed such details as the light angle in relation to the blackboards, the design of the school uniforms, and the rules about discipline. Almost in the same breath he examined offers for the jute mills (an offer for one was ten million dollars). Reports on I.P.S. schemes under consideration piled up on his desk. In 1969 there were twenty-two, involving amounts from fifty thousand dollars up. Proposals come in great numbers. "We get hundreds," Dr. Hengel says. "People think we are sitting on a pile of money." One typical request came from Sir Ahmad Yar, H.H. Beglar Beg, the Khan of Kalat, who, in November, 1968, wrote a personal letter to the Aga Khan:

My Dear Friend, I trust this letter will find Your Highness in the best of health and happiness. I am inspired to write it because your beloved grandfather and I were friends—your grandfather has been one of the pillars and builders of Pakistan whose memory has left a very deep impression on the minds of millions of Muslims. I am one among them. I am very happy to know that Your Highness is following his tradition. . . . You have undertaken various economic development projects in Pakistan and in the short time of your Imamate have been able to win the hearts of millions of your followers. As the Khan of Kalat I have a tremendous responsibility to the millions of Baluchis in our region, a very important part of Pakistan, blessed with natural resources and fertile land which has never been allowed to be developed, has in fact been completely neglected. As an admirer of the Ismaili community, I must say that their methods of handling business and trade is very methodical, satisfactory and honest, without intrigues and political ambition. . . .

The upshot of the letter was a request to the Aga Khan for help in exploiting and developing the natural resources of

Kalat. It outlined an ambitious program on which, the Khan of Kalat added, he had the general guidance and approval of the President of Pakistan.

Sometimes I.P.S. returns from investigations with figures that do not warrant an investment. When one such negative result was communicated to the local Ismailis, they appealed to the Imam and begged him to reconsider. "Go back there and start something!" the Aga Khan told his experts. "Start a hotel or a small factory." They protested, "There is no market, Your Highness, it will not pay. You will never get your money back." The Aga Khan insisted. "Never mind, my spiritual children expect me to help them—whatever the cost, we must help them." In September, 1963, he went to the Congo as a guest of the government and promised to launch a development project. "Not many people would have invested in the Congo at that time," one of his aides remarked.

Of his own enterprises, the East African newspapers seem closest to his heart. He personally supervised their reorganization and commissioned a German psychologist to carry out motivational research into what readers wanted. As a result, foreign news reporting has been stepped up, greater emphasis placed on the news behind the news, and the Fleet Street approach abandoned. Michael Curtis has carried out the changes and has taken charge of the firm's expansion into commercial and book printing and packaging, which have proved highly profitable. A Swahili-language paper, *Taifa*, was brought out, and new magazines came into being. Within a year or so the group was beginning to make money and the Aga Khan had the satisfaction of seeing the first of his own enterprises prosper. He has since left control largely in the hands of the man on the spot.

The *Daily Nation* chronicled Kenya's fast strides toward sovereignty. In December, 1963, after six months of internal self-government, the country emerged from British colonial rule. When he arrived for the official ceremonies the Aga Khan was cordially received by Kenya's President Kenyatta as an early supporter of Kenyan independence. The President attended the opening of a nurses' home and training school at the Aga Khan Platinum Jubilee Hospital in Nairobi, and Prince Karim asked him to accept Caledonian House (popularly known as Aga Khan Bungalow) as a personal present. Then the Imam of the Ismailis, who, as he said, was concerned for the whole lives of his followers, addressed a strong and unequivocal "Unto Caesar!" message to his community and asked them to give their temporal loyalty to the new state and to adopt the nationality of the country in which they lived and worked. He repeated this message in Zanzibar and Uganda, and every Ismaili in East Africa profited from it. Unlike other Asians who retained their British passports and soon found themselves between the devil of East African xenophobia and the deep blue sea of the British color problem, East African Ismailis have become citizens of their emergent countries. On the advice of the Imam they soon went a step further and associated themselves in business with indigenous East Africans, who share benefits from Ismaili industry and progress. Ismaili schools and hospitals restrict the quota of Ismaili pupils and patients to make room for Africans. Asians, even second- and third-generation Asians, are still not quite at home in East Africa, but those who are Ismailis are now being accepted as Kenyans, Tanzanians, and Ugandans.

Little of all this has percolated to Europe, where the Aga Khan continues to be regarded simply as a rich young man, less of a playboy than his father, less of a character than his grandfather—a handsome, pleasant young aristocrat eminently eligible for a place in the gossip columns. Those who kept their eyes on him, as I did, watched him at Innsbruck, Austria, early in 1964 competing in the winter Olympics under the Iranian colors, doing well but not well enough to be a medallist. He was seen at most major race meetings in England and France and the output of his studs commanded respect (he even bought a new stud, Bonneval), but on the Côte d'Azur and other pleasure capitals the long-focus lenses of the magazine reporters were still trained hopefully on him.

More and more of his time was spent in Sardinia, and in the summer of 1964 he again played host to Princess Margaret and Lord Snowdon, who were staying at one of his cottages. His house party, including his mother and his brother, swam and sunbathed much of the time. Princess Margaret showed herself adept at water-skiing; Tony Snowdon found a rich bounty for his camera. Some evenings they strolled to a discothèque and Amyn taught Margaret how to dance the "Surf." On August 26, 1964, the Aga Khan took the Princess and her husband in his yacht, *Amaloun,* on one of those leisurely Mediterranean cruises for which Sardinia is an ideal starting point. Their destination was the neighboring island of La Maddalena, but they had not gone very far when *Amaloun* hit a rock and sprung a leak. The yacht was taking on water, and two fishing smacks, seeing her in distress, hurried to the scene. The next day's papers, with a sense of the dramatic, reported that "the Aga Khan directed the operation of abandoning ship." Actually he helped Margaret and Tony into a dinghy. Then they were hoisted aboard one of the fishing boats, which landed them safely at Porto Cervo.

Amaloun was quickly repaired, but the Aga Khan soon became fascinated with the work of a French-American designer who produced a revolutionary new type of motorboat with an aircraft turbine. He bought it and named it *Silver Shark* (after his colt who was well on the way to his record stake-winning of one million francs, or nearly $200,000). But this was not a success. On one of its first outings *Silver Shark* was shaken by an explosion and the engine blew up. No one was hurt, but the boat sank without a trace.

That winter he went to Pakistan for a month for the usual round. At Dacca, in a philosophical mood, he made a speech from which Ismailis are fond of quoting this passage: "The tapestry of Islamic history is studded with jewels of civilization; these jewels poured forth their light and beauty; great statesman, great philosophers, great astronomers; but these individuals, these precious stones, were worked into a tapestry whose dominant theme was Islam, and this theme remained dominant regardless of the swallowing up of foreign lands, foreign cultures, foreign languages, and foreign people." His one weakness, due probably to his degree in history, he said, was that he liked to look backward before going forward.

Karachi gave a civic reception in his honor, in the course of which he was asked whether he would help establish a medical college in the city. The suggestion struck a chord. Only a few days earlier his Ismaili followers had told him that there was a great need for a hospital in Karachi, and the two projects seemed to go together. What followed is a good example of his modus operandi. He promptly appointed a Hospital Advisory Committee, put experts to work on estimates of the cost, and gave instructions to look for a suitable piece of land. After consulting legal experts, he then established the Aga Khan Hospital and Medical College Foundation with an advisory body of twelve leading medical men and superintendents of medical colleges.

An estimate put the cost of the scheme at between £4.5 million and £5 million. "His Highness wanted to put up the whole amount," Amirali Fancy told me, "but was persuaded to give members of the community and philanthropic institutions an opportunity to contribute." They did so generously. The Ford, Rockefeller, and Asia foundations were expected to give support, and manufacturers donated plants and machinery, one offering a cobalt unit. Several countries have sent doctors to work free of charge and to train Pakistanis. The foundation is kept open to all. A sixty-five-acre site was acquired and Pakistan's biggest hospital was in the making. (The project owed much to the Health Board of Pakistan's Ismailis, headed by Dr. Habib Patel, which is responsible for a dozen hospitals, maternity homes, children's nursing homes, and health centers for Ismailis in countless villages.

During this trip the Aga Khan was in a happy frame of mind when, in the company of several Ismailis, he went to visit Tekri Honeymoon Lodge, his grandfather's birthplace high up on a hill. At the bottom of the steps leading up to the house he asked his followers to stay behind. "He went up alone," one of them told me, "meditated, and said his prayers. He was there for about ten minutes, but when he came down, his mood had changed. He was serious, thoughtful, nostalgic. 'I want to build a house here for myself,' he said. 'It reminds me of the past.'" As if the community had long guessed his thoughts, they were ready with plans to fulfill his wish. The occasion was his twenty-eighth birthday, the first time he had spent this Ismaili holiday in Karachi. The official record has the following entry:

> December 13, 1965: A Unique Event took place at Karachi when Mowlana Hazar Imam celebrated his birthday for the first time with the jamats in the grand special Durbar held at the Aga Khan Gymkhana grounds amidst the delegations of Ismaili communities from all over the world. On this occasion, Ismailis requested Imam-e-Zaman to be graciously pleased to accept their humble gift of a bungalow to be constructed by them in Karachi at a site where Hazrat Imam Sultan Mahomed Shah of revered memory was born.

The *durbar* was an oriental affair. Followers prostrated themselves and kissed the Imam's hand. Seeing him in this setting, it was difficult to identify him as the Aga Khan Europe knew so well. He was indeed a different person, and not only because of the glittering robes and the *paqri* he wore. Even when, dressed in a lounge suit, he attended the wedding of young Zool Khanbhai, nephew of Sir Eboo Pirbhai, to Amirali Fancy's pretty daughter Naseem (a symbolic union between Ismaili communities in Asia and Africa), he was every inch the oriental

Imam. In the *gymkhana* five thousand wedding guests were as anxious to pay him homage as to congratulate the young couple. The pattern of his life and work now seems set. Peripatetic and apparently erratic, it nevertheless has a rhythm that does not change much: Paris and racing in the spring; London for the Derby, the Oaks, the Newmarket Sales, with excursions across the Irish Sea to his stud farms; Gstaad in the winter, until recently when he sold Châlet Daranoor and moved to St. Moritz; the south of France and Sardinia in the summer (Sardinia any odd time); Asia and East Africa for long tours every third year plus several brief trips in between; regular flights to the United States. There are receptions and honors wherever he goes (frequently he plays the host), meetings with heads of state (Dr. Milton Obote in Kampala, President Mobutu in the Congo, President Léopold Senghor in Senegal); religious ceremonies in mosques and *jamatkhanas;* reports from community leaders when he is in France; business conferences in his Geneva headquarters.

Contact with his family continues to be close. He sees his mother in London and Amyn in New York. Having received his Master of Arts Degree at Harvard, the Aga Khan's younger brother, a tall, studious, unhurried bachelor, inhabits a four-level three-bedroom house in New York, often cooking his own meals and sometimes dinners for guests. He joined the United Nations Department of Economic and Social Affairs but was clearly destined sooner or later to transfer to his brother's staff, where his special status in the Ismaili community would be immensely useful in intricate negotiations on the Imam's behalf. His first assignment was a study of agricultural opportunities for Ismailis in East Africa.

The United Nations also claimed Prince Sadruddin, who chose international public service as a career. As a descendant of the much-persecuted early Ismailis, it was fitting that he should become High Commissioner for Refugees, refusing to accept more than nominal payment for the job. The fortune inherited

from his father gives him substantial interests in a variety of
enterprises, a share in a major American hotel group among
them.

The death of Prince Sadruddin's ex-wife, who took her own
life, was one of two recent personal tragedies that the family
suffered. Later it was echoed when her jewels fetched over half
a million pounds at auction in Geneva. Patrick Guinness, Prince
Karim's half-brother, died in a car crash, leaving his beautiful
young wife, Dolores, and three small children. A friendship that
developed between Karim and Dolores soon began to feed the
rumor machine and marriage between them was confidently
predicted. "The God Consoles the Widow—Karim Khan's Love
Remains in the Family" was the kind of headline that made him
wince. (This one was in the German magazine *Stern.*) The
rumormongers were proved wrong, but did not give up easily.
When on one of his rare excursions to a nightclub he was seen
dancing with a pretty girl, the paparazzi were convinced they
had discovered a new "girl friend." Actually the young lady was
his half-sister Yasmin, whom he had taken for a night out in Paris.

The year 1967 was special in the Ismaili calendar, but the
Aga Khan did not change his routine and still bounced like
a shuttlecock from continent to continent. He flew to the United
States in the Mystère for a fortnight's visit, returned to Geneva
to preside over the second World Ismailia Socio-Economic Conference, and in Paris met a gathering of Ismailis resident in
Europe. In the course of a two-month tour of Africa he was
present when President Kenyatta opened the new £500,000
I.P.S. building in Nairobi. On July 11 he completed ten years
of his "Glorious Imamate," the occasion for another demonstration
of fanatical devotion from millions of followers. Going back to
the family seat in Bombay, he held a *durbar* at Hassanabad,
linking his own Imamate with that of his grandfather. But there
was no question of his being weighed in silver, gold, diamonds,
or platinum. (There is little likelihood in fact that he will ever
submit himself to the traditional ceremony.) He was only thirty-

one years of age, but the community already bore the stamp of his youthful personality.

An honor that pleased him more than most was the honorary degree of Doctor of Law which the University of Peshawar offered him in recognition of his services to education. As the Prophet Mohammed said, "To acquire education is the duty of every Muslim, man and woman!" Months before the appointed day, his staff began to collect material for his speech. He discussed the topic with them again and again before settling down to write and rewrite the text, a week's hard work during which he sometimes spent six hours a day at his desk.

At Peshawar he was received by the Governor of West Pakistan and the university's vice chancellor, who spoke glowingly of his efforts for Pakistan. The Aga Khan's response was a learned review of Peshawar's colorful history that led into the more contemporary subjects of television and the permissive society. "What has been called the permissive society," he said, "where anything goes, nothing matters, nothing is sacred or private any more, is not a promising foundation for a brave and upright world." Was he thinking of extremism and permissiveness in politics? In another year or so this was the specter that faced Pakistan. A wave of unrest and riots swept the country and President Ayub Khan stepped down. His picture by the side of Jinnah's and the Aga Khan's in many an Ismaili office and home was soon replaced by that of his successor General Yahya Khan. "Politically I am not involved, but I am a shareholder of the jute mills there," the Aga Khan told me soon after the news of the grave disturbances in East Pakistan. Like workers throughout the country, the twenty thousand employees in the mills received a pay increase of 20 percent, which could only make it more difficult for the mills to compete against chemical substitutes already threatening the industry.

There was tension in Africa, too, but although responsible for communities in several countries with widely different political systems, he has managed to keep out of political involvement with surprising dexterity. Kenya was moving toward a one-party system, and Tanzania was extending state control over the economy, but his relations with East Africa's leaders have been an asset to Ismailis, and he is full of new plans and projects from which the economy of their countries can only profit.

CHAPTER XVIII

In the winter of 1968–69 Karim Aga Khan made a break with the habit of a lifetime. He left Gstaad and put his chalet on the market. Did he want to get away from the past, from his childhood, his boyhood, his youth? He was certainly not giving up skiing, and his move, when he made it, took him no farther than St. Moritz, 150 miles away. Undecided as yet whether to build himself a house in Europe's premier winter-sport resort, he took over the chalet of Greek shipowner Stavros Niarchos. His routine was hard work, hard skiing, and more hard work, but occasionally he slipped into the Palace Hotel, where his grandfather had spent most of his time during two wars and which remains the winter rendezvous of the world's upper "four hundred."

In retrospect, he could not fix the exact moment when he first became aware of a most attractive visitor who stood out among the "beautiful people" at the hotel. At twenty-eight, she had the slim figure of a top model, the elegance of a woman of the world, features of rare line and symmetry, eyes the size of saucers, and chestnut hair in a new and striking coiffure almost every day. Friends soon introduced him. She was known as Sally Croker-Poole, although her correct name was Lady James

Crichton-Stuart. She was the former wife of the Marquess of Bute's brother, whom she had married in 1959. The marriage, which remained without issue, was dissolved in 1966, and Lord James being a Catholic, was annulled by the Vatican in 1970.

The Aga Khan soon discovered that Sally—"Lady James," as he pedantically called her—was born in New Delhi, the daughter of an English officer in the Indian army. (She speaks Urdu at least as well as he does.) Although she did not share her new friend's love of skiing—she had broken her left leg on the slopes two years earlier and her right leg the following year, and that was quite enough for her—they had a lot in common. She was a racing enthusiast and understood horses well, was deeply interested in Islam, in Muslim clothes, food, and customs. Currently she was earning a fair amount of money as a very successful photographer's model. She was amusing, gay, sensible, with the aura of a *grande dame* such as attaches to few women of the present time.

The oriental in the Aga Khan's personality invests him with a mystery and a quality of reticence hard to define. But to those close to him during those days it was no mystery that he was in love. In the past, however, whenever the subject of marriage cropped up—it had been raised in subtle hints and humble inquiries from prominent followers anxious for the Imam to take a wife and "experience the happiness of married life and the blessing of an heir"—he had brushed it aside, saying he did not want to be tethered yet.

He no longer talked in these terms. His acquaintance with Sally, struck up in St. Moritz, was renewed in London, where the Aga Khan met her parents, Lieutenant-Colonel Arthur Croker-Poole and his wife. He and Sally were seen together at the races and dining out in London, which provoked the inevitable predictions of an early marriage, although people seemed no longer to believe their own gossip about the Aga Khan. During a summer visit to Sardinia Sally met many of Prince Karim's friends, including Princess Margaret and Lord Snowdon.

As the Aga Khan has told me, by that time they had already made up their minds to get married, not an easy step for either of them to take. For him it meant a profound change in his style of life, for her the prospect of arduous ceremonial duties in many parts of the world and a change of outlook, not to say a different philosophy of life. Her interest in Islam helped. She started taking instruction with a view to adopting the Muslim faith and learned her prayers in Arabic. At the end of the instruction she found herself involved in long discussions with Si Hainza Boubaker, the imam of the Paris mosque. "I did not realize it then, but I was being quizzed," she said to me. "The object of a two hours' conversation was to find out how serious I was about my conversion." She passed the test easily, was accepted into the Muslim faith, and took the name of Salima, which means "Peace."

In the study of his Paris house overlooking the Seine the Aga Khan next put the finishing touches to a number of communal, industrial, and personal projects. For some time to come, he expected to be "otherwise engaged." Each decision involved big issues. Symbolizing the expansion of his interests, he took delivery of the new Grumman Gulfstream jet, twice the size and cost of the old Mystère. "It will enable me to visit my community more frequently," he told me. He approved plans for a building project in central London, where a new headquarters— including *jamatkhana*, social center, and shops—for his growing community in Britain would soon be going up. His East African tourist operation was already under way. To cope with the growing volume of work he initiated a reorganization of his team and recalled Michael Curtis from Nairobi to Europe.

After the initial stage, during which the infrastructure was created, and the second stage, when the accounts were balanced and the first profits made, the Aga Khan organization was now moving into third gear. A young man with power over millions of followers, with experience and the entrée in parts of the world that do not readily welcome Westerners, and with a lot of money at his disposal, he was now recognized as a leading international industrialist in his own right with whom American and other banking, hotel, and aviation interests were anxious to join forces.

Preparations for his wedding were going ahead on several levels. In Muslim law Lady James's previous marriage was no obstacle, and having remained without issue, had been declared null and void by the Vatican in any case. Plans had to be coordinated with Ismaili communities, for whom the Imam's wedding would be a tremendous event. A marriage contract had to be drawn up including financial provision for the future Begum Aga Khan. The date for the announcement of a formal engagement was fixed for October 8, 1969, to be made from Paris, where Lady James was staying with her parents.

Carefully timed to reach communities as far apart as East Africa, Syria, Pakistan, and India simultaneously, the announcement brought hundreds of reporters from all over the world to Paris. They were laying seige to the Aga Khan's house in the rue des Ursins, bombarding his associates with telephone calls, and searching for him and his elusive English bride, who took refuge in a chalet behind the well-protected gates of one of his stud farms. Only one magazine photographer and one television cameraman were admitted to take "official pictures."

Because I had been working on my account of the Aga Khan, his family, his history, and the Ismaili community, which would not be complete without the happiest chapter in his life, it was arranged for me to meet him and his fiancée "at a secret address"—the offices of Maître André Ardoin, in the Avenue de l'Opera, in Paris. The Aga Khan and Lady James came there by separate routes and staged a joyful reunion after what was obviously only a short separation.

He was wearing a smart dark suit, belying his reputation as an overcasual dresser, and Lady James wore a simple black dress, a five-row pearl necklace, and a twenty-carat pear-shaped diamond engagement ring. Her present to him was gold cuff links. "Gifts are a fairly common thing among Muslims on the occasion of betrothal or marriage," the Aga Khan explained, "but an engagement ring has no religious significance."

Our three-cornered conversation developed into a spontaneous exchange between them. "When we first met," Prince Karim said to his fiancée, "I had no idea you knew so much about Islam." Clearly they were still at the stage when they were discovering each other. They discussed the meaning and implications of a Muslim marriage, so different from the Christian tradition. "It is a practical and contractual matter," the Aga Khan said to me, adding quickly, "but nonetheless serious for that. In taking Lady James for a wife, I am entering a contract." Lady James nodded. "It is more like a civil marriage," she said.

There was no mistaking their devotion to each other. They were looking forward to a life together, and though there is no such vow in a Muslim marriage, something about them seemed to say "until death do us part." The subject of an heir came up. "Naturally I would like a boy," Prince Karim admitted. "Your future wife is dying to give you an heir," Lady James interjected, "but I also hope for lots of children!" The Aga vigorously approved. She spoke about her parents, with whom she had been living until quite recently. As a child Prince Karim, on the other hand, had not seen much of his parents. "Once I have children," Lady James said, "I could not bear to be separated from them for long."

She was not going to make changes in her husband's household. "Your house is so well run, 'K' "—she called him by the name by which he is known to his family and friends. She would be taking her place in the Ismaili community, welfare, health, and housing being a Begum's traditional spheres, and would obviously be a great help to the Imam. "I would not marry a woman who I did not believe could help me," Prince Karim said. "I hope to reorganize my life so as to have a little more time to be with my wife—and my children—though not at the expense of the community."

Our talk lasted over two hours. The wedding—two ceremonies, one civil, one Muslim—would be in the strictest privacy,
with only members of the family and leaders of the community present. The date was set for October 28.

Bringing their colorful robes and gold-threaded turbans, the
Ismaili dignitaries were soon on their way to Paris to join two
previous Begums (Yvette and Andrée), Prince Sadruddin, Princess Joan Aly Khan, Prince Amyn, and Princess Yasmin. In
East Africa and all over Asia, Ismaili communities only two
years after paying homage to the Imam on his tenth anniversary
were preparing illuminations, prayer meetings, special editions
of newspapers, and publication of little volumes to mark the
occasion.

Next came the civil ceremony. Outside the Aga Khan's house
in Paris even the most inveterate onlookers had almost given up
hope of setting eyes on the couple when he and Lady James
arrived from the Haras de Lassy, the stud farm near Chantilly,
which had been their hideout for weeks. After a few minutes
in the rue des Ursins, they emerged from a back door to be
driven to the local town hall, where they were received by
Georges Théolierre, Mayor of the fourth arrondissement, wearing his badge of office. Like his grandfather and his father
before him, Prince Karim was complying with French law,
which requires a civil ceremony to accompany marriages of all
denominations. After the brief formalities the couple, duly married in Western eyes, returned to the country.

The following Monday, the eve of the Muslim ceremony, the
Aga Khan and his bride entertained Ismaili leaders representing
his millions of followers. At the big, charming house at Lassy,
the Mir of Hunza and his Rani headed the imposing assembly
of the world's outstanding Ismailis, wealthy and influential men,
and their ladies, among them Sir Eboo Pirbhai, from Nairobi,
Amirali Fancy, and Captain Currim, from Karachi. That evening the Aga Khan gave an intimate dinner for members of the
family only.

By Tuesday morning the northern end of the narrow rue des Ursins had disappeared below a structure that allowed access to the Aga Khan's house straight from the Quai aux Fleurs. Architects had added an entrance hall, and a neighbor's garden at the back had been covered with a roof to provide additional space for the evening reception. But none of the distinguished Europeans and Americans invited to toast the couple later in the day were present at noon, when the Aga Khan and his bride entered their first-floor drawing room, where the ceremony was performed. There Si Hainza Boubaker, in white burnoose and headdress, and two other Muslim dignitaries were waiting to perform the Muslim wedding ceremony.

Wearing a long white *sherwani*, white trousers, white shoes, and a black Astrakhan hat, Prince Karim sat by the side of his bride, who looked a little pale, her small face only just showing from beneath her white sari. They meditated in prayer while the principal guests, Princess Sultan Mohammed, the former Begum, Princess Joan Aly Khan, and Mrs. Croker-Poole took their seats on a couch to the right. Crowded against the Gobelin-covered walls, the Ismaili elite stood in silent prayer.

After a recital from the Koran, the singing voice of the rector filling the room, came the signing of the marriage contract, the essential part of the ceremony. There were more prayers to Allah to bless the union and guide the couple to happiness. As Prince Karim and the Begum rose to leave the room, the Rani of Hunza, in a traditional gesture, strewed pearls in their path. The couple was garlanded and showered with orchids and rose petals. Downstairs the wedding guests were entertained with orange juice, sour milk, and almond cakes. The Aga Khan and his bride cut a mammoth, three-tier wedding cake topped with his insignia. Slices were sent to Ismaili communities around the world.

Precious stones, gold, and platinum were among the personal presents from rich followers, quite apart from the offerings of the community, to which each Ismaili had made a contribution.

In the United States, England, France, and Germany, as well
as in Africa and Asia, Ismailis staged celebrations to coincide
with the Paris ceremony. In Karachi a mammoth reception was
attended by President General A. M. Yahya Khan, who cut a
ceremonial cake, and addressing the huge gathering, praised
the Ismaili community's "zealous contribution to the improvement of Pakistan's socioeconomic life," ending with warm
wishes for the young couple's "very long and very happy married life." Sweets and traditional foods were distributed.
Jamatkhanas and Ismaili private residences were bright with
illuminations. The celebrations, which lasted three days, ended
with over a hundred community marriages.

In stark contrast with the solemn religious wedding ceremony
earlier in the day, the Aga Khan's house in Paris that evening
was the scene of a more conventional social occasion. From six
onwards, a never-ending stream of limousines passed through
the police cordon while the city's rush-hour traffic was diverted.
They brought some six hundred guests, who presently found
themselves transported into a sea of flowers. Thousands of
candles illuminated the house as the guests were greeted by
the Aga Khan and the new Begum. Tables were laden with
delicacies, and footmen served champagne but soon found it
difficult to make their way through the crowd thronging the
covered courtyards and the reception rooms.

Princess Margaret of England arrived on the arm of the
British Ambassador—Prince Karim had sent his jet to London to
bring her to Paris. Princess Ashraf, twin sister of the Shah of
Iran, represented the largest community of Shia Muslims.
Members of the former royal houses of Italy and Yugoslavia
rubbed shoulders with Barons Elie and Guy de Rothschild, who
still firmly occupy their thrones. Outstanding among the French
racing fraternity was Mme. Suzy Volterra, widow of the late
great showman and rival of the old Aga and Prince Aly in many
a classic race. Charlie and Oona Chaplin were there, and David
Niven and Danny Kaye. Henry Ford headed a strong American

contingent and a dozen ambassadors represented the Aga Khan's links with their countries. A sprinkling of extremely attractive London and Paris models among the guests testified to the new Begum's loyalty to old friends.

The couple's first official engagement together came the next day, when they were the guests of the President of France and Mme. Pompidou at an intimate luncheon in their honor, a rare privilege. They received an invitation from President Yahya Khan to stay with him during their visit to Pakistan early in 1970, when the Imam was due to introduce the Begum to the community.

That evening the Grumman Gulfstream jet took them on their "secret honeymoon." They traveled under assumed names, which did not protect them for long. It was only a day or so before they were traced to Lyford Cay in Nassau.

At the start of his married life the Aga Khan has made a brave attempt to come out of his shell. With the Begum he attended a grandiose party given by his neighbor, Baron Lopez de Rede. Guests were asked to come to the Baron's sixteenth-century Hôtel Lambert on the Île St.-Louis dressed in oriental style; Karim and Salima could be truly themselves. Unlike most of the perambulating guests, Brigitte Bardot and Salvador Dali among them, the newlyweds stayed together in their corner and did not circulate.

The forthcoming tour of Pakistan presently involved the Aga Khan in a complicated process of selection and elimination. Hundreds of invitations from scores of cities, official bodies, religious, medical, and educational institutions were pouring in. The timing, the drafting of speeches (more than two dozen of them) for different reasons and diverse audiences, briefings for himself and the Begum on places they were to visit and people they were to meet, occupied much time and thought. Prince Karim had to be armed with instant responses to greetings from the President, local governors, military authorities, university chancellors.

Ismaili couples planning to get married, even some previously undecided, hastily arranged their weddings, either holding them up or putting them forward to coincide with the Imam's presence. Children were being spruced up to be worthy of the Imam's glance when their parents held them up for his inspection. With all this in mind, Michael Curtis was again entrusted with the conduct of public relations and the duties of aide-de-camp. A small staff was selected to accompany the Aga Khan and Princess Salima in the Grumman Gulfstream.

In the middle of January, 1970, after a quick excursion to St. Moritz to breathe the mountain air, the tour got under way. The departure from Europe was as quiet and inconspicuous as the arrival in Pakistan was well publicized and tumultuous. The official welcoming party, including members of the Pakistan government, was swamped by thousands of Ismailis who came to greet the Imam and the Begum. Decorated floats, Aga Khan bands, Boy Scouts, and Girl Guides accompanied them in triumph to their residence. With a few added touches, it repeated the triumphal tours of Prince Karim's grandfather.

It was the same wherever they went. Islamabad, Rawalpindi, Lahore, Hyderabad, Peshawar, Dacca, and Karachi were the main stations on the tour, which took in scores of smaller places. Prince Karim talked to cabinet ministers, senior government officials, industrialists, educators, and medical men. At Rawalpindi he gave a dinner in honor of President Yahya Khan attended by the whole cabinet.

The Begum managed the tour, the first of many long and wearying official engagements ahead of her, with consummate skill and perfect assurance. She was at ease, charming, and very beautiful. Among themselves, Ismailis made no secret of their pleasure in seeing the mother of the Aga Khan's heir, who, in the passage of time, would follow him as Imam of the Ismailis, the fiftieth in direct line of descent from the Prophet Mohammed.

GENEALOGY

Zahir Ali	1020–1035
al-Mustansir	1035–1095
Nizar	1095–1097
Hadi	1097–1135
Mohatadi	1135–1157
Kahir	1157–1162
Hasan Zakaresalam	1162–1166
Ala Muhammad	1166–1210
Hasan	1210–1221
Alauddin Muhammad	1221–1255
Raknuddin Khurshah	1255–1256
Shamsudin Muhammad	1256–1310
Kassam Shah	1310–1370
Islam Shah	1370–1424
Muhammad bin Islam Shah	1424–1464
Mustansir billah II	1464–1476
Abdus Salaam	1476–1494
Gharib Mirza	1494–1497
Abuzar Ali	1497–1509
Murad Mirza	1509–1514
Zulfiqar Ali	1514–1516
Nurdin Ali	1516–1550
Khalilullah Ali	1550–1585
Nizar Ali Shah	1585–1629
Sayyid Ali	1629–1661
Hassan Ali	1661–1695
Kassam Ali	1695–1730
Abul Hasan Ali	1730–1780
Khalilullah	1780–1817
Shah Hasan Ali Shah, Aga Khan I	1817–1881
Ali Shah, Aga Khan II	1881–1885
H.R.H. Prince Sultan Moham-	
med, Aga Khan III	1885–1957
H.H. Prince Karim, Aga Khan IV	1957–

THE AGA KHAN'S EMPIRE

THE Aga Khan's empire, industrial and communal, can be roughly divided into seven categories. The frontiers between them are often blurred, but with minimal exceptions, the Aga Khan's control over his enterprises is absolute.

1. *Investment and Insurance*
   Diamond Jubilee Investment Trust, Kenya
   Diamond Jubilee Investment Trust, Uganda
   Diamond Jubilee Investment Trust, Tanzania
   Diamond Jubilee Investment Trust Service, Kenya
   The Aga Khan Bank in Asia (Pak Ismailia Co-op. Bank),
   controlling ten industrial enterprises, including jute mills
   and marble factory
2. *Industrial Promotion Services (I.P.S.)*
   I.P.S. Switzerland
   I.P.S. Pakistan
   I.P.S. Kenya
   I.P.S. Uganda
   I.P.S. Tanzania
   I.P.S. Congo (Kinshasa)
   I.P.S. Ivory Coast

I.P.S. companies have stakes in seventy industrial enterprises in Asia and Africa, producing textiles, cotton,
shirts, socks, blankets, shoes, suitcases, cosmetics, candy,
pharmaceutical products, screws, kitchen utensils, fish-
nets, cigarette paper.

3. *Publishing and Printing*
East African Publishers and Printers (Holding), Kenya
East African Newspapers, Kenya
Uganda African Newspapers, Uganda
Kenya Litho, Kenya
Tanzania Litho, Tanzania
Uganda Litho, Uganda
Andrew Crawford Production
Tanzania Public Relations Company
African Life Publications, Kenya

4. *Studs and Stables*
IRELAND
Gilltown
Sallymount
Sheshoon
Ballymanny
FRANCE
Marly-la-Ville
Lassy
Saint Créspin
Bonneval
350 horses (Four stallions and eighty-one brood mares listed
in the 1968 edition of H.H. Agá Khan Stud Book)

5. *Sardinia*
Societa Alberghiera Costa Smeralda (hotel group)
Agenzia Immobiliare della Costa Smeralda (real-estate
agency)
Societa Porto Cervo (harbor company)
Alimentaria Sarda (trading company and supermarket)
Alisarda Airline

Marinasarda (boat sales and hire)
Bianca Sarda (laundry)
Cerasarda Ceramics Factory ‾
Servici Tecnici Generali della Costa Smeralda (consulting firm)
6. *Community Institutions in Asia and Africa*
Five hundred schools
Hospitals
Social centers
Sports grounds
Real estate and housing colonies
Jamatkhanas
7. *Private Holdings*
Shares (oil), real estate, residences

BIBLIOGRAPHY

Aga Khan. *India in Transition.* Philip Lee Warner, 1918.

———. *The Memoirs of Aga Khan.* London: Cassell, 1954.

Aga Khan Diamond Jubilee Souvenir Book. Nairobi: 1945.

Arberry, A. J. *The Romance of the Rubaiyat.* Edward FitzGerald's First Edition reprinted with Introduction and Notes. London: George Allen & Unwin.

Bettina. *Bettina.* London: Michael Joseph, 1965.

Brown, E. G. *Literary History of Persia.* London: 1906.

Code of Conduct for the Followers of the Imam. Translated by Jawad Muscati and A. Moulvi. Mombasa: Ismailia Association for Africa, 1950.

Constitution of the Councils and Jamats of Shia Ismaili Muslims of Pakistan, The. Karachi: H.R.H. Prince Aga Khan Ismaili Federal Council for Pakistan.

Constitution of the Shia Imami Ismailis in Africa, The. His Highness the Aga Khan Imami Ismaili Supreme Council for Africa.

Donaldson, Dwight M. *The Shi'ite Religion.* London: Luzac, 1933.

Dumasia, Naoroji. *The Aga Khan and His Ancestors.* Bombay: Times of India Press, 1939.

Fielding, Daphne. *Duchess of Jermyn Street*. London: Eyre & Spottiswoode, 1967.

Flynn, Errol. *My Wicked Ways*. London: William Heinemann, 1960.

Frischauer, Paul. *Es Steht Geschrieben*. Zurich: Droemer Knaur, 1967.

————. *Der Mensch macht seine Welt*. Hamburg: Mosaik Verlag, 1962.

Gibb, H. A. R., and Kramers, J. H. *Shorter Encyclopaedia of Islam*. London: Luzac, 1961.

Greenwall, Harry J. *His Highness the Aga Khan*. London: The Cresset Press, 1952.

Hitti, Philip K. *History of the Arabs*. London: Macmillan, 1967.

Hodson, H. V. *The Great Divide*. London: Hutchinson, 1969.

Ibn Ishaq. *The Life of Muhammad*. Translated by A. Guillaume. London: Oxford University Press, 1955.

Ismailia Association. *H.R.H. Prince Aga Khan Platinum Jubilee*. Karachi: Ismailia Association, 1954.

Jackson, Stanley. *The Aga Khan*. London: Odhams, 1952.

Kassim Ali, M. J. *Ever Living Guide*. Karachi: Ismailia Association, 1955.

Koran, The. Translated by George Sale. London: Frederick Warne.

Lewis, Bernard. *The Assassins*. London: Weidenfeld and Nicolson, 1967.

Lyle, R. C. *The Aga Khan's Horses*. London: Putnam, 1938.

Malick, Qayyum A. *H.R.H. Prince Aga Khan*. Karachi: Din Muhammadi Press.

Marsh, Marcus. *Racing with the Gods*. London: Pelham Books, 1968.

Muscati, Jawad. *Life and Lectures of Al-Muayyad-Fid-Din*. Karachi: Ismailia Association, 1966.

Nehru, J. J. *Autobiography*. London: Bodley Head, 1936.

Picklay, A. S. *The History of the Ismailis*. Bombay: 1940.

Rahman, Fazlur. *Islam*. London: Weidenfeld and Nicolson, 1966.

Slater, Leonard. *Aly*. London: W. H. Allen, 1966.

Stark, Freya. *The Valley of the Assassins*. London: John Murray, 1934.

Stephens, Ian. *Pakistan*. London: Ernest Benn, 1963.

Strachey, Lytton. *Eminent Victorians*. London: Chatto & Windus, 1948.

Vanderbilt, Gloria, and Furness, Thelma. *Double Exposure*. London: Frederick Muller, 1959.

Vatikiotis, P. J. *The Fatimid Theory of State*. Orientalia.

Viner, Richard. *George of the Ritz*. London: William Heinemann, 1959.

Young, Gordon. *The Golden Prince*. London: Hale, 1955.

Zahur (magazine). Nairobi: Ismailia Students Union, July, 1945, and August, 1948.

INDEX

331

Williams, Emrys, 178, 206
Wilson, Sir Maitland, 161
Wiltshire Yeomanry Regiment, 156
Winchell, Walter, 221
Windsor, Duke of, 150, 151
Wintle, Alfred D., 160
World Bank, 288
World Ismailia Socio-Economic Conference, 310
World Muslim Conference, 213
World War I, 52, 73–78, 160
  beginning of, 73
  Pan-Islamic movement, 74
World War II, 16, 157–173
  Afrika Korps, 160, 169
  beginning of, 154
Wragg, Harry, 116, 117, 134

Yahya Khan, A. M., 311, 320, 321, 322
Yar, Sir Ahmad, 303–304
Yarde-Buller, Joan, *see* Joan, Princess
Yarovda Palace (India), 16–17, 46
Yasmin, Princess, 14, 210, 211, 218–219, 235, 238, 239, 242–243, 244–245, 286, 288, 300, 310, 318
  birth of, 207
Yorde, Primrose, 156
Young, Gordon, vii, 167–168, 197, 212
Yvette, Begum, 173, 178, 180, 182, 183, 185, 186, 188, 197, 199, 203, 205, 214, 228, 229, 233–235, 238, 244, 250, 251, 253, 254–255, 285, 318
  as advisor to Karim, 257–258, 265, 280–281
  coolness between Karim and, 280
  Ismaili title of, 3
  marriage of, 167–168, 249
  Mecca pilgrimage, 225–226
  Muslim name, 168
  at religious burial of Aga Khan III, 278–281

Zakat, 86–87, 129
  defined, 18
  percent of income for, 63
  technicalities of, 61–63
Zanzibar, Sultan of, 3